# MANUAL

OF THE

# HIGHWAY LAWS

OF THE

## STATE OF NEW YORK.

WITH AN

## APPENDIX OF FORMS.

---

By ROBLEY D. COOK,

COUNSELLOR-AT-LAW.

---

ALBANY:
JOHN D. PARSONS, Jr.,
LAW PUBLISHER,
1870.

# PREFACE.

This work is not intended as an elaborate treatise on the Law of Highways, but simply as a Manual for the use of the legal profession, and of those officers to whom are intrusted the care and management of the highways of the State.

It has been the aim of the author to confine himself exclusively to the subject of Public Highways and Private Roads. The various kinds of ways — such as rivers, canals, railways, etc., — though properly included under the generic term Highway, have been referred to only where their connection with the principal subject has rendered it necessary.

So much of the common law as remains in force has been given as succinctly as possible. The statute law has been fully and literally set forth, with such explanations and constructions as the courts of this State have furnished, and the decisions of the courts of other States and of the English courts have been cited wherever they could serve to illustrate our law. In the citation of opinions the leading cases have been chosen, and what is understood to be the established law has been stated as briefly as was consistent with perspicuity. It has been the author's aim to lay down no principles and to make no statements not fully sustained by the statutes or the decisions. That the work is perfect is not claimed; but it is hoped that it will be found reliable and sufficiently exhaustive to answer the requirements of the profession and of the highway officers.

The author would return his thanks to Messrs. G. A. Mosher and C. W. Perkins, of the Troy bar, for their valuable assistance in the preparation of the work, and to Mr. Matthew Walsh for his labors in verifying the citation of authorities.

TROY, *September*, 1870.

# CONTENTS.

# TABLE OF CASES.

Page.



## D.



## E.

## R.



## S.

## T.



## U.



## V.



## W.

# MANUAL

OF

# HIGHWAY LAWS.

---

## CHAPTER I.

### WHAT ARE HIGHWAYS?

A highway, at common law, is a right of passage for the public in general, without distinction. The term "highway" extends to all public ways, and includes carriageways, horseways, footways, streets, turnpike and plank roads, railroads, ferries, canals and navigable rivers.

These different kinds of highways are distinguished from each other only by the mode of their use, the material of which they are composed, or by the manner in which the costs of construction and maintenance are defrayed.

Public piers or landing places are highways (*Radway* v. *Briggs*, 37 N. Y. R. 256; *People* v. *Lambier*, 5 Denio, 9; *Fowler* v. *Mott*, 19 Barb. 204); so also are public squares, parks, etc.

In the statute law of this state the word "road" is used synonymously with "highway." (*Brace* v. *N. Y. Central R. R. Co.*, 27 N. Y. R. 269.)

The size of the way is not material; a public footway or bridleway is a highway for foot passengers or horse passengers (*Rex* v. *County of Salop*, 13 East, 95), and a public carriageway is not restrained because all carriages cannot pass and repass. (*Rex* v. *Lyon*, 3 Dow. & R. 497.)

There was formerly a way termed *driftway*, over which cattle were driven; but this is now included in the term "highway," since it is well settled that a public highway is open to cattle being driven from one place to another. (*Ballard* v. *Dyson*, 1 Taunt. 285.)

In this state the public have no highway along the margins of the navigable rivers and lakes, unless such a right has been acquired by express grant or by prescription. (*Ledyard* v. *Ten Eyck*, 36 Barb. 102.)

And, although a navigable river is a highway, yet, if an individual, having authority from the legislature, erect a wharf on the bank, such wharf is strictly private property, although it extend into the river and diminish the breadth of the stream, and the public cannot claim free access to it. (*Wetmore* v. *Atlantic White Lead Co.*, 37 Barb. 70.) However, if a highway terminate in a navigable river, and the owner of the fee on the bank builds a bulk-head in the river in front of his land and the street, and fills in the intervening space, the highway is not thereby cut off from the river, but continues over such bulk-head to the water. (*People* v. *Lambier*, 5 Denio, 9.)

*Extra viam.*—The right of the public to pass along a highway is, to a limited extent, paramount to the rights of adjoining owners; for it is well settled that if a highway be impassable or founderous, or even dangerous or incommodious, from being out of repair, the public may pass for the time being over the adjacent land; and it makes no difference whether it be sown with grain or not. If the adjacent land be inclosed the traveler may remove so much of the fence as will enable him to pass, doing no unnecessary injury. (3 Kent, 424; *Williams* v. *Safford*, 7 Barb. 309.) But this right of going upon adjoining lands, applies to public and not to private ways.

(*Taylor* v. *Whitehead*, Doug, 745; *Bullard* v. *Harrison*, 4 M. & S. 387.) Uninclosed lands, adjacent to a highway, are considered so far dedicated to public use that an action will not lie, at the suit of the owner, against any person traveling thereon. (*Cleveland* v. *Cleveland*, 12 Wend. 172.

*Cul de sac.*—It was, for a long time, a question of doubt in England, whether there could be a highway where there was no thoroughfare; that is, whether a *cul de sac*, or way closed at one end, could be a highway. In the case of the *Rugby Charity* v. *Merriweather* (11 East, 375, note), Lord Kenyon held that it made no difference whether or not a street was a thoroughfare, and that it was a question for the jury, whether there was a highway or not. A similar view had been before taken by Lord Ellenborough, in *Rex* v. *Lloyd* (1 Camp. 260.) The correctness of Lord Kenyon's decision was afterward strongly questioned by Lord C. J. Mansfield, in *Woodyer* v. *Hadden* (5 Taunt. 125), and by Justices Abbott, Holroyd and Best, in *Wood* v. *Veal* (5 Barn. & Ald. 454.) But the more recent English decisions entirely sustain the decision of Lord Kenyon, and hold that there may be a highway where there is no thoroughfare. In the case of *Bateman* v. *Black* (14 Eng. Law and Eq. 69), which came before the Court of Queen's Bench, in 1852, the question was directly in issue, and Lord Campbell announced his opinion as follows: "We must take it that there is a good finding on this issue, unless there cannot, in point of law, be a good highway where there is no thoroughfare. Now, such a position cannot, I think, be supported. There may be, or there may not be, a highway under such circumstances. It would be very strong to hold that there could be no highway, even where there has been an express dedication to a public purpose, because the place is no thoroughfare. There may be a large square with only one entrance to it; and if the owner allows the public to use it, without restriction, for a great many years, he cannot afterward turn round and say they are all trespassers. That would be, as said by Lord Kenyon, a trap to catch trespassers. In the *Rugby Charity* v. *Merriweather*, Lord Kenyon laid it down that there might be a public highway where there was a *cul de sac;* and that in was a question for a jury, on evidence, whether such a place was a highway or not. I do not find that this case has ever been expressly overruled. In the other cases referred to, the judges do not hold that such highway does not exist, but only say that there is no evidence of there being a highway. It seems to me that it rests on principles of convenience, that there may be a highway without a thoroughfare; and it is not inconsistent with what is laid down by Hawkins and other text writers on the subject." This was concurred in by all the judges in that case. The opinion of Earle, J., was, in brief, as follows: "The question is, whether there can be, in law, a highway where no thoroughfare exists. It seems to me clear, from the authorities, that there can be such a highway; and convenience requires that this should be so. It is for the jury to consider, whether, on the whole of the facts proved, they will presume a dedication to the public."

In this state the weight of authorities is in favor of the proposition that there can be, in law, a highway where no thoroughfare exists. A road may be laid out by the public authority which has no issue at one extremity, but abuts upon private ground. (*People* v. *Kingman*, 24 N. Y. R. 559; *Hickok* v. *Trustees of Plattsburgh*, 41 Barb. 130; *Wiggins* v.

*Tallmadge*, 11 id. 457.) The case of *Trustees of Jordan* v. *Otis* (37 id. 50), was, however, to the contrary.

A highway, terminating at one extremity in a navigable river, is not a *cul de sac;* for, the river being a highway, the right of passage is continuous; and any change in the line of the shore, whether effected by natural or artificial means, does not affect the continuity of that right; so that, if an owner of the fee of a street ending at a navigable river erect wharves or docks in front of the street terminus, the highway will extend over such erections to the water edge. (*People* v. *Lambier*, 5 Denio, 9.)

*Streets.* — A street in a city or village, common to all people, is a public highway. (*Brace* v. *N. Y. Central R. R. Co.*, 27 N. Y. R. 271; *Benedict* v. *Goit*, 3 Barb. 459; *Adams* v. *Wash. & S. R. R. Co.*, 11 id. 449.) Strictly, a street is a paved way or road, but the term is used for any way or road in a city or village. It is defined by Bouvier (Law Dic.) as "a road in a city or village;" and by Webster, "a paved way or road; a city road; hence a mainway in distinction from a lane or alley." There is, however, a distinction — so far as the uses to which they may be applied — between a highway in the country and a street in a city. The manner and extent of the uses of a highway in the country are restricted for the reason that they are needed only for passing and repassing, while in a city such is not the case. There are certain uses — such as the construction of sewers, and the laying of water and gas pipes — to which, in modern times, such streets have generally been applied. These urban servitudes, as they are called, are the necessary incidents of a street in a large city; and whether the street be laid out and opened upon property belonging to the corporation, or whether they become public streets by grant, or upon compensation being made to the owner of the fee, they have all the incidents attached to them which are necessary to their full enjoyment as streets. And whether the corporation be the owner of the fee of the streets, in trust for the public, or whether it be merely the trustees of the streets and highways as such, irrespective of any title to the soil, it has the power to authorize their appropriation to all such uses as are conducive to the public good, and do not interfere with their complete and unrestricted use as highways. (*Milhau* v. *Sharp*, 15 Barb. 210; *People* v. *Kerr*, 27 N. Y. R. 202; *White v. Cincinnati*, 6 Peters, 432; *Kelsey* v. *King*, 32 Barb. 410.)

Among the certain uses referred to is the use of water pipes for the supplying the inhabitants with water. So gas pipes are laid under the streets, through the land over which they run, and lamps are erected in the streets at the pleasure of the city. The construction of sewers is a still more marked evidence of the extent of the appropriation of the lands of individuals to the use of the public, when laid out as city streets.

However, it is thought that this doctrine does not apply to highways acquired by dedication. The question was very elaborately examined by Mr. Justice Selden in the case of *Williams* v. *The N. Y. Central R. R. Co.* (16 N. Y. R. 97), and it was there held that the legislature had no power to authorize a railroad company to lay its road in a street which had been acquired by dedication, against the will of the owner of the fee, or without the appraisal and payment of his damages in the mode provided by law. So, in the case of *Kelsey v. King* (33 Howard, 39), Davis, C. J., who delivered the opinion of the court, argued that the streets in a village or city, the easement in which had been acquired by dedication, could only be used to the same extent, and in the same manner, as highways in the country, and the court held that the city authorities of Brooklyn could not construct a sewer in a dedicated street, without the consent of the owner of the fee, or without making him adequate compensation in the manner by law prescribed. The cases decided relating to the city of New York cannot be relied upon as authorities as to the general doctrine, since most of the streets of that city are owned in fee by the corporation for public use. (*People* v. *Williams*, *supra;* *Kelsey* v. *King*, 33 How. 39; Hoff. Treatise, 289.)

*Turnpike roads.*—A turnpike road is a public highway established by public authority for public use, and is to be regarded as a public easement. The only difference between this and a common highway is, that, instead of being made at the public expense in the first instance, it is authorized and laid out by public authority, and made at the expense of individuals in the first instance, and the cost of construction and maintenance is reimbursed by a toll, levied by public authority for the purpose. Every traveler has the same right to use it, paying the toll established by law, as he would have to use any other public highway. (*Commonwealth* v. *Wilkinson*, 16 Pick. 175.)

The legislature has power to authorize chartered companies to construct turnpikes on existing highways; and the construction of such turnpikes abolishes the old roads on which they are constructed, or which run parallel with and adjoining to them. (*Nolenville Turnpike Co.* v. *Baker*, 4 Humph. [Tenn.] 315.) However, it is thought that in this state the highway appropriated to the purposes of a turnpike does not entirely cease to be a public highway. The general right of the public to use it remains unimpaired. The public, in consideration of the payment of certain tolls, is relieved from the burden of keeping it in repair; and the duties in this respect, which before belonged to the commissioners and overseers of highways, are transferred to the turnpike corporators. But these local authorities are not ousted of their jurisdiction in the particulars in which their exercise would not conflict with the purposes or with the rights of the plank road company, and which the public interests require should be exercised; and especially are they not relieved from their duties in respect to encroachments upon highways which are at the same time used as turnpike roads. (*Walker* v. *Caywood*, 31 N. Y. R. 51.)

When a plank or turnpike road is constructed upon a highway, the company succeed to the rights and powers of the commissioners of highways, and any inconvenience or damage which an owner of land suffers, by proper and reasonable repairs or improvements of the highway, is *damnum absque injuria*. (*Benedict* v. *Goit*, 3 Barb. 459; *Dexter* v. *Broat*, 16 id. 337.)

The supervisors of a county are authorized to provide for the use of abandoned turnpike, plank or macadamized roads within any town as public highways; also to provide for an alteration, reduction or change in the rate of toll charged by such roads. Laws of 1869, ch. 855.

*Plank roads.*—Plank roads, like turnpikes, are public highways when established by law, and the same general principles which apply to turnpike roads apply also to plank roads. They are common in the sense that every citizen has the right to travel on them, either on foot, on horseback, or in his carriage, subject to the payment of the legal toll.

A plank road company, which has acquired a right to use a public highway for the location and construction of their road, have no right to exclude the public from it, or interrupt the enjoyment of their right of way while the change is being made. They are bound, like town officers engaged in repairing roads, to carry on the work with as little inconvenience to the public as is reasonably practicable, and if, through their neglect, a person passing with ordinary care and prudence suffers damage, the company are liable. (*Ireland* v. *Oswego, etc., Plank Road Co.*, 13 N. Y. R. 526.)

Under the statutes of this state authorizing a plank road company to abandon its road (Laws of 1854, ch. 87), and providing that thereupon the road shall revert to the several towns through which it was constructed, it is held that plank roads constructed over lands which had not previously belonged to the town, or been used for highways, pass to the town on the dissolution of the company. (*Heath* v. *Barman*, 49 Barb. 496.)

*Railroads.* — A railroad is a public highway to be used in a particular manner. (*Rex* v. *Severn & Wye Railway Co.*, 2 Barn. & Ald. 646.)

In *Beekman* v. *Saratoga and Schenectady Railroad Company* (3 Paige, 74), Chancellor Walworth thus expresses himself: "It is objected, however, that a railroad differs from other public improvements, and particularly from turnpikes and canals, because travelers cannot use it with their own carriages, and farmers cannot transport their produce in their own vehicles; that the company are under no obligation to accommodate the public with transportation, and that they are unlimited in the amount of tolls which they are authorized to take. If the making of a railroad will enable the traveler to go from one place to another, without the expense of a carriage and horses, he derives a greater benefit from the improvement than if he was compelled to travel with his own conveyance over a turnpike road at the same expense. And if a mode of conveyance has been discovered by which the farmer can procure his produce to be transported to market at half the expense which it would cost him to carry it there with his own wagon and horses, there is no reason why the public should not enjoy the benefit of the discovery. And if any individual is so unreasonable as to refuse to have the railroad made through his land, for a fair compensation, the legislature may lawfully ap propriate a portion of his property, or may authorize an individual or a corporation thus to appropriate it upon paying a just compensation to the owner of the land for the damage sustained."

The tenure of railroad corporations in the lands taken for the construction of their road is in the nature of a trust for public use, subject to the supervision of the government. (*Swan* v. *Williams*, 2 Mich. 424.)

It is held in Pennsylvania that, when lands are acquired for a railway under the right of eminent domain, and established by law as thoroughfares of commerce, such lands will not revert to the owner on the dissolution or abandonment of the franchise by the company, but will remain a public highway, subject to the management and control of the state. (*Erie & N. E. R. R. Co.* v. *Casey*, 26 Penn. 287; see *Hayward* v. *Mayor, etc*, 7 N. Y. R. 314; *Rexford* v. *Knight*, 11 id. 308.)

*Railroads in highways and streets.* — Notwithstanding the fact that a railroad is a highway, its use is wholly unlike, and to a great degree inconsistent with, that of the latter; and it is decided that the location of a railroad, upon a public highway, is the imposition of a new servitude upon the land in addition to, and distinct from, that to which it was originally subjected, when taken for a highway, and the owner of the fee is entitled to compensation for the damage caused thereby. (*Williams* v. *N. Y. Central R. R. Co.*, 16 N. Y. R. 97; *Inlay* v. *Union Branch R. R. Co.*, 26 Conn. 249.)

The legislature have no power to authorize a railroad company to take land which has already been taken by the public as a highway, and appropriate it to construction of the railroad, without making compensation to the owner of the fee. The owner is not divested of the fee by the laying out of the highway, and the public thereby only acquire a right of way and the incidental privileges. Appropriating such highway to a railroad company is giving, not an easement to the public, but an exclusive right to a company, and they cannot be regarded as standing in the place of the public. (*Trustees of Pres. Soc. in Waterloo* v. *Auburn & Rochester R. R. Co.*, 3 Hill, 567; *Fletcher* v. *Auburn, etc., R. R. Co.*, 25 Wend. 462; *Mahon* v. *N. Y. Central R. R. Co.*, 24 N. Y. R. 658.)

One who dedicates land to the purpose of a highway does not relinquish to the public any thing more than the right of way; and the municipal or state authorities have no power to authorize the taking of such highway by a railroad company, without his consent or making compensation to him. The taking and use of the street for a railroad is not one of the modes of enjoying the public easement, but imposes an additional burden upon the soil, for which the owner is entitled to damages, and he may recover them in an action against the company, if the road is taken without compensation. (*Williams* v. *N. Y. Central R. R. Co.*, 16 N. Y. R. 97.)

It being settled that a highway cannot be taken for railroad purposes without the consent of, or compensation rendered to, the owner of the fee, it follows that the statutes, giving permission to railroad corporations to construct their road on highways, after having obtained the consent of the commissioners of highways (Laws 1835, ch. 200), or an order of the supreme court (Laws 1854, ch. 582), must be held to relate only to the public property in the road, and confers the right only so far as the public easement is concerned, leaving the companies to deal with the private rights of individuals in the ordinary way. The statutes effectually protect the company, if they comply with the conditions, from an indictment, or against any interference with their works as a public nuisance, on account of their occupation of the highway, but not against claims for private damages arising from the use and occupation of the highway. (*Fletcher* v. *Auburn, &c., R. R. Co.*, 25 Wend. 462; *Robinson* v. *N. Y. & Erie R. R., Co.* 27 Barb. 512; *Williams* v. *N. Y. Central R. R. Co.*, 16 N. Y. R. 97.)

The question was directly at issue in the case of *The Presbyterian Society* v. *Auburn, etc., R. R. Co.* (3 Hill, 567), and the court held, that the only right or interest the people had in the premises in question — a highway — was a right of way with its necessary incidents, and that the legislature had no power to enter upon and appropriate the land for purposes other than those to which it had been originally dedicated. So, in *Wager* v. *Troy Union R. R. Co.* (25 N. Y. R. 526), it was held, that the use of a street for a railroad is a new burden beyond the public easement, which cannot be taken by legislative authority without compensation to the owner of the fee; that such use, without acquiring title of the owner of the fee, or his license, is a continuing trespass, and that he may maintain ejectment to recover the land, subject to the public easement, as a highway. The same doctrine is also held in *Carpenter* v. *The Oswego, etc., R. R. Co.* (24 N. Y. R. 655); *Mahon* v. *N. Y. Central R. R. Co.* (id. 658).

So, where land has been taken for a turnpike, and afterward transferred, by legislative authority, to a railroad company, without compensation by the latter to the owner of the fee, he may maintain an action for damages resulting from such occupation. (*Mahon* v. *N. Y. Central R. R. Co.*, 24 N. Y. R. 658.)

So, the statute permitting a railroad to construct its road over or along a plank road or turnpike does not preclude such plank road or turnpike from recovering of the railroad all damages sustained by it, the company having entered upon the plank road or turnpike without causing damages to be assessed under the statute. (*Ellicotville Plank Road* v. *Buffalo, etc., Railroad*, 20 Barb. 644; *Seneca Road Co.* v. *Auburn, etc., R. R. Co.*, 5 Hill, 170.)

In ascertaining what compensation ought justly to be made to a turnpike company for granting to a railroad company an easement or right of way across their road, it should be assumed that the railroad company would, as required by law, restore the turnpike to such state as not unnecessarily to impair its usefulness. The consideration that the business of the turnpike would be diminished by the construction of a railroad along the same general line of travel should be disregarded. Every public improvement, from the necessity of the case, must affect some property favorably and some unfavorably. When this effect is merely consequential, the injury is *damnum absque injuria.* If no vested rights have been violated, and the turnpike company still enjoy all the rights and privileges secured to them by their charter, the depreciation of their property does not furnish a legal ground of remuneration. (*Troy & Boston R. R. Co.* v. *Northern Turnpike Co.*, 16 Barb. 100; *Matter of Hamilton Avenue*, 14 id. 405.) But compare *Matter of Flatbush Avenue* (1 id. 286).

In the city of New York it is held, that the fee of most of the streets is in the city, in trust for the public use of all the people of the state, and is under the unqualified control of the legislature, and that, therefore, any appropriation of them to a public use — as for a railroad — by legislative authority, is not a taking of private property so as to require compensation to the city or to adjoining proprietors. (*People* v. *Kerr*, 27 N. Y. R. 188.) But the corporate authorities of the city of New York have no power to confer upon individuals, by contract, for an indefinite period, the franchise of constructing and operating a railroad in the public streets for their private advantage. Their power in respect to the control and regulation of the streets is held in trust for the public benefit, and cannot be abrogated nor delegated to private individuals. So that a resolution of the common council authorizing private persons to construct and operate a railroad upon certain conditions, without limitation as to time, or reserving a power of revocation, is void, because it would deprive the corporation of the power to control and regulate the use of the streets. (*Milhau* v. *Sharp*, 27 N. Y. R. 611; *Davis* v. *Mayor of New York*, 14 id. 506.) Nor can the common council of the city of New York authorize the extension of a railroad in that city, irrespective of any legislative grant, except, perhaps, when it may be necessary to the enjoyment of the principal legal grant. (*People* v. *Third Avenue R. R. Co.*, 30 How. 121.)

Where a railroad company use a street or highway without making compensation to the owner of the fee, or without his license, the latter may maintain an action of ejectment to recover the street, or an action of trespass for damages. (*Wager* v. *Troy Union R. R. Co.*, 25 N. Y. R. 526; *Lozier* v. *N. Y. Central R. R. Co.*, 42 Barb. 465; *Presbyterian Church* v. *Auburn, etc., R. R. Co.*, 3 Hil. 567.) An injunction will also be granted in a proper case. (*Craig* v. *The Rochester City, etc., R. R. Co.*, 39 N. Y. R. 404.)

*Horse railroads.*—An effort has been made by some of the courts to draw a distinction between railroads operated by steam and those which are simply operated by horses as a motive power; and it has been contended that the rules laid down as to the former are not applicable to the latter class of railroads, and that the use of a street for a horse railroad approximates more closely to ordinary highways, and is consistent with the original dedication of such street. (Per Emott, J., in *People* v. *Kerr*, 27 N. Y. R. 188.)

The question, however, has recently come before the Court of Appeals; which court decided that the rule applying to steam railroads was equally applicable to horse railroads, and that the laying of a horse railroad in the streets of a city was an imposition of an additional burden upon the land of an adjoining proprietor covered by such street. (*Craig* v. *Rochester City, etc., R. R. Co.*, 39 N. Y. R. 404; *S. C.*, 39 Barb. 494.)

The public have the right to use every part of a highway for passage; and, therefore, where a horse railroad is laid upon and along the street of a city, the public have a right to travel thereon with horses and wagons. (*Fettrich* v. *Dickenson*, 22 How. 248.) But a city railroad company is entitled to the unrestricted use of its rails, for the progress of its cars, within that limit of speed which the law allows them; and the driver of any other vehicle, who may be upon their track, is bound to use greater care than if upon the common pavement. And if, through his negligence or willfulness, in this respect, a collision ensues, he should not have damages against the company, even though the latter are also in fault. (*Wilbrand* v. *Eighth Avenue R. R. Co.*, 3 Bosw. 314.)

In Massachusetts, the driver of a wagon who occupies the track of a horse railroad, and does not turn off at the request of the conductor of a car, so as to obstruct the passage of the car at its usual speed, is liable to indictment under a statute prohibiting the unlawful and malicious obstruction of the road, although he did not get upon the track with the intent of obstructing it. (*Commonwealth* v. *Temple*, 14 Gray, 69.)

*Ferries.*— A ferry, though in its nature *sui generis*, is governed by principles similar to those which govern highways. The interests of the public in a ferry are similar to their interest in highways in general. The privilege of landing at either end of a ferry crossing, is an easement upon the freehold. Some of the earlier cases held that the owner of a ferry over a navigable river had no right to land or receive freight or passengers on the adjoining bank without the owner's consent, even though the landing place was a public highway. Mr. Justice Cowen, in a most elaborate opin on, says: "The landing of wagons, horses and passengers on the shores of a river, a sea, or an ocean, even though it be upon a dedicated or recorded highway, on the land connected with the watery way, and for the direct purpose of going onward, is still a trespass on the riparian owner, unless we could suppose such acts to be performed without any contact between the vessel and the shore." (*Pearsall* v. *Post*, 20 Wend. 131; see, also, *Chambers* v. *Furry*, 1 Yeates [Penn.] 167; *Cooper* v. *Smith*, 9 Serg. & Rawle, 26.) But this *dictum* of the learned judge has been overruled by more recent decisions, and the right of the public to land in such cases established. (*Fowler* v. *Mott*, 19 Barb. 204.) The same principle is laid down also by the English writers; for, with regard to a ferry, it is stated, that a ferry is as much a highway as a bridge; and that, therefore, the public have a right to embark and disembark at the landing places, provided such landing place be a highway. (Welb. on Highways, 35; *Peters* v. *Kendal*, 6 Barn. & Cress. 703.

*Canals.*—Canals, when authorized by public law, are public highways, with the right of tolls attached. (*Robinson* v. *Chamberlain*, 34 N. Y. R. 389.)

In this state, the state takes the fee of lands taken for the canals, and, upon abandonment, the use of the lands does not revert to the original owner. (*Rexford* v. *Knight*, 11 N. Y. R. 308.)

When a canal commissioner makes an alteration in a highway, under the power conferred by Revised Statutes (p. 221, § 19), which authorizes a commissioner, in charge of constructing or repairing a canal, to discontinue or alter any highway which interferes with the work, such commissioner does not exercise any power of appropriating lands in such way as to divest the owner of his title, and vest it in the state. No power is given to a canal commissioner to appropriate lands for the mere purpose of a common highway. It is a power given to be exercised as subordinate or auxiliary merely to the main power to construct, repair or improve a canal. This auxiliary power is of the same nature and kind precisely with that exercised by highway commissioners in the discontinuance and alteration of highways; and the highway, when altered by the canal commissioner, instead of the commissioner of highways, and changed to another location, would be nothing more nor less than a common highway, as it was before. If any portion of the new location should fall within the boundaries of the appropriation for the canal, the title in fee simple to the land, as to such portion, would be in the state; but, as to all other portions, the title to the land would remain in the owner, as before, subject to the public easement. The owner would no more lose his title to lands covered by a highway, thus altered and located, than he would to land covered by a highway laid out or altered in the usual manner. The title of the owner, subject only to the easement, remains perfect, not only to the land covered by the highway, but to all the material within its boundaries, except such as may be needed to build or to maintain the road. (*Higgins* v. *Reynolds*, 31 N. Y. R. 151.)

*Navigable river.*—A navigable river, common to all men, is a public highway, by water; and, if the water change its course, and make for itself a new channel, the right of way will continue through the new course. (10 Mod. 382; 4 Com. Dig. Chimin *A*, 1.)

By the common law, the ebb and flow of the tide was adopted as the criterion for determining what rivers were navigable; that is, all rivers in which the tide flowed and reflowed were held to be technically navigable, and belonged, of right, to the public, or sovereign power; while fresh rivers, or rivers where the tide did not flow and reflow, belonged to the adjacent owners, subject to the public easement of passage, if they were, in fact, navigable. (Hale De Jure Maris; *Ex parte Jennings*, 6 Cow. 518; *Morgan* v. *King*, 35 N. Y. R. 458.) This doctrine of the common law, though it has been recognized by some of our courts, cannot be regarded as the settled law of this state. In *The People* v. *The Canal Appraisers* (33 N. Y. R. 461), Mr. Justice Davies entered into a very learned and elaborate discussion of the subject of navigable streams; and, after a careful examination of the English and American authorities, lays down the proposition that the common law criterion of navigability is not the criterion in this state; but that a river, that is navigable in fact, belongs to the state, and that adjoining proprietors own only to the margin of the stream. The point at issue in the case, however, was as to whether the Mohawk river was a navigable river, in such sense as to vest the title to the bed of the river in the state; and as that question had been before decided in the affirmative (see *The Canal Appraisers* v. *The People*, 17 Wend. 571), the argument of the learned judge may be regarded as *obiter*, and the decision in the case as restricted to and applicable only to the Mohawk river. However, his examination of the cases is very exhaustive, and his conclusions are those of an able jurist.

As to what constitutes a river navigable in fact, it was the rule at common law that capacity for floating boats, lighters, or rafts, to market, was sufficient. (De Jure Maris; *Commissioners, etc.*, v. *Kempshall*, 26 Wend. 413.) But it has also been held in this country, that the public have *a right of way* in every stream which is capable, in its natural state and its ordinary volume of water, of transporting, in condition fit for market, the products of the forests or mines, or of the tillage of the soil upon its banks.

It is not essential to the right, that the property to be transported should be carried in vessels, or in some other mode, whereby it can be guided by the agency of man, provided it can ordinarily be carried safely without such guidance. Nor is it necessary that the stream should be capable of being thus navigated against its current, as well as in the direction of its current. If it is so far navigable or floatable, in its natural state and its ordinary capacity, as to be of public use in the transportation of property, the public claim to such use ought to be liberally supported. (*Morgan* v. *King*, 35 N. Y. R. 454; *Shaw* v. *Crawford*, 10 Johns. 236.)

Nor is it essential to the easement that the capacity of the stream, as above defined, should be continuous, or, in other words, that its ordinary state, *at all seasons of the year*, should be such as to make it navigable. If it is ordinarily subject to periodical fluctuations in the volume and height of its water, attributable to natural causes, and recurring as regularly as the seasons, and if its periods of high water or navigable capacity ordinarily continue a sufficient length of time to make it useful as a highway, it is subject to the public easement. (Id. *Browne* v. *Chadbourne*, 31 Maine, 9; see, however, *Munson* v. *Hungerford*, 6 Barb. 265; *Curtis* v. *Keesler*, 14 id. 511.)

But where it appeared that a stream was not capable of floating even single logs, except during seasons of highwater, which were about two months in a year, and that then the logs, so floated, had to be aided in their passage by men in skiffs or on shore; that the current was so broken and impeded by rapids and rocks that the logs were sometimes badly injured, and the ends were always more or less bruised up; and that the stream was used only occasionally for floating logs, etc., the court of appeals decided that such stream was not, in its natural state, a public highway, even within the liberal rules above laid down. (*Morgan* v. *King*, 35 N. Y. R. 460.)

The public have likewise a right to travel on a public river on the *ice;* and, therefore, if any one cuts holes through the ice upon or near the place where there has been a *winter-way* for twenty years, he is liable to the payment of all damages sustained thereby, by those traveling upon such way, without carelessness or fault on their part. (*French* v. *Camp*, 6 Shepl. [Me.] 438.)

A riparian proprietor does not make his water-course a public one, or subject to a public easement, by making it, at his own expense, and by artificial means, boatable. (*Wadsworth* v. *Smith*, 2 Fairb. 278.)

The legislature cannot, by declaring a river navigable, which is not so in fact, deprive the riparian owners of their rights to the use of the water for hydraulic and other purposes, without rendering compensation. (*Walker* v. *Board of Public Works*, 16 Ohio, 540.) Nor has the state a right, without compensation, to destroy the property of individuals situated upon rivers, above tide waters, in making waters navigable which are not so by nature, or to appropriate such waters to the public use by artificial erections or improvements. (Per Chancellor and Senator Allen in *Canal Commissioners* v. *The People*, 5 Wend. 423; see *Canal Appraisers* v. *People*, 17 id. 571; *Commissioners, etc.*, v. *Kempshall*, 20 id. 404.)

## CHAPTER II.

### COMMISSIONERS OF HIGHWAYS.



### SECTION I.

#### ELECTION.

There shall be chosen at the annual town meeting in each town one, two or three commissioners of highways. (1 R. S. 340, as amended 1866, ch. 30.) Such commissioners are to be chosen by ballot, and are to be electors of the town. (1 R. S. 343.)

*Number and term of office.*—The electors of each town shall have power, at their annual town meeting, to determine, by resolution, whether there shall be chosen one, two or three highway commissioners, and the number so determined upon shall be balloted for and chosen; and if only one be determined upon and chosen, he shall possess all the powers, and discharge all the duties, of commissioners of highways as prescribed by law, and shall hold his office for one year. And whenever three commissioners shall be chosen in any town, they shall be divided by lot by the canvassers, upon the result of the canvass, into three classes, to be numbered one, two and three; the term of office of the first class shall be one year, of the second, two, and of the third, three; and one commissioner only shall thereafter annually be elected in such town, who shall hold his office for three years, and until a successor shall be duly elected or appointed; but, in case any commissioner shall be elected to fill a vacancy, he shall hold the office only for the unexpired term which shall have become vacant; and, if two vacancies shall be required to be filled, the canvassers shall, after the canvass, determine by lot, as aforesaid, the terms they shall respectively hold. (Laws of 1845, ch. 180, as amended 1847, ch. 455.)

*Vacancy.*—And when any vacancy shall happen, by death, removal, resignation, neglect to qualify, or refusal to serve, it shall be supplied until the next succeeding annual town meeting by an appointment in writing, under the hands of any three justices of the peace, or two justices and the supervisor of the town. (Id.) (See form No. 1.)

*To administer oath.*—And every commissioner of highways shall be authorized to administer oaths to any witnesses or juries in proceedings which may be had by or before them. (Id.)

*Number, how changed.*—And, whenever any town shall have determined upon having three commissioners, and shall desire to return two or have but one, such town shall have the power so to do by a resolution taken at an annual town meeting; and when such resolution shall have been adopted, no other commissioner shall be elected or appointed until the term or terms of those in office at the time of adopting such resolution shall expire or become vacant; and they shall have power to act until their terms shall severally become vacant or expire, as fully as if the three continued in office. (Id.)

*To give bond.*—Every commissioner of highways hereafter to be elected or appointed shall, before entering upon his duties, and within ten days after notice of his election or appointment, execute to the supervisor of his town a bond, with two sureties, to be approved by the supervisor by an indorsement thereon, and filed with him, in the penal sum of one thousand dollars, conditioned that he will faithfully discharge his duties as such commissioner, and within ten days after the expiration of his term of office pay over to his successor what money may be remaining in his hands as such commissioner, and render to such successor a true account of all moneys received and paid out by him as such commissioner. (Laws of 1845, ch. 180.) (See form No. 2.)

The sureties to the above bond will be liable only for dereliction in duty during the term for which the commissioner was chosen at the time the obligation was entered into, and not for those which happen under his re-appointment. (See *Kingston Mut. Ins. Co.* v. *Clark*, 33 Barb. 196.)

In case of default on the part of the commissioner, the bond is to be prosecuted by the supervisor of the town. (*Jansen* v. *Ostrander*, 1 Cow. 670; *Fuller* v *Fullerton*, 14 Barb. 59.)

*Vacancies, how filled.*—In case a vacancy happens from any cause, it is to be filled by three justices of the town, or two justices and the supervisor, who are to make their appointment in writing, and the appointee is to serve till the next succeeding annual town meeting. When two vacancies are to be filled, and two persons are appointed, without a designation as to the class to which they shall respectively belong, the one first named in the appointment is to be regarded as appointed to serve the shorter term. (*People* v. *Supervisors of Richmond Co.*, 20 N. Y. R. 252.)

Where there is a failure to elect commissioners at the annual town meeting in consequence of a *tie* in the vote, and the meeting adjourns without making an election, the justices may appoint a suitable person to the office, who, and a person subsequently elected at a special town meeting, is entitled to hold the office. (*People* v. *Van Horne*, 18 Wend. 515.)

At the town meeting next succeeding the appointment, a person is to be elected to fill the vacancy for the unexpired term.

*To take oath.*—Every person chosen or appointed to the office of commissioner of highways, before he enters on the duties of his office, and within ten days after he shall be notified of his election or appointment, shall take and subscribe, before some justice of the peace or commissioner of deeds, the oath of office prescribed in the sixth article of the constitution of this state. (1 R. S. 345.) Such oath shall be administered without reward, and the justice or commissioner before whom the same shall be taken shall also, without reward, certify in writing the day and year when the same was taken, and shall deliver such certificate to the person by whom the oath was taken. (Id.) The oath may also be subscribed and sworn before the town clerk of the town in which such officer shall be elected. Such oath shall be administered and certified without fee or reward. (Laws of 1838, ch. 172.) Acts designating persons to administer the oath of office to officers are held to be merely directory. (3 Hill, 42; 4 E. D. Smith, 430.) The commissioner of highways taking the oath, within eight days thereafter, shall cause the certificate to be filed in the office of the town clerk. (1 R.

S. 345.) If any person chosen commissioner of highways shall not take and subscribe such oath, and cause the certificate thereof to be filed as above required, such neglect shall be deemed a refusal to serve. (Id.) But, if he enters upon the duties of his office before he shall have taken such oath, he shall forfeit to the town the sum of fifty dollars. (1 R. S. 347.) If his name appears on the poll-list, that is to be deemed a sufficient notice of his election; but, if not, he is entitled to a notice of his election from the town clerk of the town within ten days after the meeting at which he is chosen. (See form 3.)

*Penalty for refusing to serve.*—If any person chosen or appointed to the office of commissioner of highways shall refuse to serve he shall forfeit to the town the sum of fifty dollars. (1 R. S. 347.)

*Resignation.*—One of three justices of the peace of a town may, for sufficient cause shown, accept the resignation of any commissioner of highways. (1 R. S. 348.)

*Two may act.*—Any two commissioners of highways of any town may make any order in execution of the powers conferred in this title, provided it shall appear in the order filed by them, that all the commissioners of highways of the town met and deliberated on the subject embraced in such order, or were duly notified to attend a meeting of the commissioners for the purpose of deliberating thereon. (1 R. S. 525, § 125.)

An order made by two commissioners, where there are three in office, must show *on its* face, either that the third commissioner met with his associates and that he participated in their deliberations, even if he did not concur in their conclusions, or that he was notified, not only of the intended meeting, but of the particular subject on which it was proposed to deliberate. (*People* v. *Williams*, 36 N. Y. R. 441.)

## SECTION II.

### GENERAL POWERS AND DUTIES.

The commissioners of highways in the several towns in this state shall have the care and superintendence of the highways and bridges therein; and it shall be their duty,

1. To give directions for the repairing of the roads and bridges within their respective towns:

2. To regulate the roads already laid out, and to alter such of them as they, or a majority of them, shall deem inconvenient:

3. To cause such of the roads used as highways, as shall have been laid out but not sufficiently described, and such as shall have been used for twenty years, but not recorded, to be ascertained, described and entered of record in the town clerk's office:

4. To cause the highways, and the bridges which are or may be erected over streams intersecting highways, to be kept in repair:

5. To divide their respective towns into so many road districts as they shall judge convenient, by writing under their hands, to be lodged with the town clerk, and by him to be entered into the town book; such division to be made annually, if they shall think it necessary, and in all cases to be made at least ten days before the annual town meeting:

6. To assign to each of the said road districts such of the inhabitants liable to work on highways, as they shall think proper, having regard to proximity

of residence as much as may be; provided, however, that, whenever the commissioners of any town shall have neglected, for the period of one year, at any time after any public road or highway shall have been laid out, and title thereto acquired by due process of law, to open or work the same, or any part thereof, and whenever any number of inhabitants of any town in or through which the said road has been laid out shall have given ten days' notice to the commissioners of said town that they desire to apply the whole or any part of their highway labor to the working of said road, the said commissioners shall forthwith assign the said inhabitants to such road, direct the highway labor for which they are annually assessed to be applied to the same, and cause the same to be worked and put in good order for vehicles and travelers, within one year, under the direction of any of the said inhabitants whom such commissioners may appoint as an overseer of the labor so to be applied to such road; and when the number of days of labor assessed in the current year to such inhabitants, as their annual highway tax, is not sufficient to put such road in good order, as aforesaid, then the said inhabitants may anticipate the whole or any part of the highway labor assessed, and to be assessed, against them for a period not exceeding three years; but from no one of the districts into which the said town is divided shall more than one-half of its annual labor be taken and applied to any road not embraced in said district; and,

7. To require the overseers of highways, from time to time, and as often as they shall deem necessary, to warn all persons assessed to work on highways to come and work thereon, with such implements, carriages, cattle or sleds as the said commissioners, or any one of them, shall direct. (1 R. S. 501, § 1.)

The commissioners have the general control and oversight of all highways and bridges in their town; but they have no power over other officers intrusted with duties in relation to highways, except as given by statute.

By "highways and bridges" are meant public highways and bridges; not those made by individuals, unless they have become *public* by the acts of the individuals, or by the commissioners, in the manner set forth in the statute.

By subdivision one, it is the duty of the commissioners, and they have the authority, to direct the overseer as to the general manner he shall improve the roads or bridges in his district; as, for instance, the grade of the road, how drained or leveled, or in what manner a bridge shall be repaired.

The overseer is subordinate to the commissioners. The principal duties of the overseers are to warn persons to work, to see that they do work, and to collect fines and commutation money. The commissioners have the exclusive control in directing the manner in which bridges shall be repaired; and on this subject are the persons responsible to the public, and not the overseers. (*Bartlett* v. *Crozier*, 17 Johns. 452.)

If an overseer of highways shall refuse or neglect to perform any of the duties enjoined on him by the commissioners, he shall forfeit the sum of ten dollars for each refusal or neglect, to be sued for by the commissioners, and to be by them applied in making and improving the roads and bridges in the town. (1 R. S. 504.)

An overseer, however, is liable for not removing obstructions in the highway, although not specially required by the commissioners. (*McFadden* v. *Kinsbury*, 11 Wend. 667.)

By the second subdivision, the commissioners are required to *regulate and alter*, that is, to restore, the boundaries and fences of a highway to its original lines; and if it passes by or through an inconvenient place, they may change its location; but if, in making the alteration, it is necessary to take more or other lands, damages must be paid, and the same course taken as on an original location of a new road. (*Bartlett* v. *Crozier*, 17 Johns. 447; 1 R. S. 504.)

*To ascertain, describe, and enter of record.*—The third subdivision of the above quoted section authorizes the commissioners, in their respective towns, to cause such of the roads as are not already described and recorded, to be ascertained, described, and entered of record. This authority necessarily implies and presupposes an omission of some of the requisites to the establishment of a public highway.

In the case of *The People* v. *Judges of Cortland County* (24 Wend. 491), the commissioners of highways of Cortlandville made an order adjudging that a certain road in that town, particularly designated, *had been used as a public highway for twenty years, but had not been recorded;* and they thereupon proceeded *to ascertain, describe, and enter the road of record*, in the town clerk's office. Peck appealed to the judges. From the return it appeared that the commissioners, in their order, declared the road to be *three* rods wide; and they insisted, before the judges, that this was the width originally intended. It was proved, before the judges, that the road never was opened more than *two* rods wide. Judge BRONSON says: "This provision does not authorize the commissioners to say what was 'originally intended,' either by the owner of the soil or any one else, in relation to the width or location of the road, any further than such intention has been manifested by permitting the way to be used. It is a power in relation to the road *as it actually exists*, and *has existed* for the last twenty years. It does not authorize the commissioners to create or enlarge, but only to perpetuate the evidence of a public right. Both the *extent* and *fact* of dedication depend on the user; and the public must take *secundum forma doni*. On the facts returned by the judges, it is clear that the commissioners exceeded their powers; and the only question is, whether Peck had a remedy by appeal."

A road which has been previously laid out, but not in conformity with the law, and which has been used for a number of years, though less than twenty, and is afterward ascertained and recorded by the commissioners, becomes a public highway, so as to justify one in passing over it. (*Colden* v. *Thurber*, 2 Johns. 424.)

The duty of ascertaining, describing and recording, under the above section, belongs exclusively to the commissioners, and not to a jury called to determine a disputed question of encroachment. The power of the commissioners is limited to ascertaining the boundaries of the road, according to the actual use for the twenty years. They have no right, in the exercise of this power, to alter and change the boundaries with reference to public convenience. (*Talmage* v. *Hunting*, 29 N. Y. R. 447.)

The intention of the owner of the land, in permit ting a user for twenty years, is not material. Such a user of land for that period makes it a public highway, under the statute, though the owner be a lunatic, an infant, or a married woman, and has no knowledge thereof during the entire time. (*Devenpeck* v. *Lambert*, 44 Barb. 596.)

If a road has been opened, used and worked substantially as laid out, though not of the entire width, for a period of thirty years, it is, nevertheless, a highway of full statute width; and the commissioners have the right to ascertain, describe and record it as of that width, and to open it and remove obstructions. (*Walker* v. *Caywood*, 31 N. Y. R. 51.)

The commissioners act in a ministerial capacity in ascertaining, describing and recording a road; and no appeal lies from their proceedings. (*People* v. *Judges of Cortland County*, 24 Wend. 491.) What remedy an aggrieved party would have, was referred to in the above case, but not decided.

*To cause the highways and bridges to be kept in repair.*—The fourth subdivision requires the commissioners to cause the highways and the bridges which are or may be erected over streams intersecting highways, to be kept in repair. The commissioners, as the general superintendents of the highways and bridges of the town, are primarily responsible for their condition; although it is likewise made the duty of the overseers to keep the highways within their respective districts in order. (1 R. S. 503.) All the powers of the overseers are subordinate to, and under the superior control of, the orders of the commissioners, whom they are bound to obey.

The overseers have no concern with bridges erected over streams, except so far as they are directed, generally, to execute the orders of the commissioners. In the case of *Bartlett* v. *Crozier* (17 Johns. 449), Chancellor KENT says: "In short, it appears, from a careful examination of the several provisions of the act, that the commissioners, and not the overseers, of highways, are the responsible persons in respect to the erection and repair of bridges. The overseers have nothing to do with bridges, but in the single instance in which they receive fines and commutation money, or other money, under the order of the commissioners."

The commissioners' obligation in repairing bridges extends not only to the floor of the bridge, but to the providing of proper guards or railings on the sides or borders, when necessary for the protection of the public. (*Hyatt* v. *Trustees of Rondout*, 44 Barb. 391.)

All public bridges are, *prima facie*, repairable by the commissioners of highways, without distinction of foot, horse or carriage bridges, unless they can show that others are bound to repair particular bridges. But, where a bridge has been erected solely for private use, although it may be used by the public, the one who erected it must keep it in repair; as where a man digs a ditch or canal across the highway, and makes a bridge over it. In such case, although the public would have to use the bridge in traveling the highway, yet they would derive no benefit from it, since the way was as good before the bridge was built as after it, and are not bound to maintain it. (*Dygert* v. *Schenck*, 23 Wend. 446.) But, if the bridge be built over a natural stream, and the public cross and recross thereon, the town should keep it in repair, although it was built for the private benefit of the builder. (Id.) A company lawfully cutting a canal across a highway, for its own purposes, is bound to build and keep in repair a bridge across it, and so maintain the highway. (*Heacock* v. *Sherman*, 14 Wend. 58.)

It is unquestionably true that the highway officers of a town are not required to grade the whole space within the limits of the highway, so that a traveler can safely drive his carriage over every part of it. In ordinary cases, if they provide a pathway for carriages of suitable width, and so define it as that there shall be no reasonable danger of its being mistaken, they will not be in fault if a traveler chooses to try an experiment upon the part which is not thus prepared for traveling. (*Ireland* v. *Oswego, etc., Plank Road Co.*, 13 N. Y. R. 531, per DENIO, C. J., and cases cited.)

But where a road is so constructed or altered as to present, at one point, two paths, both of which exhibit the appearance of having been used by travelers, and one of them leads to a dangerous precipice, while the other is quite safe, it is the duty of those having charge of the road to indicate, in a manner not to be mistaken by day or night, that the unsafe path is to be avoided; and, if it cannot be otherwise done, to put up such obstructions as will turn the traveler from the wrong track. (Id.)

The commissioners are not bound to build or repair highways or bridges when not in funds to defray the expense, and, in such case, a mandamus will not lie to compel them to make such repairs. (*People* v. *Comrs. of Hudson*, 7 Wend. 474; *Garlinghouse* v. *Jacob*, 29 N.Y. R. 303, and cases; *Barker* v. *Loomis*, 6 Hill, 619.)

And where there are several bridges out of repair, and the commissioners have only money enough for the repair of a part, they have a discretion as to which of the bridges they will repair, and an action will not lie against them for not repairing any particular one. (Id.)

*Liability for not keeping highways and bridges in repair.*— Whether an action will lie against the commissioners at the suit of an individual who has sustained injury by reason of their neglect to keep the highways and bridges in a proper state of repair, when they have the necessary funds, is not clearly settled in this state.

In the case of *Bartlett* v. *Crozier* (17 Johns. 437), which was an action against *overseers* of highways, for neglect to repair a bridge whereby the plaintiff was injured, Chancellor Kent, after holding that the action would not lie against the overseers, they not being responsible for the repair of bridges, expressed the opinion that such action would not lie even against the commissioners. Speaking of the duty imposed by the statute upon town commissioners in respect to roads and bridges of the town, the chancellor says: "There is no certain, stable, absolute duty in the case. It is not like the case of an individual bound by a private statute, or by a certain tenure, to keep a road or bridge in repair, nor like the case of turnpike companies. There the duty is perfect and binding at all times, and is founded on a valuable consideration. The roads and bridges must, at all events, be kept in repair, according to ordinary diligence. It is a condition of the grant. The duty is not casual or contingent, but inevitable. In the case, however, of these commissioners and overseers, the duty depends upon a train of circumstances; it is very indefinite, and is varied and regulated by their discretion. There is not that precision and certainty of duty that ought to make them responsible to individuals to any extent and for any damage. The law has not supplied them with the pecuniary means, or armed them with the coercive requisite to meet and sustain such an enormous and dangerous responsibility. The argument to be drawn from the English law on the subject is very strong against the right of action. There are officers under the English law, equally as under ours, charged with repairing the roads and bridges; they have existed and been known from ancient times, and yet there is no case in the English books, nor any precedent under our colony government, of any such private action. This affords a very strong presumption that no such action will lie."

In the case of *Adsit* v. *Brady* (4 Hill, 630), which was an action against the superintendent of repairs, for damages sustained by the plaintiff by reason of the defendant's not having kept the canal in good repair, the court laid down the broad proposition, that, "When an individual sustains an injury by the misfeasance or non-feasance of a public officer who acts, or omits to act, contrary to his duty, the law gives redress to the injured party by an action adapted to the nature of the case." Judge Sandford, in speaking of this case in *Hutson* v. *The city of New York* (5 Sandf. 289), says: "The liability was taken for granted by the distinguished judge who delivered the opinion of the court, without discussion or reference to authority, and yet, so far as we know, there is no reported adjudication, either in this state or in England, which sustains a private action in such a case; and, with much deference, we submit that a decision making such a great stride in asserting the liability of public officers is not entitled to the full weight of authority when it appears not to have been made upon grave argument and mature consideration." This commentary was approved in *West* v. *Trustees of Brockport* (16 N. Y. R. 161.) In the latter case, Judge Selden, after a careful review of the authorities, took the ground that commissioners are not liable in a civil action for a mere omission to keep the highways of their town in repair; and his opinion was adopted as the opinion of the court in the case of *Hickok* v. *Trustees of Plattsburgh*, (16 N. Y. R. 161.) The position taken is, that, where an officer has been appointed, not for the public in general, but for individuals in particular, and from each individual receives an equivalent for the services rendered, he may be responsible, in a private action, for neglect of duty; but, where the officer acts for the public in general, the appropriate remedy for his neglect of duty is a public prosecution. The proposition laid down in *Adsit* v. *Brady* (*supra*), was also disapproved of by Wright, J., in *Garlinghouse* v. *Jacobs*. After a careful review of the authorities, that learned judge says: "I am of the opinion, therefore, that town commissioners of highways are in no event liable to a private action for a mere neglect or omission to keep the highways of their towns in repair." Although the question was not necessarily involved in the case, it appearing that there were not sufficient funds, yet, from the note of the reporter added to the case, it appears that a majority of the judges concurred with Judge Wright on this point.

The case of *Smith* v. *Wright* (24 Barb. 170), however, holds a contrary doctrine, based mainly on the proposition advanced in *Adsit* v. *Brady*, above cited. The question came directly before the court at special term, and Davies, J., held that commissioners of highways were liable to a civil action at the suit of a person who had sustained injuries through their neglect to keep the highways and bridges in repair where they had, or might have had, the necessary funds for such repairs. In the late case of *Robinson* v. *Chamberlain* (34 N. Y. R. 380), the opinion of Peckham, J., sustains the doctrine of *Adsit* v. *Brady* and *Smith* v. *Wright*, though the question was not necessarily involved, and was not passed upon, in the other opinions.

Whether or not commissioners are liable to a private action for neglect to keep the highways in repair, there is no doubt about their liability to be indicted for such neglect. (Per Nelson, J., in *People* v. *Cor-*

*poration of Albany*, 11 Wend. 539; per Wright, J., in *Garlinghouse* v. *Jacobs*, 29 N. Y. R. 305; per Beardsley, J., in *Wilson* v. *Mayor of New York*, 1 Denio, 599.)

In an indictment, however, against commissioners of highways for neglect of duty in not repairing a highway or bridge, it must be averred that they had the requisite funds in their hands, or other specific means provided by law for that purpose. (*People* v. *Com'r of Highways of Hudson*, 7 Wend. 474; *People* v. *Adsit*, 2 Hill, 619; *Barker* v. *Loomis*, 6 id. 463.)

Supposing a civil action will lie against commissioners for a neglect of duty, the same allegations should be set forth in the complaint. (*Smith* v. *Wright*, 27 Barb. 621; per Sandford, J., in *Hutson* v. *City of New York*, 5 Sandf. 315; but see *Adsit* v. *Brady*, 4 Hill, 630.)

The complaint ought to state specifically every fact requisite to enable the court to judge whether there has been a breach of duty. (Per Kent, Chancellor, in *Bartlett* v. *Crozier*, 17 Johns. 456.)

A town is in no event liable to a civil action for injuries sustained through the negligence of its officers to keep the highways in repair. The obligation of a town to maintain the highways is wholly the creature of the statute, and is not of that absolute character which is essential to make them liable to a private action for an injury springing from their neglect to perform it. (*Morey* v. *Newfane*, 8 Barb. 645; *Town of Galen* v. *Clyde, etc.*, 27 id. 543.)

This, however, is not the rule with regard to incorporated villages and cities. Civil actions will lie against them for a failure to keep their streets and highways in a proper state of repair, provided it is by the charter made the duty of the city officers to maintain the highways. (*Conrad* v. *Trustees of*

*Ithaca*, 16 N. Y. R. 158; *Hickok* v. *Trustees of Plattsburgh*, id. 161: *Wendall* v. *Mayor of Troy*, 39 Barb. 329; *Hyatt* v. *Trustees of Rondout*, 44 id. 385.)

*To divide town into road districts, etc.* — Subdivision five of the section before cited requires commissioners to divide their respective towns into so many road districts as they shall judge convenient, by writing under their hands, to be lodged with the town clerk, and by him to be entered in the town book; such division to be made annually, if they shall think it necessary, and in all cases to be made at least ten days before the annual town meeting.

Whenever a highway is laid out on a line between two towns, the commissioners of each of such towns are required to divide it into two or more road districts, in such manner that the labor and expense of opening, working and keeping in repair such highway, through each of the said districts, may be equal, as near as may be, and to allot an equal number of the said districts to each of the said towns. (1 R. S. 516, § 74.)

Each district shall be considered as wholly belonging to the town to which it shall be allotted, for the purpose of opening and improving the road, and for keeping it in repair; and the commissioners shall cause such highway, and the partition and allotment thereof, to be recorded in the office of the town clerk in each of their respective towns. (Id. § 75.)

All highways heretofore laid out upon the line between any two towns shall be divided, allotted, recorded and kept in repair in the manner above directed. (Id. § 76.)

The order dividing the town into road districts must be made upon a meeting and conference of all the commissioners, though the signature of two will be sufficient. Where two only sign, however, the order should state that it had been made upon a meeting and conference of all the commissioners, or that the third had been duly notified to attend, for the particular purpose of making a division of the town. (1 R. S. 525; § 125; *People* v. *Williams*, 36 N. Y. R. 441.) (See form No. 5.)

*To divide roads between cities, towns and villages.*—Whenever a highway, street or road shall be on the line between a city, town and village, or between either of them, the officers authorized and required to repair and keep in order the highways, streets and roads in such city, town and village, shall meet together at the mayor's office in such city, if said highway, street or road be on the line between a city and town, or a city and village, or at the office of the town clerk of such town, if the same be on the line between a town and village, on the first Monday of May in each year, at twelve o'clock M., and divide such highway, street or road, and allot one part thereof to such city, and the other to such town or village, or one part thereof to such town and the other to such village, as the case may be, in such manner that the labor and expense of working and keeping in repair such highway, street or road may be equal as near as may be. (Laws of 1870, ch. 311, § 1.)

Upon the neglect or failure to attend on the part of the officers of any city, town or village, at the time or places designated in the first section of this act, for the purposes therein mentioned, the officers of the city, town or village present may perform the said duty, and, when done, the divisions thus made shall be of the same force and effect as if made by the joint action of such city and town, or such city and village, or such town and village. (Id. § 2.)

The statement of the division made pursuant to the provisions of the first or second section of this act shall be reduced to writing and properly authenticated by the officers making the same, and shall be filed, within ten days after such division is made, in the offices of the city clerk of the city, of the town clerk of the town, and of the clerk of the village, between whom such division has been made. (Id. § 3.)

*To assign inhabitants to work.*—Subdivision six requires the commissioners to assign to each of the said road districts such of the inhabitants liable to work on highways as they shall think proper, having regard to proximity of residence as much as may be: *provided, however*, that whenever the commissioners of any town shall have neglected for the period of one year, at any time after any public road or highway shall have been laid out, and title thereto acquired by due process of law, to open or work the same, or any part thereof; and whenever any number of inhabitants of any town, in or through which the said road has been laid out, shall have given ten days' notice to the commissioners of said town that they desire to apply the whole or any part of their highway labor to the working of said road, the said commissioners shall forthwith assign the said inhabitants to such road, direct the highway labor for which they are annually assessed to be applied to the same, and cause the same to be worked and put in good order for vehicles and travelers within one year, under the direction of any of the said inhabitants whom such commissioners may appoint as an overseer of the labor so to be applied to such road; and when the number of days' labor assessed in the current year to such inhabitants, as their annual highway tax, is not sufficient to put such road in good order, as aforesaid, then the said inhabitants may anticipate the whole or any part of the highway labor assessed, and to be assessed, against them for a period not exceeding three years; but from no one of the districts into which the said town is divided shall more than one-half of its annual labor be taken and applied to any road not embraced in said district.

*To require overseers to give warning.*—Subdivision seven directs the commissioners to require the overseers of highways from time to time, and as often as they shall deem necessary, to warn all persons assessed to work on highways to come and work thereon, with such implements, carriages, cattle or sleds as the said commissioners, or any one of them, shall direct.

This duty is usually performed by delivering the tax list to the overseers. Where the overseers neglect to perform their duty, the commissioners should give them a special requirement.

*To lay out and discontinue roads.*—The commissioners of highways shall have power, in the manner and under the restrictions hereinafter provided, to lay out, on actual survey, such new roads in their respective towns as they may deem necessary and proper; and to discontinue such old roads and highways as shall appear to them, on the oaths of twelve freeholders of the same town, to have become unnecessary. (1 R. S. 502, § 2.) See, *post*, chapters on laying out and discontinuing highways.

*To render account to board of auditors.*—The commissioners of highways of each town shall render to the board of town auditors, at their annual meeting for auditing the accounts of town officers, an account in writing, stating,

1. The labor assessed and performed in such town.

2. The sums received by such commissioners for fines and commutations, and all other moneys received under this chapter.

3. The improvements which have been made on the roads and bridges, in their town, during the year immediately preceding such report, and an account of the state of such roads and bridges; and,

4. A statement of the improvements necessary to be made on such roads and bridges, and an estimate of the probable expense of making such improvements, beyond what the labor to be assessed in that year will accomplish. (1 R. S. 503, § 3.) (See form No. 6.)

The annual meeting of the town auditors referred to is that held on the Tuesday preceding the annual town meeting.

*To account for moneys.*—The commissioners of highways in each town of this state, and all town officers who receive or disburse any moneys belonging to their respective towns, shall, on the last Tuesday preceding the annual town meeting of their town, account with the board of town auditors of such town for all moneys received and disbursed by them by virtue of their offices. (Laws of 1863, ch. 172.)

The said board of town auditors shall make a statement of such accounts, and append thereto a certificate, to be signed by a majority of the board, showing the state of the accounts of the said highway commissioners and other officers at the date of the certificate; which statement and certificate shall be filed with the town clerk of the town, and be by him produced at the next annual town meeting, and publicly read. (Id.) (See form No. 7.)

## SECTION III.

### MONEY FOR REPAIR, HOW RAISED.

The commissioners of highways of each town shall deliver to the supervisor of such town a statement of the improvements necessary to be made on the roads and bridges, together with the probable expense thereof; which supervisor shall lay the same before the board of supervisors at their next meeting. The board of supervisors shall cause the amount so estimated to be assessed, levied and collected, in such town, in the same manner as other town charges; but the moneys to be raised in any such town shall not exceed, in any one year, the sum of two hundred and fifty dollars. (1 R. S. 502, § 4.) (See form No. 8.)

It is the duty also of the supervisor to lay before the board of supervisors the statements of the commissioners of highways in relation to the improvements necessary to be made on the roads and bridges; and it is the duty of the board to raise the amount as estimated, provided it be within the sum limited.

In 1832 the following provision was made for raising an additional sum:

Whenever the commissioners of highways of any town in this state shall be of opinion that the sum of two hundred and fifty dollars, as now allowed by law, will be insufficient to pay the expenses actually necessary for the improvement of roads and bridges, it shall be lawful for such commissioners to apply, in open town meeting, for a vote authorizing such additional sum to be raised as they may deem necessary for the purpose aforesaid, not exceeding two hundred and fifty dollars, in addition to the sum now allowed by law. (Laws of 1832, ch. 274, § 1.)

Before making such application, it shall be the duty of the commissioners to give notice of their intended application, by posting the same in a conspicuous manner, in at least five of the most public places in such town, at least four weeks next preceding the annual town meeting; such notice shall specify the amount to be applied for, and the purposes to which the same is to be appropriated, with the probable amount necessary to be expended at each place, if there shall be more than one. (Id. § 2.) (See form 9.)

Whenever any application for a grant of moneys for the purposes mentioned in the first section of this act, shall be made to any town meeting, it shall be the duty of the commissioners making the same to exhibit a statement of their accounts, and an estimate of the expenses necessary for the improvement of roads and bridges in such town the ensuing year. (Id. § 3.)

If the town meeting shall, by their votes, determine that a sum, over and above the amount now allowed by law, will be necessary for the improvement of roads and bridges, or to pay any balance that may be due, the clerk shall enter such resolution as shall be agreed to in the minutes of the meeting, and deliver a copy thereof to the supervisor of the town, who shall lay the same before the board of supervisors, at their next annual meeting; and it shall be their duty to cause the amount specified in such resolution to be levied and collected in the same manner as other town charges of such town. (Id. § 4.)

If any town shall, at an annual meeting, have already voted to raise a sum exceeding two hundred and fifty dollars, for the purposes aforesaid, it shall be the duty of the board of supervisors of the county in which such town is situated to assess, levy and collect the sum so voted to be raised upon said town. (Id. § 5.)

Again, by subdivision five of section first of chapter 314 of the Laws of 1838, it is provided, that the board of supervisors of each county shall have power "to cause to be levied, collected and paid, in the manner now provided by law, such sum of money, in addition to the sum now allowed by law, not exceeding five hundred dollars in any one year, as a majority of the qualified voters of any town may, at any legal town meeting, have voted to be raised upon their town, for constructing or repairing roads and bridges in such town."

No money shall be raised under the authority conferred by the fifth subdivision of the preceding section (which is the subdivision cited above), unless a written notice of the application to such town meeting to raise such amount shall be posted on the door of the house where the town meeting is to be held, and also at three public places in such town, for two weeks before the town meeting, and be also openly read to the electors present immediately after the opening of the meeting. (Id. § 2.) (See form No. 9.)

In 1857, a further act was passed, which provides that,

"Whenever the commissioners of highways of any town in this state shall be of opinion that the sum now provided by law will be insufficient to pay the expenses actually necessary for the improvement of roads and bridges, and to pay any balance that may be due for such improvement, it shall be lawful for such commissioners to apply in open town meeting for a vote authorizing such additional sum to be raised as they may deem necessary for the purposes aforesaid, not exceeding seven hundred and fifty dollars in addition to the sum now allowed by law. The same notice shall be given by the commissioners of their intention to apply for the raising of such additional sum as is now required by law for the raising of money for roads and bridges above the amount of two hundred and fifty dollars." (Laws of 1857, ch. 615, § 1.) (See form No. 9.)

*Supervisors may authorize town to borrow money.* In 1849 the board of supervisors in each county were empowered "to authorize any town in such county, by a vote of such town, to borrow any sum of money, not exceeding four thousand dollars in one year, to build or repair any roads or bridges in such town, and prescribe the time for payment of the same, which time shall be within ten years, and for assessing the principal and interest upon such town." (Laws of 1849, ch. 194, § 4, sub. 9.)

Such authority can be granted by the board only on a vote of a majority of all the members elected in the county. (Id. § 5.)

Again, an act passed in 1869 (chapter 855), "To extend the powers of boards of supervisors," provides as follows:

The boards of supervisors of each county in this state, except New York and Kings, shall have power, at their annual meeting, or at any other regular meeting, to authorize the supervisors of any town in such county, by and with the consent of the commissioner or commissioners of highways, town clerk and justices of the peace of such town, to borrow such sums of money, for and on the credit of such town, as the said town officers may deem necessary to build or repair any road or roads, or bridge or bridges, in such town, or which shall be partly in such town and partly in an adjoining town, or to pay any existing debt incurred in good faith by or on behalf of such town for such purpose before the passage of this act; and the said board of supervisors shall have power to prescribe the form of obligation to be issued on any such loan, and the time and place of payment, the time not to exceed ten years from the date of such obligation, and the rate of interest thereon not exceeding seven per cent per annum. And the said board of supervisors shall have power and it shall be their duty from time to time, as the said obligation shall become due and payable, to impose upon the taxable property of such town sufficient tax to pay the said principal and interest of such obligations according to the terms and conditions thereof.

*In case roads and bridges are damaged or destroyed.*—In case any road or roads, bridge or bridges shall be damaged or destroyed by the elements or otherwise, after any town meeting shall have been held, and since the fifteenth day of February, A. D. eighteen hundred and sixty-five, then, and in that case, it shall be lawful for the commissioner or commissioners of highways, by and with the consent of the board of town auditors, or a majority thereof, of the town or towns in which such road or roads, bridge or bridges shall be situated, to cause the same to be immediately repaired or rebuilt, although the expenditure of money required may exceed the sum now authorized to be raised by law upon the taxable property of the town or towns for such purposes; and the commissioners of highways shall present the proper vouchers for the expense thereof to the town auditors, at their next annual meeting, and the said bill shall be audited by them, and the amount audited thereon shall be collected in the same manner as amounts voted at town meetings as now required. The commissioners acting under this act, shall be entitled to receive for each day's service actually rendered, two dollars. (Laws, 1858, ch. 103, as amended 1865, ch. 42.)

The board of town auditors may be convened in special session by the supervisor, or, in his absence, the town clerk, upon the written request of any commissioner of highways, and the bills and expenses incurred in the erection or repairs of any such roads or bridges may then be presented to and audited by such board of town auditors; and the supervisor and town clerk shall issue a certificate, to be subscribed by them, setting forth the amount so audited and allowed, and in whose favor, and the nature of the work done and material furnished; and such certificate shall bear interest from its date, and the amount thereof, with interest, shall be levied and collected in the same manner as other town expenses. (Id. § 2.)

No account for services rendered or material furnished according to the provisions of this act, shall be allowed by such board, unless the same shall be accompanied by the affidavit of the party or parties performing such labor or furnishing such material, nor unless the commissioner or commissioners shall certify that such service has been actually performed, and such material was actually furnished, and that the same was so performed or furnished by the request of said commissioner or commissioners, and such board of auditors may require and take such other proof as they may deem proper to establish any claim for such labor and material and the value therefor. (Id. § 3.)

## SECTION IV.

### THEIR DUTY AS FENCE VIEWERS.

The commissioners of highways and assessors elected in every town shall, by virtue of their offices, be fence viewers of their town. (1 R. S. 340.)

The duties of fence viewers pertain to division and other fences, to floating timber, to strays, and to sheep killed by dogs. These duties will be described in the order in which they are stated.

The statute provides that where two or more persons shall have lands adjoining, each of them shall make and maintain a just and equal proportion of the division fence between them, in all cases where one-half or more of each of such adjoining farms or lands shall be cleared or improved. (1 R. S. 353, § 30, as amended 1866, ch. 540.)

The provisions of this statute are not limited to *owners*, but are for the benefit of any persons interested—as tenants. (*Bronk* v. *Becker*, 17 Wend. 320.)

Where two or more persons shall have lands adjoining, and not within the provisions of section thirty of said article, as hereby amended, each of them shall make and maintain a just and equal proportion of the division fence between them, except the owner or owners of either of the adjoining lands shall choose to let such land lie open to the public. If he shall afterward inclose it, he shall refund to the owner of the adjoining land a just proportion of the value, at that time, of any division fence that shall have been made and maintained by such adjoining owner, or he shall build his proportion of such division fence. (Id.)

Before a party can claim that he has chosen to let his lands lie open to the public, he must give the adjoining owners, or the fence viewers, notice that he has so chosen, upon his being requested to build his share of the fence. The fact that he has never fenced his land, and has only used it for a wood and timber lot, will not establish that he has elected to let the same lie open. (*Perkins* v. *Perkins*, 44 Barb. 134.)

There must be some act that amounts to a license to the people of the town, to go upon it and allow their cattle to feed upon it without being trespassers. (Id.)

Where a person shall have a farm or land lying open, one-half or more of such farm or land being cleared or improved, he shall refund to the owner of the adjoining land a just proportion of the value at the time this act shall take effect, of any division fence that shall have been made and maintained by such adjoining owner, or he shall build his proportion of such division fence. (1 R. S. 353, § 32, as amended, Laws of 1866, ch. 540.)

The Revised Statutes (1 R. S. 353, § 32) provides that two of the fence viewers may determine the value of the fence already built, where an owner inclosed his lands after letting them lie open. (See *Hewitt* v. *Watkins*, 11 Barb. 409.) But the section quoted above, substituted for the thirty-second section, makes no such provision, and the value can probably only be recovered by action.

*Disputes, how settled.*—If dispute arises between the owners of adjoining lands, concerning the proportion or particular part of fence to be maintained or made by either of them, such dispute shall be settled by any two of the fence viewers of the town. (1 R. S. 353.)

The only disputes which fence viewers are empowered to settle are such as respects the proportion or particular part of the fence which is to be maintained or made by the respective owners of adjoining lands. Where one of the parties is bound by grant, covenant, presumption, or in any other way, to build the whole of the fence, the fence viewers have no jurisdiction. (*Adams* v. *Van Alstyne*, 25 N. Y. R. 232.)

This statute is for the benefit of tenants as well as *owners*, and they may take the same proceedings as land owners for an apportionment of a division fence. (*Bronk* v. *Becker*, 17 Wend. 320.)

*Proceedings.*—When any of the above mentioned matters shall be submitted to fence viewers, each party shall choose one; and if either neglect, after eight days' notice, to make such choice, the other party may select both. (1 R. S. 353.)

The fence viewers shall examine the premises, and hear the allegations of the parties. In case of their disagreement, they shall select another fence viewer to act with them, and the decision of any two shall be final upon the parties to such dispute, and upon all parties holding under them.

The decision of the fence viewers shall be reduced to writing, shall contain a description of the fence, and of the proportion to be maintained by each, and shall be forthwith filed in the office of the town clerk. (1 R. S. 354.) (See form No. 10.)

*On sale of land.*—Where two or more persons shall own lands adjoining, in case either of them shall sell, convey or devise such lands, or any portion thereof, the owner of any division fence that shall have been theretofore made and maintained by him, shall not be deprived of his interest therein in consequence of such sale, except so far as it relates to the grantor; and in all cases where such sale or devise shall interfere with or affect the division fences existing between such adjoining owners at the time of such sale, or on receiving such devise, a subdivision of such division fence shall then be made by all the adjoining owners affected thereby, and each adjoining owner shall refund to the owner of the adjoining land a just proportion of the value at the time of such sale, or, on receiving such devise of any division of fence that shall have been theretofore made and maintained by such adjoining owner, or that shall have been made and maintained by the persons from whom he received such title, or the adjoining owner, shall build his proportion of such division fence. The value of such fence, and the proportion thereof to be paid by such person, and the proportion of the division fence to be built by him, shall be determined by any two of the fence viewers of the town. (Laws of 1866, ch. 540.)

The statute empowering fence viewers to fix the just proportion of the fence to be maintained refers to the state of things existing when they are called upon to act, and has no relation to any former ownership of the adjoining property. The just proportion of the fence is, of course, changed whenever a change takes place in the extent which each owner has in the lands which adjoin, and then a new adjustment becomes necessary. (*Adams* v. *Van Alstyne*, 25 N. Y. R. 232.)

*Neglect to build.*—If such neglect or refusal shall be continued for the period of one month after request, in writing, to make or repair such fence, the party injured may make or repair the same, at the expense of the party so neglecting or refusing, to be recovered from him, with costs of suit. (1 R. S. 354.)

An appraisement by the viewers is not necessary under this section. (*Bronk* v. *Becker*, 17 Wend. 320.)

*When fence may be removed.*—If any person who shall have made his proportion of a division fence shall be disposed to remove his fence and suffer his land to lie open to the public, he may do so, provided such farm or lands are not one-half or more cleared or improved, at any time between the first day of November in any one year, and the first day of April following, but at no other time, giving ten days' notice to the owner or occupant of the adjoining land of his intention to apply to the fence viewers of the town for permission to remove his fence; and if, at the time specified in such notice, any two of such fence viewers, to be selected as aforesaid, shall determine that such fence may with propriety be removed, he may remove the same (1 R. S. 354, as amended 1866, ch. 540.)

If any such fence shall be removed without such notice and permission, the party removing the same shall pay to the party injured all such damages as he may sustain thereby, to be recovered with costs of suit. (Id.)

The only effect of a permission from the fence viewers to remove the fence is to remit the parties to their common law rights; and if the cattle of the owner so removing his fence pass through the opening on to the land of his neighbor, he is liable for the damages committed by them. (*Holladay* v. *Marsh*, 3 Wend. 142.)

*Fences destroyed by floods.*—Whenever a division fence shall be injured or destroyed by floods, or other casualty, the person bound to make and repair such fence, or any part thereof, shall make or repair the same, or his just proportion thereof, within ten days after he shall be thereunto required by any person interested therein. Such requisition shall be in writing, and signed by the party making it.

If such person shall refuse or neglect to make or repair his proportion of such fence, for the space of ten days after such request, the party injured may make or repair the same, at the expense of the party so refusing or neglecting, to be recovered from him, with costs of suit. (1 R. S. 354.)

*Examination of witnesses — costs.* — Witnesses may be examined by the fence viewers on all questions submitted to them; and either of such fence viewers shall have power to issue subpœnas for, and to administer oaths to, said witnesses; and each fence viewer and witness thus employed shall be entitled to one dollar and fifty cents per diem; such fence viewers, or a majority of them, shall determine what proportion thereof shall be paid by each of the parties interested in such division fence, and reduce their determination to writing, and subscribe the same and file it in the office of the town clerk where such fence viewers shall reside; the party refusing or neglecting to pay such fence viewers, or either of them, shall be liable to be sued for the same, with costs of suit. (1 R. S. 355, as amended, ch. 540.) For forms of subpœna and determination, see forms Nos. 10 and 11.)

*When damages may be recovered.* — If any person liable to contribute to the erection or reparation of a division fence shall neglect or refuse to make and maintain his proportion of such fence, or shall permit the same to be out of repair, he shall not be allowed to have and maintain any action for damages incurred, but shall be liable to pay to the party injured all such damages as shall accrue to his lands, and the crops, fruit trees and shrubbery thereon, and fixtures connected with the said land, to be ascertained and appraised by any two fence viewers of the town, and to be recovered with costs of suit; which appraisement shall be reduced to writing, and signed by the fence viewers making the same, but shall be only *prima facie* evidence of the amount of such damages. (Laws of 1838, ch. 261.)

Though not, in terms, an amendment of the Revised Statutes, yet, in fact, it is a substitute for section thirty-seven of the statute on division fences, and is here given in place of that. The fence viewers are limited in their action, under the above section, to the damages occurring to the lands, crops, fruit trees, etc., and they cannot assess the value of cattle which escape through a defective fence into a cornfield, and eat so much corn that they die. (*Clark* v. *Brown*, 18 Wend. 213.)

If an owner permit his portion of the division fence to get out of repair, and the cattle of the adjoining owner escape from his field through such defective portion of the fence, and damage the former, he can recover no damage, as he contributes to the injury by not keeping his fence in repair. (*Cowles* v. *Balzar*, 47 Barb. 562.)

Whenever the electors of any town shall have made any rule or regulation, prescribing what shall be deemed a sufficient fence in such town, any person who shall thereafter neglect to keep a fence according to such rule or regulation shall be precluded from recovering compensation, in any manner, for damages done by any beast, lawfully going at large on the highways, that may enter on any lands of such person, not fenced in conformity to the said rule or regulation, or for entering through any defective fence. (1 R. S. 355.)

The statute of 1867 (ch. 814) practically repeals this section, by rendering it unlawful for any cattle, etc., to run at large in the highways, at any time.

*Presumption of sufficiency.* — When the sufficiency of a fence shall come in question, in any suit, it shall be presumed to have been sufficient, until the contrary be established. (1 R. S. 356.)

*Compensation of fence viewers.* — Each fence viewer is entitled to receive one dollar and fifty cents per day for the time occupied in relation to fences; and they are to determine what proportion thereof shall be paid by each of the parties interested in such division fence, and reduce their determination to writing, and subscribe the same, and file it in the office of the town clerk where such fence viewers shall reside; the party refusing or neglecting to pay such fence viewers, or either of them, shall be liable to be sued for the same, with costs. 1 R. S. 355, as amended 1866, ch. 540.)

*As to floating timber.* —The duty of fence viewers, as to floating timber, is prescribed in the Revised Statutes, as follows:

Whenever any logs, timber, boards or plank, in rafts or otherwise, shall have been drifted upon any island in any of the waters within this state, or upon the bank or shore of any such waters, the owner of such logs or other lumber may take the same away, on his first paying or tendering to the owner or possessor of the land on which the same shall have been drifted, the amount of the damages which such owner or possessor shall have sustained by reason thereof, and which may accrue in the removal of such logs or other lumber. (1 R. S. 697.)

If the parties cannot agree as to the amount of such damages, either party may apply to any two of the fence viewers of the town or city in which such lumber may be found, whose duty it shall be, after hearing the proofs and allegations of the parties, to determine the same, at the expense of the owner of the lumber, and their decision shall be conclusive. (Id.)

The fence viewers, or either of them, shall have power to issue process for such witnesses as may be desired by either party, and to administer oaths to all witnesses produced before them. (Id.)

In case the owner does not appear within a prescribed time, the statute authorizes the timber to be sold, and directs that a portion of the proceeds be paid to the owner of the lands for damages. But it provides that, before such money be paid, such damages shall be assessed by any two fence viewers of the city or town, and a specification thereof, signed by such fence viewers, shall be filed in the office of the clerk of the city or town. (1 R. S. 899, § 9.)

The above provisions do not apply to that kind of lumber called drift-wood. (Id. § 21.)

*In relation to strays.* — There are two methods prescribed by statute for the recovery of damages occasioned by cattle straying into an inclosure. That prescribed by chapter 814 of the Laws of 1867, providing for the summary seizure and disposition of such cattle; and that provided by the Revised Statutes, given below. These remedies are concurrent; and every person damaged may resort to either, at his discretion. The provisions of the Revised Statutes, regarding strays, are as follows:

Whenever any person shall, at any time, have any strayed horse upon his inclosed land, or shall, between the first day of November, in any year, and the first day of April thereafter, have any strayed neat cattle or sheep upon his inclosed lands, such person shall, within ten days after the coming of any such stray thereon, deliver to the clerk of the town within which such lands shall be, a note in writing, containing the name and place of abode of such person, and the age, color and marks, natural and artificial, of each stray, as near as may be. (1 R. S. 351, § 17.)

If any person, upon whose inclosed lands any such neat cattle, horses or sheep shall come, shall neglect to deliver such note in writing to the town clerk within the time above required, he shall be precluded from the benefits of this article, and from all claim to compensation for keeping such strays. (Id. § 18.)

The town clerk, on the receipt of every such note, shall enter the same at large in a book to be provided by him for that purpose; for which entry he shall receive six cents each for all neat cattle and horses, and three cents for each sheep, to be paid by the person delivering the note. (Id. § 20.)

The book in which such entries shall be made shall always be kept open to inspection; and no fee shall be taken by the clerk for any search therein. Id. § 20.

The person delivering the note shall be entitled to receive therefor nine cents each for all neat cattle and horses, and three cents for each sheep, described in the note; and he may detain such strays until the owner thereof shall appear and pay such fees, together with the fees paid or due to the clerk, and all reasonable charges for keeping the strays; such charges being first ascertained by two of the fence viewers of the town, to be selected by the person claiming the same, in case he and the owner of the stray cannot otherwise agree. (Id. § 21.)

Each fence viewer shall be entitled to receive six cents for every mile he shall be obliged to travel, from his house to the place where such strays are kept, and twenty-five cents for a certificate of the charges as ascertained by him; such fees to be paid by the owner of the strays. (Id. § 22.)

Every person who shall deliver any such note, and keep any stray described therein, shall, if the same be not sooner claimed and redeemed, between the first day of May and the twentieth day thereafter, give notice to one of the fence viewers of the town, whose duty it shall be to ascertain, according to the best of his knowledge and judgment, the reasonable charges of keeping such stray, a certificate whereof shall be given by him to the person applying for the same. The fence viewer shall be entitled to the like fees as above provided, to be paid by the person applying for the certificate. (Id. § 23.)

If no owner shall appear to claim such stray on or before the first day of May next after the making of such entry, or if the owner shall refuse or neglect to pay the sums charged on such stray, then the person who shall have delivered such note, and kept such stray, may proceed to sell the same by public auction, to the highest bidder. (Id. § 24.)

Such person shall give at least twenty days' previous notice of the time and place of such sale, by advertisement, to be posted up at three of the most public places in the town where the strays shall have been kept. (Id. § 25.)

Out of the moneys arising from such sale, he shall retain for his own use the sums charged on such strays for the aforesaid note in writing, entry and certificate, together with the sum specified in the certificate for keeping such strays, and the like charges for such sale as are allowed on sales under executions issued out of justices' courts. He shall pay the residue of said moneys, on demand, to the owner of the strays, if he shall appear to demand the same. (Id. § 26.)

If the owner shall not appear and demand the residue of such moneys, within one year after the sale, he shall be forever precluded from recovering any part of such moneys; and the aforesaid residue shall be paid to the supervisor of such town, for the use of the town; and his receipt shall be a legal discharge to the keeper of such strays. (Id. § 27.)

If the person who shall have sold such strays shall not, within thirty days after the expiration of the year, pay such residuary moneys to the supervisor of the town, he shall forfeit to the town double the sum so remaining in his hands, together with the amount of such residuary moneys. (Id. § 28.)

Each of the cities of this state shall be considered towns for the purposes of this article. (Id. § 29.)

*In relation to sheep killed by dogs.*—It is also the duty of fence viewers to assess, when required, the damage arising from the killing of sheep by dogs. That part of the statute relating to such duties is as follows:

The owner of any sheep or lambs that may be killed or injured by any dog may apply to any two fence viewers of the town, or assessors of the city, or of the ward of the city, who shall inquire into the matter, and view the sheep injured or killed, and may examine witnesses in relation thereto, for which purpose either of them shall have power to administer oaths. If they are satisfied that the same were killed or hurt only by dogs, and in no other way, they shall certify such fact, the number of the sheep killed or hurt, and the amount of the damages sustained thereby by the owner, together with the value of the sheep hurt or killed. (1 R. S. 704, § 10, as amended 1862, ch. 244.) See form No. 12.

*Their certificate evidence.* — The said certificate shall be presumptive evidence of the facts therein contained, in any suit that may be brought by the party injured against the owner or possessor of any dog, if it shall appear on the trial of such suit that notice in writing of the time and place of such view shall have been served at least twenty-four hours before, on the said owner or possessor, either personally or by leaving at his dwelling-house with a person who usually dwells therein, and who shall have arrived at the age of sixteen years. (Id. § 11.)

In addition to the provisions of the revised statutes, there was an act passed in 1864 (ch. 197) relating to tax upon dogs in Ontario county, which contained a provision that such act may be extended to any county, by a resolution to that effect passed by the supervisors of such county. Among the provisions of that act are the following:

The owner or owners of any sheep or lambs that may be killed or injured by dogs may apply to any two fence viewers of the town, who shall inquire into the matter and examine witnesses in relation thereto, for which purpose either of them shall have power to administer oaths, and if they shall be satisfied that the same were killed by dogs, and in no other way, they shall certify such fact, the number of such sheep killed and the number injured, the value of the sheep killed or injured immediately previous to such killing or injury, together with the value of the sheep after being killed or injured, together with the amount of their fees. (Laws of 1864, ch. 197, § 3.)

Such certificate shall be presented to the board of town auditors, at their annual meeting for auditing town accounts, who shall have the same power in auditing or allowing the same as in regard to town accounts, and if such board shall be satisfied, by the oath of the person claiming such damages, that such claimant has not been able to discover the owner or possessor of the dog or dogs by which such damage was done, or that he has failed to recover his damages of such owner or possessor, they shall give an order on the supervisor of the town for the amount which they shall allow, who shall pay such order out of the funds arising from the provisions of this act. (Id. § 4.)

## SECTION V.

### MISCELLANEOUS PROVISIONS — COMPENSATION.

*May consent to use of highway by railroad.*— Whenever any association or individual shall construct a railroad, upon land purchased for that purpose, on a route which shall cross any road or other public highway, it shall be lawful for the commissioners of highways, having the supervision thereof, to give a written consent that such railroad may be constructed across or on such road or other public highway; and, thereafter, such association or individual shall be authorized to construct and use such railroad across or on such roads or other highways as the commissioners aforesaid shall have permitted; but any public highway, thus intersected or crossed by a railroad, shall be so restored to its former state as not to have impaired its usefulness. Laws of 1835, ch. 300.

Railroad corporations have power,

To construct their road across, along or upon any stream of water, water-course, street, highway, plank road, turnpike or canal, which the route of its road shall intersect or touch; but the company shall restore the stream or water-course, street, highway, plank road and turnpike thus intersected or touched, to its former state, or to such state as not unnecessarily to have impaired its usefulness. Every company formed under this act shall be subject to the power vested in the canal commissioners by the seventeenth section of chapter two hundred and seventy-six of the session laws of eighteen hundred and thirty-four. Nothing in this act contained shall be construed to authorize the erection of any bridge, or any other obstructions across, in or over any stream or lake navigated by steam or sail boats, at the place where any bridge or other obstructions may be proposed to be placed; nor to authorize the construction of any railroad not already located in, upon or across any streets in any city, without the assent of the corporation of such city. (Laws 1850, ch. 140, § 28.)

Nor to authorize any such railroad company to construct its road upon and along any highway, without the order of the supreme court of the judicial district in which said highway is situated, made at a special term of said court, after at least ten days' notice in writing of the intention to make application for said order shall have been given to the commissioners of highways of the town in which said highway is situated. (Laws of 1850, ch. 140, § 26, subd. 5, as amended 1864, ch. 582.)

The consent of the commissioners, or the order of court permitting a railroad company to occupy a highway, does not deprive the owner of the fee of his right to compensation for the extra burden imposed. The statute provides for obtaining the consent of the public to an interference with its easement; but the private interests of the adjoining owner are to be protected in other ways. (*Davis* v. *Mayor of New York*, 14 N. Y. R. 521; *Fletcher* v. *Auburn, etc., R. R. Co.*, 25 Wend. 462.)

Neither the consent of the commissioners nor the order of the court authorizes a company to use a highway without making compensation to the owner of the fee. (*Williams* v. *N. Y. Central R. R.*, 16 N. Y. R. 197.)

*May agree with turnpike or plank road company for use of highway.*—Whenever it shall become necessary for any such company to use any part of a public highway for the construction of a plank or turnpike road, the supervisor and commissioners of highways of the town in which such highways is situated, or a majority, if there be more than one such commissioner in such town, may agree with such company, upon the compensation and damages to be paid by said company for taking and using such highway for the purposes aforesaid. Such agreement shall be in writing, and shall be filed and recorded in the town clerk's office of such town. In case such agreement cannot be made, the compensation and damages for taking such highway for such purpose shall be ascertained in the same manner as the compensation and damages for taking the property of individuals. Such compensation and damages shall be paid to the said commissioners, to be expended by them in improving the highways of such town. (Laws of 1847, ch. 210, § 26.)

No supervisor or commissioner of highways of any town shall make any agreement with any plank road company, or turnpike road company, under the first section of "An act in relation to plank road and turnpike road companies," passed November 24, 1847, for the right to take and use any part of any public highway for a plank road or a turnpike road, without they first obtain the consent in writing of at least two-thirds of all the owners of land along such highway who shall actually reside on that part of the highway on which such plank road or turnpike road is to be constructed. (Laws of 1850, ch. 71, § 5.)

The supervisor and commissioners cannot agree to the use of a highway by a plank road or turnpike company without receiving a pecuniary consideration for such use; a mere condition, as not to put toll gates within certain limits, is not sufficient. (*Palmer* v. *Fort Plain, etc., Plank Road Co.*, 11 N. Y. R. 376.)

The supervisor and commissioners of highways cannot join in an action on an agreement made by them with a plank road company. (Id.)

*To erect mile stones.*—It shall be the duty of the commissioners of highways of each town to cause mile boards or stones to be erected, where not already erected, on the post roads, and such other public roads in their town as they may think proper, at the distance of one mile from each other, with such fair and legible inscriptions as they may think proper. (1 R. S. 503, § 5.)

*Guide posts.*—The commissioners of highways of each town shall cause guide posts, with proper inscriptions and devices, to be erected at the intersections of all the post roads in their town, and at the intersection of such other roads therein as they may deem necessary. (1 R. S. 503, § 9.)

*Penalty for injury.*—Whoever shall destroy, remove, injure or deface any mile board or mile stone erected on any highway shall forfeit for every offense the sum of ten dollars; he shall also be deemed guilty of a misdemeanor, and, on conviction, shall be fined not exceeding fifty dollars, or imprisoned not exceeding three months, at the discretion of the court. (1 R. S. 526.)

Whoever shall injure or deface any description affixed to a guide post erected on any highway, or destroy or injure any such guide post, shall be liable to all the penalties provided in the last preceding section. (Id.)

All penalties or forfeitures given in this title, and not otherwise specially provided for, shall be recovered by the commissioners of highways of the town in which the offense shall be committed, and, when recovered, shall be applied by them in improving the roads and bridges in such town. (Id.)

*To procure scraper and plough.*—The commissioners of highways, whenever they shall think it necessary or useful, may direct and empower any overseer of highways in their respective towns to procure a good and sufficient iron or steel shod scraper and plough, or either of them, for the use of his road district, to be paid for by the moneys arising from commutations and fines within such district. (1 R. S. 504.)

In case such moneys shall be insufficient for the purpose, the deficiency shall be assessed by the overseers upon the inhabitants of the districts in the proportion they are respectively assessed on the assessment roll of said town; and if any one so assessed shall neglect or refuse to pay such assessment, the same may be sued for and recovered by the overseer. (Id.)

*Duty in case of fire in woods.*—Whenever the woods in any town shall be on fire, it shall be the duty of the justices of the peace, the supervisor and the commissioners of highways of such town, and each of them, to order such and so many of the inhabitants of such town, liable to work on the highways, and residing in the vicinity of the place where such fire shall be, as they shall severally deem necessary, to repair to the place where such fire shall prevail, and there to assist in extinguishing the same, or in stopping its progress. (1 R. S. 697.)

If any person, so ordered to repair to and assist in manner aforesaid, shall refuse or neglect to comply with any such order, he shall forfeit and pay the sum of fifty dollars, and shall also be deemed guilty of a misdemeanor, and, on conviction, shall be punished by fine or imprisonment, or both, at the discretion of the court; such fine not to exceed one hundred dollars, and such imprisonment not to exceed sixty days. (Id.)

Every forfeiture recovered under the last section shall be applied as a reward to such person or persons as the officers above mentioned, or a majority of them, shall deem best entitled thereto, for superior exertions in extinguishing or stopping the progress of such fire. (Id.)

*To account to town auditors.*—The commissioners of highways of each town shall render to the board of town auditors, at their annual meeting for auditing the accounts of town officers, an account in writing, stating,

1. The labor assessed and performed in such town.

2. The sums received by such commissioners for fines and commutations, and all other moneys received under this chapter.

3. The improvements which have been made on the roads and bridges in their town, during the year immediately preceding such report, and an account of the state of such roads and bridges; and,

4. A statement of the improvements necessary to be made on such roads and bridges, and an estimate of the probable expense of making such improvements, beyond what the labor to be assessed in that year will accomplish. (1 R. S. 502, § 3.)

The meeting for auditing the accounts of town officers is held on the Tuesday next preceding the annual town meeting.

*To account for moneys.*—The commissioners of highways in each town of this state, and all town officers who receive or disburse any moneys belonging to their respective towns, shall, on the last Tuesday preceding the annual town meeting of their town, account with the board of town officers of such town for all moneys received and disbursed by them by virtue of their office. (Laws of 1863, ch. 172.)

*To deliver records, books, papers, etc., to successor.*—Whenever the term of office of the commissioners of highways of any town shall expire, and another or others shall be elected or appointed, it shall be the duty of the persons so elected or appointed, immediately after they shall have entered on the duties of their office, to demand of their predecessors or predecessor all the records, books and papers, under their or his control, belonging to such office. (1 R. S. 359.)

Whenever a commissioner of highways shall resign, and another person shall be elected or appointed in his stead, the person so appointed or elected shall make such demand of the person so resigning. (Id. § 6.)

It shall be the duty of every person so going out of office, whenever thereto required pursuant to the foregoing provisions, to deliver, upon oath, all the records, books and papers in his possession, or under his control, belonging to the office held by him; which oath may be administered by the officer to whom such delivery shall be made. It shall also be the duty of every commissioner of highways so going out of office, at the same time, to pay over to such successor the balance of moneys remaining in his hands, as ascertained by the auditors of town accounts. (Id. § 7.)

Upon the death of any of the officers above enumerated, the successors or successor of such officer shall make such demand as above provided of the executors and administrators of such deceased officer; and it shall be the duty of such executors or administrators to deliver, upon the like oath, all records, books and papers in their possession, or under their control, belonging to the office held by their testator or intestate. (Id. § 8.)

If any person so going out of office, or his executors or administrators, shall refuse or neglect, when thereunto lawfully required, to deliver such records, books or papers, he shall forfeit to the town, for every such refusal or neglect, the sum of two hundred and fifty dollars; and it shall also be the duty of the officer or officers entitled to demand such records, books and papers, to proceed to compel the delivery thereof in the manner prescribed in the sixth title of the fifth chapter of this act, and, to that end, the fiftieth, fifty-first, fifty-second, fifty-third, fifty-fourth and fifty-fifth sections of that title shall be deemed to apply to the officers above enumerated, and their executors or administrators. (Id. § 9.)

The proceedings to compel delivery above referred to are as follows:

Whenever any person shall be removed from office, or the term for which he shall have been elected or appointed shall expire, he shall, on demand, deliver over to his successor all the books and papers in his custody as such officer, or in any way appertaining to his office. Every person violating this provision shall be deemed guilty of a misdemeanor. (1 R. S. 125, § 50.)

If any person shall refuse or neglect to deliver over to his successor any books or papers, as required in the preceding section, such successor may make complaint thereof to the chancellor, any justice of the supreme court, any circuit judge of the circuit, or the first judge of the county where the person so refusing shall reside; and if such officer be satisfied by the oath of the complainant, and such other testimony as shall be offered, that any such books or papers are withheld, he shall grant an order directing the person so refusing to show cause before him, within some short and reasonable time, why he should not be compelled to deliver the same. (Id. § 51.)

At the time so appointed, or at any other time, to which the matter may be adjourned, upon due proof being made of the service of the said order, such officer shall proceed to inquire into the circumstances. If the person charged with withholding such books or papers shall make affidavit before such officer, that he has truly delivered over to his successor all such books and papers in his custody, or appertaining to his office, within his knowledge, all further proceedings before such officer shall cease, and the person complained against shall be discharged. (Id. § 52.)

If the person complained against shall not make such oath, and it shall appear that any such books or papers are withheld, the officer before whom such proceedings shall be had shall, by warrant, commit the person so withholding to the jail of the county, there to remain until he shall deliver such books and papers, or be otherwise discharged according to law. (Id. § 53.)

In the case stated in the last section, if required by the complainant, such officer shall also issue his warrant, directed to any sheriff or constable, commanding them, in the day time, to search such places as shall be designated in such warrant, for such books and papers as belonged to the officer so removed, ot whose term of office expired, in his official capacity, and which appertained to such office, and seize and bring them before the officer issuing such warrant. (Id. § 54.)

Upon any books and papers being brought before such officer, by virtue of such warrant, he shall inquire and examine whether the same appertain to the office from which the person so refusing to deliver was removed, or of which the term expired, and he shall cause the same to be delivered to the complainant. (Id. § 55.)

The motion to compel delivery, as provided in section 51, is to be made before a justice of the supreme court, out of court; and any justice of that court has jurisdiction. (*Welch* v. *Cook*, 7 How. 282.) A county judge of the county also has jurisdiction. A warrant to compel delivery should not be granted, unless the applicant's title to the office is clear. (5 Hill, 63, note; 5 Abb. 73; Id. 281.)

*Compensation.*—The commissioners of highways in any town in this state shall be allowed the sum of two dollars per day for each day actually and necessarily spent in the discharge of their official duties. (Laws of 1857, ch. 615, as amended 1870, ch. 242.)

## SECTION VI.

### LEGAL PROCEEDINGS BY OR AGAINST COMMISSIONERS.

Actions may be brought by the commissioners of highways of the several towns, upon any contract lawfully made with them, or their predecessors, in their official character; to enforce any liability or any duty enjoined by law to such officers, or the body which they represent; to recover any penalties or forfeitures given to such officers, or the bodies whom they represent; and to recover damages for any injuries done to the property or rights of such officers, or of the bodies represented by them. (2 R. S. 473, § 92.)

Such actions may be brought by such officers in the name of their respective offices, notwithstanding the contract or obligation on which the same is founded may have been made with or to any predecessors of such officers, in their individual names or otherwise, and notwithstanding any right of action may have accrued previous to the time when the officers commencing such suit entered upon the execution of the duties of their office. (Id. § 93.)

But in cases where, by special provision of law, actions are directed to be brought by or against any public bodies, in the name of any such body, the same shall be brought or defended in such name by the persons representing such body then in office. (Id. § 94.)

This statute was intended to provide for cases where these officers, in the performance of their official duties, should take from others contracts running in terms to such officers by their names of office. (*Palmer* v. *Fort Plain, etc., Plank Road Company*, 11 N. Y. R. 390.) Therefore, neither the commissioners, separately or jointly with the supervisor, can maintain an action on a contract made by them on behalf of the town with a plank road company for the use of a highway. (Id.) Nor does the 86th statute authorize them to maintain a civil action against a turnpike company which has taken possession of a highway before making compensation. (*Cornell* v. *Butternut, etc., Turnpike Company*, 25 Wend. 365.)

*Actions against railroads.*—The commissioner or commissioners of highways in each of the towns of this state are hereby empowered to bring any action against any railroad corporation that may be necessary or proper to sustain the rights of the public in and to any highway in such town, and to enforce the performance of any duty enjoined upon any railroad corporation in relation to any highway in the town of which they are commissioners, and to maintain an action for damages or expenses which any town may sustain, or may have sustained, or may be put to, or may have been put to, in consequence of any act or omission of any such corporation in violation of any law in relation to such highway. (Laws of 1855, ch. 255, § 1.)

Nothing in the above act, however, is to be construed as in any manner impairing the rights of any person or officer to bring any action now authorized by law. (Id. § 2.)

Where a railroad company constructs their road across a highway, injuring the highway, and neglecting to restore it to its former state of usefulness, such company is liable in an action by the commissioners of highways, both to damages, under the general railroad act requiring crossings to be constructed without injury to the road, and also to treble damages, under 1 Revised Statutes, 526, § 130, respecting injuries to highways. (*Sipperly* v. *Troy & Boston Railroad Co.*, 9 How. 83.)

*Action against successors.*—Where any contract shall have been entered into, or any liability shall have been incurred by or in behalf of any town by any officer thereof, within the scope of his authority, the same remedies may be had upon any successor of such officer, in his official character, as might have been against such officer if he had continued in office. (2 R. S. 474.)

Where, however, the officer has exceeded his authority in entering into a contract or in incurring the liability, such contract or liability is not obligatory on his successor.

A commissioner of highways has no general authority, as such commissioner, to borrow money, or to give promissory notes, and thereby bind his successors in office. (*Van Alstyne* v. *Freday*, 41 N. Y. R. 177.)

The commissioners have no authority to bind a town, unless such power is expressly conferred by statute, or is such as is necessarily implied from the power conferred. (*Mather* v. *Crawford*, 36 Barb. 564.) The statute neither expressly nor impliedly authorizes them to pledge the credit of the town to borrow money to build bridges or repair roads, and, where they have thus pledged the credit of the town, their successors are not liable in an action brought against them in their official capacity on the indebtedness. (Id.; *Barker* v. *Loomis*, 6 Hill, 463; *Van Alstyne* v. *Freday*, 41 N. Y. R. 174.)

Where commissioners borrow money without authority, for repair of roads and bridges, they are personally liable therefor. (*Palmer* v. *Vandenburgh*, 3 Wend. 197.)

However, the commissioners may give notes in their official character for a liability incurred by them on behalf of the town within the scope of their authority, and the law gives the same remedy against their successors as might have been had against those who signed the note if they had remained in office. (*Potter* v. *Davis*, Hill & D. Supp. 394.)

The commissioners have the implied authority to adjust controversies in relation to encroachments on highways, and may take security for payment of the damages fixed for such encroachment, and may maintain actions on such securities. (*Commissioners of Courtlandville* v. *Peck*, 5 Hill, 215.)

Commissioners have also the power to invest public moneys lying in their hands, and to enforce the security in their official name. (Id.)

But they have no power to take a bond assuming the expense of laying out a highway, and indemnify the town against such expense. (*Webb* v. *Albertson*, 4 Barb. 51; *Palmer* v. *Fort Plain, etc., Plank Road Co.*, 11 N. Y. R. 376.)

*Action, how brought.*—Actions against the commissioners of highways shall be brought against them individually, specifying in the process, pleadings and proceedings, their name of office; and such actions may be commenced in the same manner as against individuals; but the defendants shall not be held to bail in any case, unless upon the order of a judge of the court in which the action is commeneed, founded upon proof by affidavit that the same is brought for some personal misconduct in office, or upon some personal liability assumed or incurred by such defendants in their official character. (2 R. S. 474, § 96.)

In actions by and against commissioners, the complaint should show by proper averments that the action is brought against them in their official capacity, and not individually.

*May employ counsel.*—Commissioners of highways may employ counsel to assist in the preparation and trial of an indictment for obstructing a public highway, and to render other legal services in relation to matters connected with the control and management of public highways; and a recovery can be had for such services against the successors in office of the commissioners employing such counsel. (*Duntz* v. *Duntz*, 44 Barb. 459.)

Where a commissioner of highways, who has employed counsel within the scope of his authority, advanced the amount of such counsel's bill, he may recover the amount from his successor in office. (Id.)

*Actions not to abate.*—No suit commenced by or against any commissioner of highways shall be abated or discontinued by his death, removal from, or resignation of, his office; nor by the expiration of his term. The court in which any such action shall be pending shall substitute the name of the successor in such office upon the application of such successor or of the adverse party. (2 R. S. 474, § 100.)

But before any new defendant shall be so substituted without his consent, at least fourteen days' notice of the application for that purpose shall be personally served on him. (Id. § 101.)

Under these provisions, if no substitution is made, the suit proceeds in the name of the original commissioners. (Seld. Notes, No. 5, 64.) It is no objection to substituting a successor in office as plaintiff in a suit brought by his predecessor that he is himself the defendant in the suit. (*Thayer* v. *Lewis*, 4 Den. 269.)

The above provisions of the statute do not extend to justices' court. A justice has no power to compel an appearance; and, if the successor do not voluntarily appear in such a case, the action should proceed against the original defendants, and the plaintiff may recover judgment against them. (*Colegrove* v. *Breed*, 2 Den. 125.)

*Judgment, how collected.*—In suits by and against commissioners of highways, the debt, damages or costs recovered against them shall be collected in the same manner as against individuals; and the amount so collected shall be allowed to them in their official accounts.

Where highway commissioners pay a judgment in a suit against them in their official capacity, they should include the amount paid in their account presented to the town auditors.

*Mandamus against commissioners.* — A mandamus may be had to compel commissioners of highways to perform any duty enjoined upon them by statute, but which they neglect or refuse to do. (*People* v. *Commissioners of Salem*, 1 Cow. 23; *People* v. *Collins*, 19 Wend. 56.) But when the duties to be performed are judicial, or where the commissioners are vested with a discretion in the performance of a duty, they may be required to act, but not directed *how* to act. (*Judges Oneida C. P.* v. *The People*, 18 Wend. 96; *People* v. *Contracting Board*, 27 N. Y. R. 378.)

Commissioners may be compelled by mandamus to lay out, open or discontinue a highway. (*People* v. *Commissioners of Salem*, 1 Cow. 23.) But they should not be compelled to lay out a road where the necessary effect would be to subject them to an action of trespass. If, therefore, the facts shown on the application are of a character to establish a want of jurisdiction, so as to make the proceedings entirely void, they furnish a sufficient ground for not awarding a peremptory mandamus, unless for some good reason the parties are estopped from inquiring into these facts. (*People* v. *Commissioners of Seward*, 27 Barb. 94; *ex parte Clapper*, 3 Hill, 458.) Where commissioners were appointed by statute to lay out a road, commencing "at or near E.," and terminating "at or near" the house of W., it was held that their determination of the route and its termini was a judicial act, and, even though it was injudicious, the town highway officers were bound by it, and might be compelled by mandamus to open the road accordingly. (*People* v. *Collins*, 19 Wend. 56; see *People* v. *Finger*, 24 Barb. 341.)

Where the referees simply reverse an order of the commissioners of highways, refusing to lay out a highway, without giving orders for the laying out of such highway, the commissioners will not be compelled by a mandamus to proceed to lay out the road. (*People* v. *Commissioners of Cherry Valley*, 8 N. Y. R. 476.) Nor will a mandamus lie to compel commissioners to lay out a highway, unless it appear that they have the funds requisite for the purpose. (*Garlinghouse* v. *Jacobs*, 29 N. Y. R. 303, and cases.)

A mandamus to commissioners will be granted without regard to the near approach of the expiration of their term of office; when the term of office expires, their successors must obey the command of the writ. (*People* v. *Collins*, 19 Wend. 56.) The writ need not in the first instance be directed to the commissioners by their individual names; it is only in case of disobedience to the writ that they are to be proceeded against personally. (*People* v. *Champion*, 16 Johns. 61.)

*Injunctions against commissioners.* — Where the commissioners of highways have a right to lay out a highway, but fail to acquire jurisdiction, or where their proceedings are irregular, a suit for an injunction will not lie, since persons entering under the order for the purpose of opening the road would be trespassers, and the evil could be remedied by an action at law; but, where they attempt to lay out a road where they have no right—as over grounds acquired by a railroad company for the site of a depot; or through an inclosure—an injunction will be granted. (*Albany Northern R. R. Co.* v. *Brownell*, 24 N. Y. R. 345.) An action cannot be maintained by a tax payer to declare void the proceedings of the commissioners of highways in laying out a road, and to restrain their further proceedings on the ground that their proceedings are fraudulent and increased the taxes of the plaintiff and others, and that the officers themselves were unqualified to act as such. (*Thatcher* v. *Dusenberry*, 9 How. 32.) Nor will an injunction be granted restraining the commissioners from carrying out an order made by them removing an encroachment, either on the ground that they had not jurisdiction, or that their decision was unjust or irregular. (*Hyatt* v. *Bates*, 35 Barb. 308.)

## CHAPTER III.

### OVERSEERS OF HIGHWAYS.

*Appointment.*—From and after the passage of this act, the commissioner or commissioners of highways, in each town in this state, shall have the power, and it shall be their duty, within one week after such annual town meeting, by an instrument, in writing, under their hands, to be filed with the town clerk, to appoint as many overseers of highways in their respective towns as there are road districts therein, to hold their office during one year, and it shall be the duty of the town clerk to notify each overseer of his appointment, as now required by law in case of elections, and all provisions of law now applicable to overseers of highways heretofore elected under the provisions of the sections above amended shall apply to overseers of highways appointed under the provisions of this act. (Laws of 1865, ch. 522, § 7.) (See form No. 16.)

The law referred to as requiring town clerk to give notice of election, was as follows: The clerk of every town meeting, within ten days thereafter, shall transmit to each person elected to any town office, whose name shall not have been entered on the poll-list as a voter, a notice of his election. (1 R. S. 344.)

When a vacancy in any town office is filled by the justices, the town clerk is to give notice of the appointment to the person appointed. (Id. 347.)

The persons appointed must be electors of the town (1 R. S. 345), and the order making the appointment must be signed by all the commissioners or else must show upon its face that all the commissioners met and deliberated upon the subject, or were notified to attend the meeting for the purpose of making the appointments. (1 R. S. 525.) Great care should be used where only two concur, in order to specify in the order either that all the commissioners were present and *deliberated* on the subject, or that all were notified, not only of the intended meeting, but of the particular subject on which it was proposed to deliberate. (*People* v. *Williams*, 36 N. Y. R. 441; *Fitch* v. *Commissioner of Kirkland*, 22 Wend. 132.)

*Notice of acceptance.* — Formerly every person so appointed, within ten days after he was notified of his appointment, and before he entered on the duties of his office, was required to cause to be filed in the office of the town clerk a notice, in writing, signifying his acceptance of such office. (1 R. S. 345.) And in case he did not cause such notice of acceptance to be filed, such neglect was to be deemed a refusal to serve (id.); but by section 1 of chapter 791 of the Laws of 1868, it was provided that "the appointment of overseers of highways, by the commissioners of highways, as prescribed in section 7 of chapter 522 of the Laws of 1865 (above cited), and the notice therein prescribed to be given by the several town clerks to the persons so appointed, shall constitute the several persons thus appointed overseers of highways in their respective districts and wards; and no acceptance of the office or appointment as overseer shall be necessary to authorize the persons so appointed to perform the duties required of and enjoined upon overseers of highways." From this provision it appears that a notice of acceptance is no longer necessary, but that the appointment and notice thereof imposes upon the persons appointed all the powers and duties of overseers.

*Penalty for refusing to serve.*—If any person appointed to the office of overseer of highways, either to fill a vacancy or otherwise, shall refuse to serve, he shall forfeit to the town the sum of ten dollars. (1 R. S. 347.)

*General duties.*—It shall be the duty of overseers of highways in each town:

1. To repair and keep in order the highways within the several districts for which they shall have been elected.
2. When so required by the commissioners of highways, or any one of them, to warn all persons assessed to work on the highways in their respective districts, to come and work thereon.
3. To cause the noxious weeds on each side of the highway within their respective districts, to be cut down or destroyed twice in each year, once before the first day of July, and again before the first day of September; and the requisite labor shall be considered highway work; and,
4. To collect all fines and commutation money, and to execute all lawful orders of the commissioners. (1 R. S. 503.)

It is the duty of the overseer to diligently repair and work the roads within his district, to the amount of the tax assessed by the commissioners, and he is not bound to do more. The overseer is subordinate to the commissioners, and is bound to obey their directions with regard to the repair of roads. The duties of the overseer do not extend to bridges, unless directed by the commissioners to repair them. (*Bartlett* v. *Crozier*, 17 Johns. 447.)

What shall be deemed a bridge is a question to be determined according to the ordinary meaning of the word. Culverts and sluices over small brooks and ditches, and even bridges of some extent, in a road district, are under the care of the overseer, and he is to repair them.

Undoubtedly the performance of the duty enjoined by subdivision 3 rests in the sound discretion of the overseer. If such weeds are so situated as it is not likely they will do injury, and in cases where the road is very bad and little work in the district, it would be absurd to expend it in destroying weeds instead of doing necessary work.

The fines which the overseer is directed to collect are for idleness (1 R. S. 510, § 39); for not working (id. § 40); and for refusing to pay assessment for scraper and plough. (1 R. S. 504, § 12.)

It shall be the further duty of the overseers of highways, once in every month, from the first day of April until the first day of December, to cause all the loose stones lying on the beaten track of every road within their respective districts to be removed; and to cause the monuments erected, or to be erected as the boundaries of highways, to be kept up and renewed, so that the extent of such roads may be publicly known. (1 R. S. 503.)

Some of the duties of the overseers are to be performed without any special order or direction from the commissioners; it is their duty, among other things, to keep the roads in repair; to destroy noxious weeds; to collect fine and commutation money, and to remove loose stones from the beaten track of the road, without any special order from the commissioners. It would seem from sub. 2, that they are not to warn persons assessed to work without being required by the commissioners to do so; but this requisition relates to the general warrant directed to them by the commissioners.

And the court decided that an overseer is bound to remove obstructions from the highways within his district, although not specially directed by the commissioners. (*McFadden* v. *Kingsbury*, 11 Wend. 667.)

In that case the court say, that "by the sixth section it is made the duty of overseers to repair and keep in order the highways within his district. What is meant by keeping a road in order? If a fence is built across a road in any district, any person may remove it; but is it not the duty of overseers to see that it is done? If logs are thrown in the road, or rubbish of any description placed in it, which deprive the public of the use of the road, whose duty is it to remove those obstacles to the public enjoyment of the right of passage upon the road? It is undoubtedly the duty of the overseer. It is no answer to say that the commissioners have the care and superintendence of the highways, and give directions for the repairing of roads and bridges; it is none the less the duty of the overseers to repair and keep in order the road in their districts; they are bound to do it, whether they receive especial instructions or not; it is their duty without special orders."

The obligation imposed upon overseers to repair highways, while it does not require them to grade the whole space from fence to fence, does require them to provide a good and sufficient carriageway, and to properly guard it, by railings, etc., in all dangerous places. (*Wendell* v. *Mayor, etc., of Troy*, 39 Barb. 335; *Ireland* v. *Oswego, etc., Plank Road Co.*, 13 N. Y. R. 531; *Hyatt* v. *Trustees of Rondout*, 44 Barb. 391.)

*To erect guide-posts and mile boards.*—It is also the duty of overseers to erect guide-posts and mile boards, with proper inscriptions and devices, at the intersection of roads, when ordered so to do, and to maintain and keep in repair such guide-posts at the expense of the town. (1 R. S. 503.) If any person shall destroy, remove, injure or deface such mile boards or guide-posts, he shall forfeit for each offense the sum of ten dollars, and be deemed guilty of a misdemeanor, and on conviction, shall be fined not exceeding fifty dollars, or imprisoned not exceeding three months, at the discretion of the court. (1 R. S. 525, § 128.)

*To purchase scraper and plough.*—Every overseer is also, when ordered by the commissioners, to purchase a good and sufficient iron or steel shod scraper and plough, or either of them, for the use of his road district; to be paid for by the moneys arising from commutations and fines within his district. In case such money shall be insufficient for the purpose, the deficiency shall be assessed by the overseer upon the inhabitants of the district in the proportion they are respectively assessed on the assessment roll of said town; and if any one so assessed shall neglect or refuse to pay such assessment, the same may be sued for and recovered by the overseers. (1 R. S. 504.) (For form see No. 18.)

These duties are to be performed upon the order of the commissioners, and no overseer is liable for a neglect of them without such order. (*McFadden* v. *Kingsbury*, 11 Wend. 667.)

*To deliver list.*—Each of the overseers of highways shall deliver to the clerk of the town, within sixteen days after his election or appointment, a list, subscribed by such overseer, of the names of all the inhabitants in his road district, who are liable to work on the highways. (1 R. S. 506, § 21.)

This list the town clerk is to deliver to the commissioners of highways, who are to proceed to assess the highway labor thereon. As to who are liable to work on the highways, see post on "assessment of highway labor."

*Penalties on overseers.*—Every overseer of highways who shall refuse or neglect, either:

1. To warn the people assessed to work on the highways, when he shall have been required so to do by the commissioners, or either of them.

2. To collect the moneys that may arise from fines or commutations; or,

3. To perform any of the duties required by this chapter, or which may be enjoined on him by the commissioners of highways of his town; and for the omission of which a penalty is not hereinafter provided, shall, for every such refusal or neglect, forfeit the sum of ten dollars, to be sued for by the commissioners of highways of the town, and when recovered, to be applied by them in making and improving the roads and bridges therein. (1 R. S. 504, § 16.)

There are some things, such as keeping roads in repair, destroying noxious weeds, collecting fines and commutation money, and removing loose stones from the road, that the overseers are absolutely required to perform; but there are others, such as warning people to work, repairing bridges, etc., that are only required when directed by the commissioners, and no penalty attaches for a neglect to perform them without such direction. A delivery of the assessment roll to overseers has been held to be a sufficient order to warn people to work. (*McFadden* v. *Kingsbury*, 11 Wend. 669.)

It shall be the duty of the commissioners of highways of each town, whenever any person resident in their town shall make complaint that any overseer of highways in such town has refused or neglected to perform any of the duties enumerated in the last preceding section, and shall give or offer to such commissioners sufficient security to indemnify them against the costs which may be incurred in prosecuting for the penalty annexed to such refusal or neglect, forthwith to prosecute such overseer for the offense complained of. (1 R. S. 505, § 17.)

If such commissioners of highways shall refuse or neglect to prosecute for such penalty, they shall, in every such case, forfeit the sum of ten dollars, to be recovered by the person who shall have made such complaint and given or offered such security. (Id. § 18.)

*To account and pay over moneys.*—Every overseer of highways shall, on the second Tuesday next preceding the time of holding the annual town meeting in his town, within the year for which he is elected or appointed, render to one of the commissioners of highways of the town, an account in writing, verified by his oath, and containing:

1. The names of all persons assessed to work on the highways in the district of which he is overseer.

2. The names of all those who have actually worked on the highways, with the number of days they have so worked.

3. The names of all those who have been fined, and the sums in which they have been fined.

4. The names of all those who have commuted, and the manner in which the moneys arising from

fines and commutations have been expended by him.

5. A list of all persons whose names he has returned to the supervisor, as having neglected or refused to work out their highway assessments, with the number of days and amount of tax so returned for each person, and a list of all lands which he has returned to the supervisor for non-payment of taxes, and the amount of tax on each tract of land so returned. (1 R. S. 512, § 51, as amended 1865, ch. 522.) The commissioners of highways are authorized to administer the oath required to the above account. (Laws of 1833, ch. 149.)

Every such overseer shall also then and there pay to the commissioner all moneys remaining in his hands unexpended, to be applied by the commissioners in making and improving the roads and bridges in the town, in such manner as they shall direct. (1 R. S. 512, § 52.)

If any overseer shall refuse or neglect to render such account, or if, having rendered the same, he shall refuse or neglect to pay any balance which may then be due from him, he shall, for every such offense, forfeit the sum of ten dollars, to be recovered, together with any balance of moneys remaining in his hands, by the commissioners of highways, to be applied to making and improving the roads and bridges in said district; and it shall be the duty of said commissioners to prosecute for such penalty in every instance in which no return is made, or such delinquency occurs. (1 R. S. 512, § 53, as amended 1865, ch. 522.)

*Compensation.*—If any overseer shall be employed more days in executing the several duties enjoined on him by this chapter than he is assessed to work on the highways, he shall be paid for the excess at the rate of one dollar per day, and be allowed to retain the same out of the moneys which may come into his hands for fines under this chapter; he shall not be permitted to commute for the days he is assessed. (1 R. S. 504, § 13, as amended 1864, ch. 395.)

## CHAPTER IV.

### ASSESSMENT OF LABOR ON HIGHWAYS, AGAINST WHOM AND HOW MADE.

*Who and what property liable to be assessed for highway labor.*— Every person owning or occupying land in the town in which he or she resides, and every male inhabitant above the age of twenty-one years residing in the town when the assessment is made, shall be assessed to work on the public highways in such town; and the lands of non-residents, situated in such town, shall be assessed for highway labor, as hereinafter directed. (1 R. S. 505, § 19.)

Since the case of *Beach* v. *Furman* (9 Johns. 229) in which a doubt was expressed as to the liability of females owning or occupying lands to assessment for highway labor, the above section has been so amended as to exclude such doubt by inserting the words *or she* in the second line.

Lands of non-residents within any town, occupied and improved by the owner or owners, or his or their servants or agents, shall be liable to the same assessments for highways as if the owner or owners were residents. (Laws of 1832, ch. 107, § 1.)

The real property of non-resident owners, improved or occupied by a servant or agent, shall be subject to assessment of highway labor, and at the same rate as the real property of resident owners. (Laws of 1835, ch. 154, § 1.)

*List of those liable to assessment.*—Having ascertained who are actual residents of the town and liable to assessment (1 R. S. 505, § 19), it is made the duty of each of the overseers of highways to deliver to the clerk of the town, within sixteen days after his election or appointment, a list, subscribed by such overseer, of the names of all the inhabitants in his road district, who are thus liable to work on the highways. (1 R. S. 506.)

*Delivered to the commissioners.*—The town clerk shall deliver the lists filed by the overseers to the commissioners of highways of the town, who shall proceed, at their next meeting, or at some subsequent meeting, to ascertain, estimate and assess the highway labor to be performed in their town the then ensuing year. (1 R. S. 506, § 23.)

*When and where commissioners' meetings held.*—The commissioners of highways of each town shall meet, within eighteen days after they shall be chosen, at the place of town meeting, on such day as they shall agree upon, and afterward at such other times and places as they shall think proper. (1 R. S. 505, § 20.)

*Land of non-residents appraised.*—The commissioners of highways of each town, at their first or any subsequent meeting, are required to make out a list and statement of the contents of all lots, pieces or parcels of land within such town, owned by non-residents therein.

Every lot so designated shall be described in the same manner as is required from assessors, and its value shall be set down opposite to such description; such value shall be the same as was affixed to such lot in the last assessment roll of the town, and if such lot was not separately valued in such roll, then in proportion to the valuation which shall have been affixed to the whole tract of which such lot shall be a part. (1 R. S. 506, § 22, as amended 1835, ch. 154, § 2.) (See form 21.)

The following is the manner in which assessors are required to describe non-resident lands.

If the land to be assessed be a tract which is subdivided into lots, or be part of a tract which is so subdivided, the assessors shall proceed as follows:

1. They shall designate it by its name, if known by one, or if it be not distinguished by a name, or the name be unknown, they shall state by what other lands it is bounded.

2. If they can obtain correct information of the subdivisions they shall put down in their assessment rolls, and in a first column, all the unoccupied lots in their town or ward, owned by non-residents, by their numbers alone and without the names of their owners, beginning at the lowest number and proceeding in numerical order to the highest.

3. In a second column, and opposite to the number of each lot, they shall set down the quantity of land therein liable to taxation.

4. In a third column, and opposite to the quantity, they shall set down the valuation of such quantity.

5. If such quantity be a full lot, it shall be designated by the number alone; if it be a part of a lot, the part must be designated by boundaries, or in some other way by which it may be known. (1 R. S. 391, § 12.)

If the land so to be assessed be a tract which is not subdivided, or if its subdivisions cannot be ascertained by the assessors, they shall proceed as follows:

1. They shall enter in their roll the name or

boundaries thereof, as above directed, and certify in the roll that such tract is not subdivided, or that they cannot obtain correct information of the subdivisions, as the case may be.

2. They shall set down, in the proper column, the quantity and valuation as above directed.

3. If the quantity to be assessed be the whole tract, such a description by its name or boundaries will be sufficient; but if a part only is liable to taxation, that part, or the part not liable, must be particularly described.

4. If any part of such tract be settled and occupied by a resident of the town or ward, the assessors shall except such part from their assessment of the whole tract, and shall assess it as other occupied lands are assessed; and if they cannot otherwise designate such parts, they shall notify the supervisor of the town, who shall cause a survey and two manuscript maps to be made, for the purpose of ascertaining the situation and quantity of every such occupied part.

5. One of those maps shall be delivered by the supervisor to the county treasurer, to be by him transmitted to the comptroller, and the other shall be delivered, in like manner to the assessors.

6. The assessors shall then complete the assessment of the tract, and shall deposit the map in the town clerk's office, for the information of the future assessors. And the expense of making such survey and maps shall be immediately repaid to the supervisor, out of the county treasury; and shall be added by the board of supervisors to the tract, distinguishing it from the ordinary tax. (1 R. S. 391, § 13.)

*Proceedings in estimating and making assessments.*—After receiving from the town clerk the lists filed by the overseers, the commissioners of highways shall proceed to estimate and assess the highway labor to be performed in their town, as follows:

1. The whole number of days' work to be assessed in each year shall be ascertained, and shall be at least three times the number of taxable inhabitants in such town.

2. Every male inhabitant being above the age of twenty-one years (excepting ministers of the gospel and priests of every denomination, paupers, idiots and lunatics) shall be assessed at least one day.

3. The residue of such days' work shall be apportioned upon the estate, real and personal, of every inhabitant of such town, as the same shall appear by the last assessment roll of the said town, and upon each tract or parcel of land, of which the owners are non-residents, contained in the list made as aforesaid.

4. If, after such apportionment, there shall be any deficiency in the number of days' work determined by the commissioners to be performed in their town, the then ensuing year, such deficiency shall be assessed upon the estates, real and personal, of the inhabitants of the town, and upon each tract or parcel of land of which the owners are non-residents, according to the last assessment roll.

5. The commissioners shall affix to the name of each person named in the lists furnished by the overseers, and also to the description of each tract or parcel of land contained in the list prepared by them, of non-resident lands, the number of days which such person or tract shall be assessed for highway labor, as herein directed, and the commissioners shall subscribe such lists, and file them with the town clerk. (1 R. S. 507, § 24, as amended 1835, ch. 154, § 3.) (See form No. 22.)

*Corporations to be assessed.*—In making the estimate and assessment of the residue of the highway labor to be performed in their town, after assessing at least one day's work upon each of the male inhabitants therein, above the age of twenty-one years, as provided in the sixteenth chapter of the first part of the Revised Statutes, entitled "Of highways and bridges," the commissioners of highways shall include among the inhabitants of such town, among whom such residue is to be apportioned, all moneyed or stock corporations, which shall appear on the last assessment roll of their town to have been assessed therein. (Laws 1837, ch. 431, § 1.)

This provision of the act of 1837 is quite fully discussed by Judge Emott, in the case of The People against Pierce, reported in 31 Barb. 138. He there holds that the commissioners of highways "are to take the last assessment roll for a guide, and to include in their assessment every corporation which they find assessed therein; and they cannot tax by name, as an inhabitant of the town, any corporation which is not so assessed upon the roll." "The error, if there be one, can only be corrected by correcting the town roll."

Associations formed under the general banking law, like other moneyed or stock corporations deriving an income or profit, are liable to taxation on their capital. In ascertaining the sum to be inserted in the assessment roll, no regard should be had either to accumulations or losses of capital in the course of the business of the company, but only to the amount of the capital stock paid in and secured to be paid, after deducting expenditures for real estate, and such of the stock as the statute exempts from taxation. (*People* v *Supervisors*, 4 Hill, 20.)

Railroad companies are to be taxed upon their real estate in the town. (*People* v. *Supervisors of Niagary*, 4 Hill, 20.) And should be assessed as residents of the several lines through which their roads extend. (*People* v. *Fredericks*, 48 Barb. 173.)

*Copies of lists.*—After the commissioners of highways have filled out the lists furnished by the overseers, and subscribed and filed them with the town lerk, as provided in the 1 R. S. 507, they shall direct the clerk of the town to make a copy of said lists, and shall subscribe such copies, after which they shall cause the several copies to be delivered to the respective overseers of highways of the several districts in which the highway labor is assessed, and the acceptance of such list by any overseer to whom the same may be delivered, shall be deemed conclusive evidence that such overseer is duly chosen or appointed to such office, although the acceptance required by section 18, article 2, title 3, chapter 11, has not been filed as required by said section. (1 R. S. 507, as amended 1863, ch. 444.)

The names of persons left out of any such list, and of new inhabitants, shall from time to time be added to the several lists, and they shall be rated by the overseers in proportion to their real and personal estate, to work on the highways, as others rated by the commissioners on such lists, subject to an appeal to the commissioners. (1 R. S. 507, § 26.) (See form No. 23.)

*When assessments to be separate.*—Whenever the commissioners of highways shall assess the occupant for any land not owned by such occupant, they shall dist nguish, in their assessment lists, the amount charged upon such land, from the personal tax, if any, of the occupant thereof. But when any such land shall be assessed in the name of the occupant, the owner thereof shall not be assessed during the same year to work on the highways on account of the same land. (1 R. S. 508, § 30.)

*Private roads.*—It shall be the duty of the commissioners of highways of each town, to credit such persons as live on private roads, and work the same, so much on account of their assessments as such commissioners may deem necessary to work such private road; or to annex such private roads to some of the highway districts. (1 R. S. 508, § 29.)

*Labor, how assessed on plank roads.*—Every person liable to do highway labor, living or owning property on the line of any plank road of this state, may, on making application in writing, to the commissioner or commissioners of their respective towns, on any day previous to the time of making the highway warrants by such commissioners, be assessed the apportionment of highway labor for such property upon such plank road; and the commissioner or commissioners shall assess such person for the land or property owned by him in or upon the line of such plank road, as a separate road district. (Laws 1853, ch. 626, § 1, as amended 1855, ch. 495.)

It shall be the duty of the highway commissioner or commissioners of such town, to make a separate list of such persons and such land or property so assessed, as commissioners are now by law required to make for every separate road district, which shall be delivered to some one of the directors of such road, who shall proceed to have said highway labor worked on such road, in the same manner that overseers of highways are required by law to do. (Id. § 2.)

The said directors shall possess all the powers and have the same authority to compel the performance of such highway labor, or the payment of such highway tax as the overseers of highways now have by law, and shall make like return to the commissioners of highways. (Id. § 3.)

Any person so assessed may commute for the tax assessed upon him or his property, by paying the sum now fixed by law to any of said directors. (Id. § 4.)

*Appeal from assessment.*—Whenever any non-resident owner shall conceive himself aggrieved by the assessments of any commissioners of highways, in carrying into effect the provisions of this article, it shall be lawful for such owner, or his agent, within thirty days after such assessment, to appeal to any three judges of the court of common pleas of the county in which such land is situated. (1 R. S. 507, § 27. By the Laws 1847, ch. 280, § 29, and Code, § 30, sub. 11), county judges are invested with all the powers and jurisdiction conferred by statute upon the late courts of common pleas of the county, or the judges or any judge thereof, respecting appeals from the determination of commissioners of highways, etc.

*Proceedings before the judge.*—It is made the duty of the county judge, to whom the appeal must be made within thirty days after the assessment is made, to decide within twenty days thereafter, on such appeal, the said owner or agent giving notice to the commissioners of the time of hearing said appeal, and his decision shall be final and conclusive in the premises. (1 R. S. 507, § 28, as changed by Laws 1847, ch. 280, § 29, and Laws 1857, ch. 564.)

*Grading, etc., by anticipation of assessment.*— It shall be lawful for the inhabitants residing in any road district in this state, to grade, gravel or plank the road or roads in such district, by anticipating the highway labor of such road district for one or more years, and applying it to the immediate construction of such plank or gravel road, and after the completion of such plank or gravel road, the said inhabitants shall be exempted from the labor so anticipated and applied, except so far as their labor may be necessary to keep their said road or roads in repair; such road to be in all cases a free road. (Laws 1849, ch. 250, § 12.)

*Omissions in assessments, how rectified.*—Whenever the assessors of any town shall have omitted to assess any inhabitant or property in such town, the commissioners of highways shall assess the persons and property so omitted, and shall apportion highway labor upon such persons or property, in the same manner as if they had been duly assessed upon the last assessment roll. (Laws 1837, ch. 431, § 6.)

*Tenant may deduct assessment.*—Whenever any tenant of any land for a less term than twenty-five years, shall be assessed to work on the highways, for such land, pursuant to the last preceding section, and shall actually perform such work, or commute therefor, he shall be entitled to a deduction from the rent due, or to become due, from him, for such land, equal to the full amount of such assessment, estimating the same at the rate of one dollar per day; unless otherwise provided for by covenant or agreement between such tenant and his landlord. (1 R. S. 508, § 31, as amended 1864, ch. 395.)

*Cemetery lands exempt from assessment.*—The cemetery lands and property of any association formed pursuant to the act entitled "An act authorizing the incorporation of rural cemetery associations," passed April 27, 1847, are exempt from all public taxes, rates and assessments, so long as the same shall remain dedicated to the purposes of a cemetery. (Laws 1869, ch. 708.)

## CHAPTER V.

### PERFORMANCE OF LABOR UPON HIGHWAYS.

*Notice to work: where to be done.*—It shall be the duty of the overseers of highways to give at least twenty-four hours' notice to all persons assessed to work on the highways, and residing within the limits of their respective districts, of the time and place when and where they are to appear for that purpose, and with what implements; but no person being a resident of the town, shall be required to work on any highway, other than in the district in which he resides, unless he shall elect to work in some district where he has any land; and in such case he may, with the approbation of the commissioners of highways, apply the work assessed in respect to such land, in the district where the same is situated. (1 R. S. 509, § 32.)

The overseers are liable to a penalty of ten dollars for every refusal or neglect to warn persons to work (1 R. S. 504, § 16), but they are not liable to such penalty until they have been required by the commissioners to give such warning. The delivery by the commissioners of the assessment roll to the overseers, is a sufficient requirement to give the warning. Notice to work need not be in writing.

It requires no formal application to the commissioners to obtain their consent to work in another district, nor need they express their approbation in any formal manner; but to avoid any controversy, it will be well to obtain this written consent.

Let the applicant work the number of days, and bring a receipt or certificate from that overseer to the one where he resides, who will give him credit accordingly.

From and after the passage of this act the highway tax upon any land or property, shall be worked out or commuted for in the district in which said land or property is situated; and if commuted for, the money shall be paid to the overseer of said district for the benefit of the roads and bridges in said district; but this act shall not apply to or affect any county, city, village, town or district where the disposition of the highway tax has been provided for by a special enactment. (Laws 1866, ch. 770.)

*Labor on plank roads.*—Every person liable to do highway labor, living or owning property on the line of any plank road of this state, may, on making application in writing to the commissioner or commissioners of their respective towns, on or before any day previous to the time of making the highway warrants by such commissioners, be assessed the apportionment of highway labor for such property upon such plank road; and the commissioner or commissioners shall assess such person for the land or property owned by him in or upon the line of said plank road, as a separate road district. (Laws 1853, ch. 626, § 1, as amended 1855, ch. 495.)

It shall be the duty of the highway commissioner or commissioners of such town to make a separate list of such persons and such land or property so assessed, as commissioners are now by law required to make for every separate road district, which shall be delivered to some one of the directors of such road, who shall proceed to have said highway labor worked on such road, in the same manner that overseers of highways are required by law to do. (Id. § 2.)

The said directors shall possess all the powers and have the same authority to compel the performance of such highway labor, or the payment of such highway tax, as the overseers of highways now have by law, and shall make like returns to the commissioners of highways. (Id. § 3.)

Any person so assessed may commute for the tax assessed upon him or his property, by paying the sum now fixed by law to any of said directors. (Id. § 4.)

*Notice to non-residents.*—It shall be the duty of the several overseers of highways to notify the agent of every non-resident landholder, whose lands are assessed (if such agent reside in the town where such assessment is made), of the number of days such non-resident is assessed, and of the time when, and the place where, the labor is to be performed; which notice shall be given at least five days previous to the time appointed. (1 R. S. 509, § 33.)

It is not necessary that this notice should be in writing; but as a matter of prudence it may be well to serve a written notice; the agent may forget, and may not inform his principal, and as he can be a witness, the overseer had better serve notice and take from him an admission of service.

If the overseer cannot ascertain that such non-resident has an agent within such town, he shall affix a written notice on the outer door of the building in which the last town meeting in such town was held, containing a list of the names of such non-residents, when known, and a description of the tracts of land comprised in his list, together with the number of days' labor assessed on each tract, and a specification of the time when, and place where, such labor is to be performed; which notice shall be posted at least twenty days before the time appointed for performing such labor. (Id. § 34.)

*Commutation for work.*—Every person liable to work on the highways shall work the whole number of days for which he shall have been assessed, but every such person, other than an overseer, may elect to commute for the same, or for some part thereof, at the rate of one dollar for each day, in which case such commutation money shall be paid to the overseer of highways of the district in which the person commuting shall reside, to be applied and expended by such overseer in the improvement of the roads and bridges in the same district. (1 R. S. 509, § 35, as amended 1866, ch. 180.)

Every person intending to commute for his assessment, or for any part thereof, shall, within twenty-four hours after he shall be notified to appear and work on the highways, pay the commutation money for the work required of him by such notice; and the commutation shall not be considered as complete until such money be paid. (1 R. S. 509, § 36.)

*May require teams, etc.*—Every overseer of highways shall have power to require a team, or a cart, wagon or plough, with a pair of horses or oxen, and a man to manage them, from any person having the same within his district, who shall have been assessed three days or more, and who shall not have commuted for his assessment; and the person furnishing the same upon such requisition shall be entitled to a credit of three days for each day's service therewith. (Id. § 37.)

*Substitutes; hours to work.*—Every person assessed to work on the highways and warned to work may appear in person or by an able bodied man as a substitute; and the person or substitute so appearing shall actually work eight hours in each day, under the penalty of twelve and a half cents for every hour such person or substitute shall be in default, to be imposed as a fine on the person assessed. (1 R. S. 510, § 38.)

*Penalty for neglect to work, and how collected.*—If any such person or his substitute shall, after appearing, remain idle, or not work faithfully, or hinder others from working, such offender shall for every offense forfeit the sum of one dollar. (Id. § 39.)

Every person so assessed and duly notified, who shall not commute, and who shall refuse or neglect to appear as above provided, shall forfeit for every day's refusal or neglect, the sum of one dollar. If he was required to furnish a team, carriage, man or implements, and shall refuse or neglect to comply, he shall be fined as follows:

1. For wholly omitting to comply with such requisition, three dollars for each day.
2. For omitting to furnish a cart, wagon or plough, one dollar for each day.
3. For omitting to furnish a pair of horses or oxen, one dollar for each day.

4. For omitting to furnish a man to manage the team, one dollar for each day. (Id. § 40.)

It shall be the duty of every overseer of highways, within six days after any person so assessed and notified shall be guilty of any refusal or neglect for which a penalty or fine is prescribed in this title, unless a satisfactory excuse shall be rendered to him for such refusal or neglect, to make complaint, on oath, to one of the justices of the peace of the town. (Id. § 41.)

The complaint can only be made by an overseer (5 Denio, 102), and to a justice of the peace; not to a justice's court. (7 Barb. 337.) An overseer will not be liable for rendering an unreasonable complaint, unless he acts maliciously. (1 Johns. 515; 10 id. 470.)

The justice to whom such complaint shall be made shall forthwith issue a summons directed to any constable of the town, requiring him to summon such delinquent to appear forthwith before such justice, at some place to be specified in the summons, to show cause why he should not be fined according to law for such refusal or neglect; which summons shall be served personally, or by leaving a copy at his personal abode. (1 R. S. 510, § 42.)

It must be served by a constable of the same town. These proceedings are very summary. The justice is authorized to proceed on the return of summons served by copy; the constable should therefore be careful and make a personal service, if in his power. (9 Johns. 229.)

If, upon the return of such summons, no sufficient cause shall be shown to the contrary, the justice shall impose such fine as is provided in this title for the offense complained of, and shall forthwith issue a warrant under his hand and seal, directed to any constable of the town where such delinquent shall reside, commanding him to levy such fine, with the costs of the proceedings, of the goods and chattels of such delinquent. (1 R. S. 510, § 43.)

It is thought that no property is exempt from levy under this warrant. It is not an execution within 2 R. S. 367, § 22.

The constable to whom such warrant shall be directed shall forthwith collect the moneys therein mentioned. He shall pay the fine, when collected, to the justice who issued the warrant, who is hereby required to pay the same to the overseer who entered the complaint, to be by him expended in improving the roads and bridges in the district of which he is overseer. (1 R. S. 511, § 44.)

When the summons is returned, the justice should allow a reasonable time for the party to appear and defend; and when it is returned, served by copy, he should see that all has been fair in the attempt to serve it. No adjournment can be granted; but the justice can exercise a reasonable discretion in holding open the court for the appearance of the delinquent, or to allow him to procure witnesses. The justice has a large discretion in passing upon the sufficiency of the excuse. He is the sole judge, and his decision is final. No appeal or certiorari will lie to his decision.

By the former highway acts the complaint of the overseer was final and conclusive, and the justice had no discretion, and acted merely as a ministerial officer. (See 9 Johns. 229; 3 id. 474.)

By the act of 1784, § 7, the overseer was authorized to impose the fine and issue the warrant. The revision of the act in 1801 required the overseer to make complaint to a justice of the peace, who proceeded *ex parte*, and acted ministerially in enforcing the penalty. The act of 1813 required a summons substantially as is now required by the act.

The proceeding is necessarily summary. It must be had before a justice of the peace as justice, and not before a justice's court. (7 Barb. 337.) The overseer can judge who is in default, and demand the warrant, and although the complaint is unjust, no action can lie against the justice

*Penalties to be set off.*—Every penalty collected for a refusal or neglect to appear and work on the highways shall be set off against the assessment upon which it was founded, estimating every dollar collected as a satisfaction for one day's work. (1 R. S. 511, § 45.)

*Excuses.*—The acceptance by an overseer of any excuse for refusal or neglect shall not, in any case, exempt the person excused for commuting for or working the whole number of days for which he shall have been assessed during the year. (Id. § 46.)

*Proceedings to collect non-resident labor unpaid.* Every overseer of highways shall, on or before the first day of October in each year, make out and deliver to the supervisor of his town a list of all resident landholders residing in his district who have not worked out their highway assessment or commuted for the same, with the number of days not worked or commuted for by each resident of his district, charging for each day in such list at the rate of one dollar and fifty cents per day; and also a list of all the lands of non-residents and of person unknown, which were assessed on his warrant by the commissioner of highways, or added by him according to law, on which the labor assessed has not been performed or commuted for, and the number of days' labor unpaid by each, charging for the same at the rate of one dollar and fifty cents per day; which list shall be accompanied by the affidavit of the overseer, duly certified, that he has given the notice required by the thirty-second, thirty-third and thirty-fourth sections of this title, and that the labor for which such residents and such land is returned has not been performed or commuted. (1 R. S. 511, § 47, as amended 1870, ch. 461.) (See form No. 20.)

Sections thirty-second, thirty-third and thirty-fourth, referred to, are given in the first part of this chapter.

If any overseer shall refuse or neglect to deliver such lists to the supervisor as provided in the last preceding section, or shall refuse or neglect to make the affidavit, as therein directed, he shall, for every such offense, forfeit the sum of ten dollars; and, also, the amount of tax or taxes for labor remaining unpaid, at the rate of one dollar for each day assessed, to be recovered by the commissioners of highways and applied to making and improving the roads and bridges in said district. (1 R. S. 511, § 48, as amended 1865, ch. 522.)

It shall be the duty of the supervisors of the several towns to receive the lists of the overseers of highways, when delivered pursuant to the preceding forty-seventh section, and to lay the same before the board of supervisors of the county. (1 R. S. 511, § 49.)

It shall be the duty of each board of supervisors, at their annual meeting in each year, to cause the amount of such arrearages for highway labor returned to them severally, as provided in the preceding section, estimating each day's labor at one dollar and fifty cents a day, to be levied on the lands of all residents and non-residents, returned as aforesaid, as returned by the assessors of the several towns, and to be collected in the same manner that the contingent charges of the county are levied and collected, and to order the same, when collected, to be paid over to the commissioners of highways of the towns, respectively, to be by them applied to the construction, repair, and improvement of the roads and bridges in the district in which the labor was originally assessed. (Id. § 50, as amended 1870, ch. 461.)

*Labor of moneyed and stock corporations; commutation for; penalties, how collected.* — All moneyed or stock corporations shall be notified to furnish the amount of highway labor assessed to them in the same manner as individuals residing in such town, by giving oral or written notice to the president, cashier, agents, treasurer or secretary of such corporation, or any clerk or other officer thereof, at the principal office or place of transacting the business or concerns of the said company, which labor shall be performed in such district or districts as the commissioners of highways of the town shall direct, and any number of days' work, not exceeding fifty, may be required to be performed by any such corporation in any one day. (Laws of 1837, ch. 431, § 2.)

Every such corporation may commute for the highway labor assessed upon it, in the same manner and at the same rate as is allowed by law to individuals or by paying such commutation to a commissioner of highways of the town, and the commutation money so paid may be expended by the commissioners of highways upon any district or districts in the town; and for that purpose the said commissioners shall be entitled to demand and receive from the overseers to whom any such commutation may have been paid, the whole or any portion thereof, but in every case where any such corporation shall be located in any city, village or town, where by law the road tax is now payable in money, the road tax imposed on any such corporation shall be paid in money, according to the provisions of the several laws affecting said city, village or town. (Id. § 3.)

Such corporation shall be liable to the same penalties for every day's work required, and for every default of any substitute sent by them, as is provided by law in the case of individuals required to work on highways, which shall be collected in the same manner, and paid over to the commissioners of highways of the town by the constable collecting the same, and may be expended by them in the same manner as herein provided for the commutation money received from any such corporation. The summons issued by any justice according to this act may be for any number of penalties incurred by any such corporation previous thereto, and may be served in the manner provided by law for the service of writs or summons issuing out of courts of record against corporations. (Id. § 4.)

In case any such penalty cannot be collected as herein provided, the commissioners of highways of the town may file a bill in the court of chancery against any such delinquent corporation for the discovery and sequestration of its property; whereupon the same proceedings shall be had as are provided by law for the collection of county taxes assessed against incorporated companies; and the chancellor shall possess the like powers in respect to the same: and the said commissioners may also recover such penalties, or any number of them that may have been incurred, with costs, from such delinquent company in any court of record in this state. (Id. § 5.)

*Overseers to make annual return and pay over moneys.*—Every overseer of highways shall, on the second Tuesday next preceding the time of holding the annual town meeting in his town, within the year for which he is elected or appointed, render to one of the commissioners of highways of the town an account in writing, verified by his oath, and containing,

1. The names of all persons assessed to work on the highways in the district of which he is overseer.
2. The names of all those who have actually worked on the highways, with the number of days they have so worked.
3. The names of all those who have been fined, and the sums in which they have been fined.
4. The names of all those who have commuted, and the manner in which the moneys arising from fines and commutations have been expended by him.
5. A list of all lands which he has returned to the supervisor for non-payment of taxes, and the amount of tax on each tract of land so returned. (1 R. S. § 51.) (See form No. 24.)

The commissioners of highways are authorized to administer the oath required by the above section. (Laws of 1833, ch. 149.)

Every such overseer shall also then and there pay to the commissioner all moneys remaining in his hands unexpended, to be applied by the commissioners in making and improving the roads and bridges in the town, in such manner as they shall direct. (1 R. S. 512, § 52.)

If any overseer shall refuse or neglect to render such account, or if, having rendered the same, he shall refuse or neglect to pay any balance which may then be due from him, he shall, for every such offense, forfeit the sum of five dollars, to be recovered, with the balance of moneys remaining in his hands, by the commissioners of highways of the town, and to be applied in making and improving the roads and bridges. It shall be the duty of the commissioners of highways to prosecute for such penalty in every instance in which no return is made. (Id. § 53.)

Whenever it shall appear, from the annual return of any overseer of highways, made in pursuance of the fifty-first section of the sixteenth chapter of title first of the first part of the Revised Statutes, that any person who was assessed to work on the highways (other than non-residents) has neglected to work the whole number of days to him assessed, and has not commuted for, or otherwise satisfied such deficiency, then it shall be the duty of the commissioners of highways to re-assess such deficiency to the person so delinquent, at the next assessment of work for highway purposes, and to add to it his annual assessment. (Laws of 1832, ch. 107.)

Such re-assessment shall not exonerate any overseer of highways from any penalty which he may have incurred under the sixteenth section of the last aforesaid chapter. (Id. § 3.)

The penalties prescribed by section sixteen, above cited, are given ante, chapter iii.

*Extent of overseer's authority in performing work.* What control has the overseer in improving the road over the soil, and materials within the limits of the road? The general rule is, that the public have a right to all the earth and materials that are necessary for the improvement of the road. Such earth and materials may be removed from one part of a highway to another, even beyond the boundaries of the land opposite which they were taken (*Fish* v. *Mayor of Rochester*, 6 Paige, 272); but this rule does not apply to trees standing or lying upon a highway. Such trees belong to the owner of the land, except such as may be requisite to make or repair the highways and bridges on the same land. (1 R. S. 525, § 126.) But if trees have been left or set out for shade, the overseer has no right to cut them, even for the purpose of repairing the roads and bridges on the same land. (1 R. S. 525, § 27.) The powers of the highway officers are co-extensive with the highway, and they may cut down, level, grade and alter every portion of the space included in the highway, for the improvement of the road, being only responsible for a wanton or malicious injury to the rights of adjacent owners. (*Graves* v. *Otis*, 2 Hill, 470; *Radcliff's Executors* v. *Mayor of Brooklyn*, 4 N. Y. R. 203; *Benedict* v. *Goit*, 3 Barb. 469.)

In Maine it has been decided that a surveyor, which answers to an overseer, has no authority to appropriate any land not laying within the lines of the road. He has no authority to make a ditch through adjoining improved lands, for the purpose of having water turned off from the highway, however important to the public it may be to have it done; and for such an act the owner of the land may maintain trespass against him. (*Plummer* v. *Sturtevant*, 32 Maine R. 325.)

So the highway officers have no right to precipitate the water from a highway upon the adjoining lands.

Where a highway crosses or passes alongside of a natural stream, the road must be so worked as not to obstruct the natural flow of the water. (*People* v. *Kingman*, 24 N. Y. R. 559.)

*Abatement of tax for shade trees.*—Any inhabitant liable to highway tax, who shall transplant by the side of the public highway, any forest shade trees or fruit trees, of suitable size, shall be allowed by the overseers of highways, in abatement of his highway tax, one dollar for every four trees set out; but no row of elms shall be placed nearer than seventy feet; no row of maples or other forest trees nearer than fifty feet, except locust, which may be set thirty feet apart; fruit trees must also be set at least fifty feet apart; and no allowance, as before mentioned, shall be made, unless such trees shall have been set out the year previous to the demand for said abatement of tax, and are living and well protected from animals at the time of such demand. (Laws of 1869, ch. 322, § 1, as amended 1870, ch. 595.)

Any trees transplanted by the side of the public highways, as aforesaid, in the place of trees which have died, shall be allowed for in the same manner and on the same conditions as in the preceding section. (Laws of 1869, ch. 322, § 2.)

No person shall be allowed an abatement of his highway tax, as aforesaid, more than one-quarter of his annual highway tax, and no one shall recover any abatement of tax for trees transplanted previous to the passage of this act. (Id. § 3.)

*Abatement for watering trough.*—The overseer of the highways in the several road districts of this state shall abate three dollars from the highway tax of any inhabitant in his district who shall construct, and, during the year previous, keep in repair, a watering trough beside the public highway, well supplied with water, the surface of which shall be two and a half feet or more above the level of the ground, and easily accessible for horses with vehicles; but the said overseers of highways respectively may designate the number necessary for the public convenience in each district, and no others but those designated shall be allowed this abatement of tax. (Laws of 1869, ch. 131.)

*Additional labor to remove snow.* — Whenever the labor in any ward or district has been worked out, commuted for or returned to the supervisor, and the highways are obstructed by snow, or otherwise, and written notice has been given to the overseer by any two or more inhabitants of the town, liable to payment of highway tax, requesting the removal of such obstruction, it shall be the duty of the overseer of highways in such district, and they are hereby required, to immediately call upon all persons liable to highway tax in their respective districts, to assist in removing such obstructions; and such labor, so called for by the overseer, shall be assessed upon those liable to perform the same, in proportion to their original assessments, and all persons so called out and failing to appear at the place designated by the overseer, or to commute at a dollar a day, within twenty-four hours after due notice, shall be liable to fine at the rate of one dollar and fifty cents a day, for each day's labor they may be required to perform, which fine shall be collectible by the overseer as such, by suit in justices' court, and shall be applied by said overseer to the purposes specified in this section. And if the said overseer of highways, after receiving the written notice, as aforesaid, neglects, without good and sufficient reasons, to have such highways opened, without delay, he shall be liable to a penalty of five dollars per day for every day he neglects such duty, the penalty to be collected in justice's court, with costs, by any one suing for the same, and the said penalty shall be paid over to the commissioners of highways for the use of the town. (Laws 1869, ch. 593.)

## CHAPTER VI.

### OF THE LAYING OUT OF PUBLIC ROADS.

*Application, by whom and how made.*—Every person liable to be assessed for highway labor, may apply to the commissioners of highways of the town in which he shall reside, to alter or discontinue any road, or to lay out any new road. Every such application shall be in writing, addressed to the commissioners, and signed by the person applying. (1 R. S. 513, § 54.)

Every person liable to be assessed for highway labor, and owning lands in a town in which he is not a resident, may apply to the commissioners of highways of the town in which the lands are situated, to alter, discontinue, or to lay out any road through the same. (Laws of 1836, ch. 122.) (See form No. 25.)

The word "same," in the above act, refers to the town and not to the lands of the non-resident. (*People* v. *Eggleston*, 13 How. 123.)

A petition for laying out a highway may lawfully include a portion of a highway already in existence, and the new highway may, for a portion of its distance, be laid out upon and be identical with an existing highway. It is a question of discretion and convenience, to be determined by the commissioners or referees. (*People* v. *Commissioners of Milton*, 37 N. Y. R. 360.)

The application to lay out a new road and discontinue an old one may be in one, and whether the proceedings to discontinue the old road are valid or not, will not effect the new road, if that is properly laid out. (*People* v. *Robertson*, 17 How. 74.) It is no objection to proceedings to lay out a highway, that they were taken on the application of a person not liable to assessment for highway labor. (*Marble* v. *Whitney*, 28 N. Y. R. 297; *Aspinwall* v. *Supervisors of Richmond*, 20 id. 252.) The language of the above sections is held to be permissive only, and does not deprive the commissioners of the power to lay out roads on their own motion. (*Gould* v. *Glass*, 19 Barb. 188. See, however, *Harrington* v. *People*, 6 Barb. 607.)

*Power of commissioners to lay out.*—The commissioners of highways shall have power, in the manner and under the restrictions hereinafter provided, to lay out, on actual survey, such new roads in their respective towns, as they may deem necessary and proper; and to discontinue such old roads and highways as shall appear to them, on the oaths of twelve freeholders of the same town, to have become unnecessary. (1 R. S. 502, § 2.)

Commissioners may, upon their own motion and without application, lay out a highway. (*Marble* v. *Whitney*, 28 N. Y. R. 297; *Aspinwall* v. *Supervisors of Richmond*, 20 id. 252.)

The commissioners exercise a special and limited jurisdiction in laying out highways, and although it may be presumed that their acts were legal until the contrary appear, their acts may be impeached. (*Ex parte Clapper*, 3 Hill, 458.)

The order laying out a highway may be made by any two of the commissioners, without the concurrence of the third, but in such case it *must show on* its face, not only that the third met with his associates, but that he participated in their deliberations, even if he did not concur in their conclusions; or else that he was notified, not only of the intended meeting, but of the particular subject on which it was proposed to deliberate. (1 R. S. 525, § 125; *People* v. *Williams*, 36 N. Y. R. 441; *People* v. *Hynds*. 30 id. 470; *Stewart* v. *Wallis*, 30 Barb. 344; *Fitch* v. *Commissioners of Kirkland*, 22 Wend. 132.)

*Survey to be made.* — Whenever the commissioners of highways shall lay out, alter or discontinue any road, either upon application to them or otherwise, they shall cause a survey to be made of such road, and shall incorporate such survey in an order to be signed by them, and to be filed and recorded in the office of the town clerk, who shall note the time of recording the same. (1 R. S. 513, § 55.) (See form No. 26.)

The survey need not specify the width of the proposed road; it is sufficient to run a single line, which will be regarded as the centre of the road. (*People* v. *Commissioners of Salem*, 1 Cow. 23.) A specification of the quantity of land which the road will take from each proprietor over whose ground it passes, will ascertain its width. (*People* v. *Commissioners of Redhook*, 13 Wend. 310; *Lamlin* v. *Commissioners of Cambridge*, 2 Caine's, 178.) The survey is merely a ministerial act, which does not require the presence of all the commissioners to give validity to an order of the commissioners laying out a highway. (*Marble* v. *Whitney*, 28 N. Y. R. 297.) Nor is it essential that the survey should be signed by all. (*Tucker* v. *Rankin*, 15 Barb. 471.)

The clerk is bound to record the survey as presented. He cannot refuse to record it by reason of some supposed omission or mistake therein. (*People* v. *Collins*, 7 Johns. 549.)

*Order to be posted.*—It shall be the duty of the town clerk, whenever any order of the commissioners for laying out, altering or discontinuing a road shall be received by him, to post a copy of such order on the door of the house where the town-meeting is usually held; and the time hereinafter limited for appealing from any such order shall be computed from the time of recording the same. (1 R. S. 513, § 56.)

*Consent of owner, when necessary.*—No public or private road shall be laid out through any orchard or garden without the consent of the owner thereof, if such orchard be of the growth of four years or more, or if such garden have been cultivated for four years or more, before the laying out of such road. Nor shall any such road be laid out through any buildings, or any fixtures or erections for the purposes of trade or manufactures, or any yards or inclosures necessary to the use and enjoyment thereof, without the consent of the owner. (1 R. S. 514, § 57.) (See Form No. 27.)

The consent need not be in writing. A parol consent is valid, provided it be acted upon immediately by the commissioners, and the road laid out before any revocation of such consent. (*People* v. *Goodwin*, 5 N. Y. R. 568; *Noyes* v. *Chapin*, 6 Wend. 461; *Marble* v. *Whitney*, 28 N. Y. R. 297; *People* v. *Albright*, 23 How. 306.) Such consent may, however, be revoked before the commissioners have acted thereon, and laid out the road or made the alteration. After they have so acted, the owner is estopped from denying the legality of the act. (*Marble v. Whitney, supra.*) When such consent has been given under a mistake of either law or fact, and acted upon, no relief can be given. (Id.) A sale of the land, in good faith, will amount to a revocation of parol consent, if made before the laying out of the road, even during the pendency of an appeal to the county court from a decision of the commissioners in relation to such road. (*People* v. *Goodwin, supra.*) The consent of the owner may also be inferred from his acts. Thus, if he appear on appeal, and contests the question of damage, his consent will be presumed. (*Lansing* v. *Caswell*, 4 Paige, 523.)

The restrictions on the powers of the commissioners in laying out roads apply only to cases where the owner withholds his consent. The commissioners may lay out a road through any kind of property, with the consent of the owner. (*Lansing* v. *Caswell, supra.*) In the five cases enumerated, the commissioners have no power, without such consent, to lay out a road: 1st, through orchards; 2d, gardens; 3d, buildings; 4th, fixtures and erections for trade, etc.; and, 5th, yards and inclosures necessary for use of buildings and manufactures.

1. ORCHARDS.—To be within the prohibition, the orchard must be of the growth of four years or more, and the road proposed must injure the usefulness of the premises as an orchard by taking some part where the fruit-trees grow.

In *The People* v. *The Judges of Dutchess* (23 Wend. 360), the road was laid through a lane where two apple-trees stood that had formerly belonged to the orchard, but they had been separated from it by a fence for several years. The road also, as laid out, passed over the circular corner of a lot or field in which there was an orchard, including in the road a piece of ground about fifty feet long and eight feet wide; but no apple-trees in the orchard situated near the road. The court said the road could not be laid out in such a manner as to deprive the owner, either in whole or in part, of the beneficial enjoyment of his fruit-trees. "But we are, in effect, asked to go further, and say that a road cannot be laid over an inclosed field, if there are fruit-trees in any part of it, however distant they may be from the highway. To this doctrine we cannot subscribe. It does not follow that the whole field is an orchard, because there are fruit-trees in some part of it."

It is thought, also, that an old road cannot be increased in width, so as to take in any part of an orchard, if the owner be thereby deprived of the benefit of his fruit-trees. (*Snyder* v. *Plass*, 28 N. Y. R. 465; *Snyder v. Trumpbour*, 38 id. 355.)

2. GARDEN. — It must have been cultivated as a garden four years previous to laying out. What constitutes a garden is a question of fact. The general definition is, a plat of ground appropriated to the cultivation of herbs or plants, fruits and flowers.

3. BUILDINGS. — They must be buildings erected previous to the application and notice for the highway. If, after such application and notice, the owner of the land puts buildings or erections thereon, it will not prevent the commissioners from going on and laying out the highway. It is the fault of the party himself, who cannot thus defeat the operation of the law. (*Caris* v. *Commissioners of Waterloo*, 2 Hill, 443.)

4. FIXTURES OR ERECTIONS. — Only such as are for the purpose of trade and manufactures are excepted. Over other fixtures and erections, by the oath of freeholders, a road may be laid, if the erections do not amount to buildings. Tenter-bars, erected for the purpose of carrying on the business of a fulling-mill,

are within the prohibition. (*Clark* v. *Phelps*, 4 Cow. 190.)

Neither a public nor a private road or way can be laid out across the fixtures and erections upon the inclined plane of a railroad which are used for the drawing or letting down cars for the conveyance of merchandise or passengers. (*Mohawk, etc., R. R. Co.* v. *Archer*, 6 Paige, 83.)

What are and are not fixtures and erections, for the purpose mentioned in this section, is a question of fact, and must be judged of in reference to the situation and nature of the property.

A ditch or canal for conducting water to a mill is not a fixture or erection. The term "erection" implies some structure above ground. (*People* v. *Kingman*, 24 N. Y. R. 559.)

5. YARDS OR INCLOSURES. — In *Ex parte Clapper* (3 Hill, 458), the highway, as laid out, passed through the *door-yard* of one man, and left his *well*, *cow-shed*, and a part of his *corn-crib*, in the highway. It also encroached on the *garden* and *cow-shed* of another man. It was decided by the court that the commissioners had exceeded their powers, no consent being given. And they further decided that the words *yards* or *inclosures* apply to "buildings" as well as to "fixtures or erections for the purpose of trade."

It is not every court-yard or inclosure which is appurtenant or contiguous to a dwelling-house or a manufacturing establishment, through which the commissioners are prohibited from laying out a road or highway. It is only such yards or inclosures as are necessary to the use and enjoyment of the dwelling-house or manufacturing establishment. This clause must be construed in reference to the situation and nature of the property to which the yard or inclosure is appurtenant. (*Lansing* v. *Caswell*, 4 Paige, 523.)

Grounds adjoining a saw-mill, and used for piling logs, but whose limits are not fixed by fences or other visible marks, nor by definite occupation, are not within the prohibition. (*People* v. *Kingman*, 24 N. Y. R. 559.) The commissioners should, however, leave a sufficient area for the use of the mill-owners; and their discretion as to the question is not reviewable. (Id.)

A highway cannot be laid out over grounds acquired by a railroad corporation for the site of an engine-house, station-house, turn-table, etc., necessary for use at the station. (*The Albany Northern R. R. Co.* v. *Brownell*, 24 N. Y. R. 345.) The commissioners have no power to lay out a road through a court-yard contiguous to a dwelling, nor grounds adjoining a factory and actually used and occupied by its machinery and appurtenances. (*Clark* v. *Phelps*, 4 Cow. 190; *Lansing* v. *Caswell*, 4 Paige, 519.) The words "yards and inclosures," in the 57th section, above cited, include those of any building, as well as of trade fixtures or erections. (*Ex parte Clapper*, 3 Hill, 458.) It is not necessary that the yard should be protected by fences, but it must be defined in some way, either by an inclosure, by visible marks, or by a definite occupation within certain exterior lines. (*People* v. *Kingman*, 24 N. Y. R. 562.)

6. VINEYARDS.—Private lands on which grape vineyards have been planted and have had one or more year's growth, shall not be taken for public highways or private roads, except with the consent of the owner or owners thereof. This act shall only apply to lands used in good faith for vineyard purposes and shall not apply to lands within the corporate

limits of any city or village, nor to any lands on which a vineyard shall hereafter be planted, after an application for the opening of a road therein shall have been made. (Laws of 1869, ch. 24.)

7. BURYING GROUND.—No private or public road shall be laid out or constructed upon or through any grave yard or burying ground in this state, unless the remains therein contained are first carefully removed and properly reinterred in some other burying ground, at the expense of the persons desiring such road. (Laws of 1868, ch. 843.) So highways are not to be laid through the lands of an incorporated soldiers' monument association, without the consent of the trustees of such association, except by special permission of the legislature. (Laws of 1866, ch. 273, § 461.)

If the commissioners exceed their jurisdiction by laying out a road through a building, fixture, yard, etc., without the owner's consent, the order is void, and is not helped by the affirmance of the judges on appeal. (*Ex parte Clapper*, 3 Hill, 458.)

And the commissioners of highways and their agents will be trespassers, if they enter upon the premises to open and work such highway. (*Harrington* v. *The People*, 6 Barb. 612.)

The commissioners, in laying out highways, exercise a special and limited jurisdiction; and although it may be presumed, until the contrary appear, that they have acted legally, it is quite clear that their acts may be impeached by showing that they exceeded their powers. (*Ex parte Clapper*, 3 Hill, 461.)

*Oath of freeholders, when necessary.*—No highway shall be laid out through inclosed, improved or cultivated land, without the consent of the owner or occupant thereof, unless certified to be necessary by the oath of twelve reputable freeholders of the town, in the manner hereinafter provided. (1 R. S. 514, § 58.)

The terms "improved or cultivated land," are to be taken in the popular sense, according to the general understanding of the community when distinguishing what is called wild land or land in a state of nature from that which has been cultivated or improved. When speaking of improved land, it is generally understood to be such as has been reclaimed, is used for the purposes of husbandry, and is cultivated as such, whether the appropriation is for tillage, meadow or pasture. (*Clark* v. *Phelps*, 4 Cow. 202.)

Many of the remarks as to consent of owners, made under the last section, apply equally to this. A written consent is not necessary. (*People* v. *Albright*, 23 How. 306.) Nor is it within the statute of frauds. (*People* v. *Goodwin*, 5 N. Y. R. 568.)

This section uses the words owner or *occupant*. This does not mean that the consent of a tenant only can confer the right to take the premises upon the commissioners. If the occupant has an interest in the lands, his consent, as well as the owner's, must be obtained. This is thought to be the correct view of the section, although there is no adjudication on the subject.

*Notice of application.*—Every person who shall apply for the laying out of a highway through any such land shall cause notices in writing to be posted up at three of the most public places of the town, specifying, as near as may be, the route of the proposed highway, the several tracts of land through which the same is proposed to be laid, and the time and place at which the freeholders will meet to examine the ground. Every such notice shall be posted up at least six days before the time specified therein for the meeting of the freeholders. (1 R. S. 514, § 59.) (See form No. 28.)

If the *termini* and general route of the proposed road are given, without specifying the course and distances, it will be a sufficient compliance with the statute. That is the business of the commissioners or judges if they conclude to lay out the road. (*People* v. *The Judges of Dutchess*, 23 Wend. 360.)

*Proceedings thereon.*—If twelve reputable freeholders of the town, not interested in the lands through which the road is to be laid, nor of kin to the owner thereof, shall appear at the time and place specified in the notice, they shall then be sworn by a justice of the peace or any officer authorized to administer oaths, well and truly to examine and certify, in regard to the necessity and propriety of the highway applied for. (1 R. S. 514, § 60.) It may be presumed by the court that the freeholders are reputable. (*Clark* v. *Phelps*, 4 Cow. 190.)

By the term "freeholders," is meant such as have the *legal* title to real estate. (*People* v. *Hynds*, 30 N. Y. R. 472.)

Persons related to the owner within the ninth degree, are "of kin," and therefore incompetent to act (*People* v. *Cline*, 23 Barb. 197); but a person holding a legal title in a purely fiduciary capacity, as one of the trustees of a religious society, although he might be deemed *interested* within the provision as to the qualifications of the freeholder, is not "*an owner*," so as to exclude those of kin to him from certifying. (Id.)

The oath may be administered by one of the commissioners. (Laws of 1847, ch. 455.)

The certificate must be signed by twelve *qualified* freeholders, or the proceeding based on it will be void. (*Town of Gallatin* v. *Loucks*, 21 Barb. 578; *People* v. *Hynds*, 30 N. Y. R. 472; *People* v. *Commissioners of Seward*, 27 Barb. 94.)

It is no objection that the certificate is signed by more than twelve freeholders; and in a case where the certificate was signed by twenty freeholders, the fact that five of them were of kin to the owner of the land, it was held that it did not vitiate it, there being still twelve who were properly qualified to sign. (*Carmel* v. *Judges of Putnam*, 7 Wend. 264; *People* v. *Cline*, 23 Barb. 197.)

A recital in the order laying out a road, that twelve freeholders have certified as to its necessity, is not conclusive evidence of the fact. That being a jurisdictional fact, is open to contradiction. (*People* v. *Commissioners of Seward*, 27 Barb. 94.)

*Certificate of freeholders.*—They shall then personally examine the route of such highway, and shall hear any reasons that may be offered for or against laying out the same. If they shall be of opinion that such highway is necessary and proper, they shall make and subscribe a certificate in writing to that effect, which shall be delivered to the commissioners of highways of the town. (1 R. S. 514, § 61.) (See form No. 29.)

The freeholders act upon the notice of the applicant and the general description of the route therein, and have no authority to locate it with greater particularity. (*Hallock* v. *Woolsey*, 23 Wend. 328.) They are to certify whether or not a road is necessary between certain specified points on the line mentioned in the application. (*People* v. *Judges of Dutchess*, 23 Wend. 360.)

No compensation shall be allowed any juror for examining and certifying in regard to the necessity and propriety of any highway being laid out, altered or discontinued, nor for appearing to make such examination. (Laws of 1845, ch. 180, § 14.)

The certificate of the freeholders is to be filed with the town clerk, and the commissioners may be compelled to file it by an attachment. (*People* v. *Vail*, 1 Cow. 589; 2 id. 623.) But omitting to file the certificate at the time of making the order laying out a road does not affect the proceedings. (*Commissioners of Bushwick* v. *Meserole*, 10 Wend. 122.)

*Notice to occupant.*—Before the commissioners shall determine to lay out the highway so applied for and certified, they shall cause notice in writing to be given to the occupant of the land through which the road is to run, of the time and place at which they will meet to decide on the application. The notice shall be served by delivering the same to such occupant, or if he be absent, by leaving the same at his dwelling-house; and in either case, at least three days before the time of meeting. (1 R. S. 514, § 62.) (See form No. 30.)

This notice in writing to occupants is necessary before the commissioners will have jurisdiction to proceed to lay out the road. The appearance, by the occupant, as a witness before the referees, will not be deemed a waiver of notice. (*People* v. *Judges of Herkimer*, 20 Wend. 186; *People* v. *Robertson*, 17 How. 74; *People* v. *Supervisors of Allegany*, 36 id. 544.)

Notice given to the actual occupant of the lands required will be sufficient to give the commissioners jurisdiction. It need not be given to an owner who is not in occupation. (*People* v. *Supervisors of Allegany*, *supra*.) A highway was proposed to be laid out through a field owned by a railroad company, but leased as a pasture, and in which was a large reservoir covered by plank and turf and fed by springs, the water from which was drawn by pipes for the use of the railroad; but the reservoir being covered, cattle in the pasture stood upon and passed over it as over other portions of the lot, and it was proposed to lay out a highway directly over the reservoir. *Held*, that notice served upon the occupant of the lot for pasturage only was sufficient to confer jurisdiction upon the proper authorities to proceed and lay out the highway. (Id.) The statute provision requiring notice to the occupant contemplates those holding occupancy of the surface as distinguished from those carrying on sub-surface operations. (Id.)

The proceedings to lay out a highway through improved lands are not void merely on account of the fact that the notice of the meeting of the commissioners to decide on the application, erroneously stated that some of the improved lands were unimproved. It is sufficient to confer jurisdiction under the act, that the party had notice and abundant opportunity to be heard. (*Snyder* v. *Trumpbour*, 38 N. Y. R. 355.)

*Order laying out road.*—The commissioners shall meet at the time specified in the notice, and shall hear any reasons that may be offered for or against laying out the highway. If they shall determine to lay out such highway, they shall make out and subscribe a certificate of such determination, describing the road so laid out, particularly, by routes and bounds and by its courses and distance, and shall deposit the same with the town clerk. (1 R. S. 314, § 63.) (See form No. 31.)

The commissioners may refuse to lay out a road even after the freeholders have certified to its necessity.

Their determination must be confined to the highway applied for; but they are not limited to the precise *route* specified in the application; they may, in the exercise of a sound discretion, make such *variations* as they may judge proper. The departure must not, however, be so great as to induce the belief that the preliminary proceedings have been wholly disregarded; the general course of the road must be preserved. By section 63 the applicant is to specify "*as near as may be, the route of the proposed highway.*" The freeholders act only upon the notice of the applicant, and the general description of the route therein, and have no authority to locate it with greater particularity. They determine only whether such highway is necessary and proper. The commissioners, by this section, are required to describe it *particularly, by routes and bounds, courses and distance.* (*Woolsey* v. *Tompkins*, 23 Wend. 324; *Hallock* v. *Woolsey*, id. 328.)

The certificate required by this section will be, however, sufficiently conformable to it, if, in the description of the road, a *single line* is given which will be intended as the center of the highway, and it contain a specification of the quantity of land which the road will take for each proprietor over whose ground it passes. By this its width can be ascertained. (*The People* v. *Commissioners of Highways of Red Hook*, 13 Wend. 310; *Herrick* v. *Stover*, 5 id. 580.)

It was also decided in *Woolsey* v. *Tompkins* (23 Wend. 324) to the same effect, that it will be sufficient if this certificate state the *termini* (that is, its beginning and end) of the road, and its route by *courses and distance.* It is not necessary to state the bounds of each course.

Since the statute prescribes the width of highways, an order laying out a road is sufficiently explicit if it specify the central line. (*Lawton* v. *Commissioners of Cambridge*, 2 Caines, 179; *People* v. *Commissioners of Salem*, 1 Cow. 23.) If the commissioners run a single line it will be intended as the center of the road, unless something appear from their record to show that it was not their intention. (*People* v. *Commissioners of Red Hook*, 13 Wend. 310.)

A writing purporting to be a survey of a road, describing the center line, and stating where the road is to commence and terminate, and filed with the town clerk as a part of the record, is a substantial compliance with the above section. (*Tucker* v. *Rankin*, 15 Barb. 471.) It is no objection to the order of commissioners laying out a road, that it does not incorporate the survey, if the survey be referred to in the order and attached thereto, and recorded with it. (*Van Bergen* v. *Bradley*, 36 N. Y. R. 316.) But the proper course is to incorporate the survey in the order itself. A description of a portion of the new highway by reference to an established highway is a description by "routes and bounds," within the requirements of the above section. (*People* v. *Commissoiners of Milton*, 37 N. Y. R. 360.)

*Order by two commissioners.*—The order laying out a highway may be made by two of the three commissioners; but, in that event, it must *show on its face*, either that the third commissioner met with his associates, and that he participated in their deliberations, even if he did not concur in their conclusions; or that he was notified, not only of the intended meeting of the commissioners, but of the particular subject on which it was proposed to deliberate. (1 R. S. 525, § 125; *People* v. *Williams*, 36 N. Y. R. 441; *People* v. *Hynds*, 30 id. 470.) Where an order was made by two commissioners, laying out a road, in which it was recited that all the commissioners of highways of the town met and deliberated on the subject embraced in the order, and the referee found as fact that all three of the commissioners met and viewed the proposed route, and that, subsequently, two of them caused it to be surveyed, and made the order of that date laying out the road, and that one of the commissioners was not present at the survey, nor notified to attend the same, it was held that the order was valid in the absence of any finding that the third commissioner did not meet with the others and deliberate on the subject of laying out the highway, the presumption being that all the commissioners did meet and deliberate on that subject, and that the act was legal until the contrary appeared. The survey was a mere ministerial act, not requiring the presence of the third commissioner to give validity to the order laying out and establishing the highway. (*Marble* v. *Whitney*, 28 N. Y. R. 297.) The order must be sufficient on its face, and cannot be sustained by parol evidence. (*People* v. *Hynds*, 30 N. Y. R. 470; *Stewart* v. *Wallis*, 30 Barb. 344.)

*Papers to be filed.*—All applications, certificates and other papers relating to the laying out, altering or discontinuing of any road shall be filed by the commissioners of highways, as soon as they shall have decided thereon, in the office of the town clerk of the town. (1 R. S. 518, § 83.)

The clerk, in recording such papers, acts ministerially, and cannot refuse to record any of them on the ground that they are not in conformity with the requirements of the statute. (*People* v. *Collins*, 7 Johns. 549.)

*Width of road.*—All public roads, to be laid by the commissioners of highways of any town, shall not be less than three rods wide, and all private roads shall not be more than three rods wide. (1 R. S. 517, § 80.)

Where roads are claimed because they have been used twenty years, they may be more or less than three rods wide: that will depend on their actual *user*. When public roads are laid out under the statute, they will be deemed to be at least three rods in width, and a person will be liable for an obstruction within that width. (*Harlow* v. *Humiston*, 6 Cow. 189.)

It shall be the duty of the commissioners of highways to order overseers of highways to open all roads to the width of two rods at least, which they shall judge to have been used as public highways for twenty years. (1 R. S. 521, § 101.)

Where a road is ordered by the commissioners to be laid out, for a part of the distance, *three* rods in width, and for the residue of the distance, which is on the bed or track of an old road used for more than twenty years, *two* rods in width, the proceedings are not vitiated and rendered void by the provision in the order allowing a road to be opened which is only two rods wide. Regarding the first part of the order, laying out the road up to the point of intersection with the old road, as one in perfect accordance with the powers of the commissioners, and the residue, which follows the old road, as a description of the old road to be recorded, and for the purpose of having it opened two rods in width by a subsequent order to that effect; the whole is consistent and harmonious, and entirely within the power of the commissioners. (*Snyder* v. *Plass*, 28 N. Y. R. 465; re-affirmed, *Snyder* v. *Trumpbour*, 38 id. 355.)

The jury, which is called to determine the disputed question of an encroachment, have no power to determine the question of the width and boundaries of a highway, according to the previous dedication or use, which has been neither laid out nor ascertained and described by the commissioners of highways. That duty belongs exclusively to the commissioners, and is to be performed by them in an entirely different manner. (*Talmage* v. *Huntting*, 29 N. Y. R. 447.)

A road laid out under the statute is at least three rods wide, and the public have a right to the use of it for the full width at any time; and any thing which interferes with that right is an obstruction of, and encroachment upon, the road. (*Walker* v. *Caywood*, 31 N. Y. R. 51.)

*How laid out across railroad tracks.*—It shall be lawful for the authorities of any city, village or town in this state, who are by law empowered to lay out streets and highways, to lay out any street or highway across the track of any railroad now laid, or which may hereafter be laid, without compensation to the corporation owning such railroad; but no such street or highway shall be actually opened for use until thirty days after notice of such laying out has been served personally upon the president, vice-president, treasurer, or a director of such corporation. (Laws of 1853, ch. 62, § 1.) (See Form No. 32.)

*Railroad corporations to take road across their tracks.*—It shall be the duty of any railroad corporation across whose track a street or highway shall be laid out as aforesaid, immediately after the service of said notice, to cause the said street or highway to be taken across their track, as shall be most convenient and useful for public travel, and to cause all necessary embankments, excavations and other work to be done on their road for that purpose; and all the provisions of the act passed April second, eighteen hundred and fifty, in relation to crossing streets and highways, already laid out, by railroads, and in relation to cattle guards, and other securities and facilities for crossing such roads, shall apply to streets and highways hereafter laid out. (Id. § 2.)

*Penalty for neglect or refusal.*—If any railroad corporation shall neglect or refuse, for thirty days after the service of the notice aforesaid, to cause the necessary work to be done and completed, and improvements made on such streets or highways across their road, they shall forfeit and pay the sum of twenty dollars for every subsequent day's neglect or refusal, to be recovered by the officers laying out such street or highway, to be expended on the same; but the time for doing said work may be extended, not to exceed thirty days, by the county judge of the county in which such street or highway, or any part thereof, may be situated, if in his opinion the said work cannot be performed within the time limited by this act. (Id. § 3.)

A highway cannot be laid out over grounds acquired by a railroad corporation for the site of an engine-house, etc., necessary for its use at a station. (*Albany Northern R. R. Co.* v. *Brownell*, 24 N. Y. R. 345.)

*How laid out between different towns or counties.* When the commissioners of highways of any town shall disagree with the commissioners of any other town in the same county, relating to the laying out of a new road, or the alteration of an old road, extending into both towns; or when the commissioners of a town in one county shall disagree with the commissioners of a town in another county, relative to laying out a new road, or altering an old road, which shall extend into both towns, the commissioners of both towns shall meet together, at the request of either disagreeing commissioners, and make their determination upon the subject of such disagreement. (1 R. S. 516, § 72.)

Whenever it shall become necessary to have a highway upon the line between two towns, such highway shall be laid out by two or more of the commissioners of highways of each of said towns, either upon such line, or as near thereto as the convenience of the ground will admit, and they may so vary the same, either to the one or to the other side of such line, as they may think proper. (Id. § 73.)

It shall be the duty of the same commissioners, when they lay out such highway, to divide it into two or more road districts, in such manner that the labor and expense of opening, working and keeping in repair such highway, through each of the said districts, may be equal as near as may be, and to allot an equal number of the said districts to each of the said towns. (Id. § 74.)

Each district shall be considered as wholly belonging to the town to which it shall be allotted, for the purpose of opening and improving the road, and for keeping it in repair; and the commissioners shall cause such highway, and the partition and allotment thereof, to be recorded in the office of the town clerk in each of their respective towns. (1 R. S. 517, § 75.)

Where an encroachment has occurred upon a highway running on the line between two towns, the commissioners of both towns cannot unite as plaintiffs, and bring an action to recover the penalty or forfeiture. (*Bradley* v. *Blair*, 17 Barb. 480.)

All highways heretofore laid out upon the line between any two towns shall be divided, allotted, recorded and kept in repair in the manner above directed. (1 R. S. 517, § 76.)

*Roads along division lines.*—Whenever a public or private road shall be laid along the division line between the lands of two or more persons, and wholly upon one side of said line, and the lands upon both sides of said division line shall be cultivated or improved, then, and in that case, the person owning or occupying the lands joining said road shall be paid for building and maintaining such additional fence as he may be required to build or maintain by reason of the laying out and opening said road; which said damages shall be ascertained and determined in the same manner that other damages are now ascertained and determined in the laying highways on private roads. (Laws of 1853, ch. 174, § 16.)

*Special commissioners to lay out highways.*—The act of 1838 (ch. 314), to enlarge the powers of boards of supervisors, provides that the supervisors of each county have power, at their annual meeting, or when lawfully convened, at any other meeting, to appoint special commissioners to lay out public highways in those cases where they shall be satisfied that the road applied for is important, and that the authority now conferred by law upon commissioners of highways cannot or will not be exercised to accomplish the laying out of such road. But such power shall not be exercised by any board of supervisors unless the applicant therefor shall prove to such board of supervisors the service of a notice in writing on a commissioner of highways of each town through and into which any such highway is intended to be laid, at least six days previous to presenting such application, specifying therein the object thereof, and names of persons proposed to be appointed such commissioners. (Laws of 1848, ch. 164.)

The supervisors shall have power to provide for the payment of the special commissioners appointed under the above provisions, for their time and expenses. The decision made by said commissioners may be appealed from and reviewed in the same manner and with the like authority as is allowed by law in the cases of roads laid out by the commissioners of highways of any town. The roads so to be laid out by such special commissioners, or the same as settled on appeal, shall be recorded, opened and worked as a public highway of the town in which they are respectively situated, in the same manner as other highways of the town are now required by law to be recorded, opened and worked. (Laws of 1838, ch. 314.)

*Fences to be removed.* — Whenever the commissioners of highways shall have laid out any public highway, through any inclosed, cultivated or improved lands, in conformity to the provisions of this title, and their determination shall not have been appealed from, they shall give the owner or occupant of the land through which such road shall have been laid, sixty days' notice, in writing, to remove his fences. If such owner shall not remove his fences within the sixty days, the commissioners shall cause such fences to be removed, and shall direct the road to be opened and worked. (1 R. S. 520, § 96.)

If the determination of the commissioners shall have been appealed from, then the sixty days' notice shall be given after the decision of the referees upon such appeal shall have been filed in the office of the town clerk of the town. (1 R. S. 520, § 97, as amended by Laws of 1847, ch. 455, § 8.)

The notice prescribed must be given, or the commissioners and all persons proceeding to open the road will be trespassers. Actual notice must be shown, as it will not be presumed. (*Case* v. *Thompson*, 6 Wend. 634.)

*When roads to be opened and worked.*—Every public highway and private road already laid out, and dedicated to the use of the public, that shall not have been opened and worked within six years from the time of its being so laid out, and every such highway hereafter to be laid out, that shall not be opened and worked within the like period, shall cease to be a road for any purpose whatever; but the period during which any suit, mandamus, certiorari or other proceeding shall have been, or shall be pending, in regard to any such highway, shall form no part of said six years; and all highways that have ceased to be traveled or used as highways for six years shall cease to be a highway for any purpose. (1 R. S. 520, § 99, as amended 1861, ch. 311.)

The provisions of this act apply to every public highway and private road laid out and dedicated to the use of the public within the last six years, and to every such highway hereafter to be laid out. (Laws of 1861, ch. 311, § 2.) This statute applies only to those cases where there has been a failure to open and work the road at all, and not where the highway has been in full use for the whole time, though not opened in all places to its full width. (*Walker* v. *Caywood*, 31 N. Y. R. 51; *Marble* v. *Whitney*, 28 id. 297.)

The road must be both opened *and worked.* It is not necessary that every part of it should be worked. This might be impossible. Where the country is new and the population thin, there might not be highway labor sufficient in the district to work all the road.

It should be embraced in a road district, and worked as far as there is necessity for work or highway labor to expend upon it.

*What roads are highways.*—All public highways now in use, heretofore laid out and allowed by any law of this state, of which a record shall have been made in the office of the clerk of the county or town; and all roads not recorded, which have been or shall have been used as public highways, for twenty years or more, shall be deemed public highways, but may be altered in conformity to the provisions of this title. Roads that have not been laid out nor used for twenty years or more are not public highways, and the town is not bound to keep them in repair. In the case of *Oswego* v. *Oswego Canal Co.* (6 N. Y. R. 262), Justice Ruggles says:

Any individual may lay out a way or thoroughfare through his own land, and may dedicate it as such to the public use. But such dedication does not impose upon the towns in which the lands lie the duty of improving, or of keeping in repair as a public highway, the land so dedicated. This will conclusively appear from a reference to the provisions which have been in force in our highway acts for half a century. The power of laying out, altering and discontinuing highways has been conferred exclusively on the commissioners of highways of the respective towns. It has been their duty to cause to be described in the town clerk's office all public highways not already on record; to assess the highway labor upon the inhabitants of the town; to divide the town into road districts; and to assign a due proportion of the labor to each district. It was the evident intent of these statutes that the labor assessed should be bestowed exclusively upon the highways established by the town authorities and recorded in the town clerk's office. The duty of causing roads to be described and recorded evidently applied to such roads as had previously been laid out by public authority, and to such as had been used as highways for twenty years, and not to roads which had been laid out by individuals on their own lands. The whole structure of the highway acts forbids the idea that the town is bound to adopt and to keep in repair every road which an individual may think proper to open through his own land, although he may dedicate it to public use in such manner as to preclude himself from shutting it up. Streets and roads dedicated by individuals to public use, but not adopted by the local public authorities, or declared highways by statute, are not highways within the meaning of the highway acts, and there is no law by which any one can be compelled to keep them in repair.

Whenever any turnpike corporation shall become dissolved or the road discontinued, its road shall become a public highway, and be subject to all the legal provisions regulating highways. (Laws of 1838, ch. 262, § 1.)

The board of supervisors have power to provide for the use of abandoned plank or turnpike roads as public highways. (Laws of 1869, ch. 855, § 2.)

## CHAPTER VII.

### OF THE ALTERATION AND DISCONTINUANCE OF HIGHWAYS.

*Commissioners may alter or discontinue.*—Section 1 of 1 R. S. 501 (ante, p. 27) authorizes the commissioners of highways "to regulate the roads already laid out, and to alter such of them as they or a majority of them shall deem inconvenient." This power should only be exercised when the road can be made more convenient by such change. In making such alteration they may remove encroachments of fences and restore the road to its original lines; change the grade of the road to take so much of the lands of adjoining proprietors as is necessary to make the desired change, but in taking such lands the owners thereof must be compensated the same as on the original location.

The commissioners are also empowered to discontinue such old roads and highways as shall appear to them on the oaths of twelve freeholders of the same town to have become unnecessary. (1 R. S. 502, § 2.)

This does not authorize the commissioners to reverse an order laying out a new road by discontinuing it, but only to discontinue such roads as have been found to be useless. (*People* v. *Pike*, 18 How. 70.)

*Application to alter or discontinue.*—Every person liable to be assessed for highway labor may apply to the commissioners of highways of the town in which he shall reside, to alter or discontinue any road, or to lay out any new road. Every such application shall be in writing, addressed to the commissioners, and signed by the person applying. (1 R. S.

513, § 54.) So every person liable to be assessed for highway labor and owning lands in a town in which he is not a resident may apply to the commissioners of highways of the town in which the lands are situated, to alter, discontinue or to lay out any road through the same. (Laws of 1836, ch. 122.)

The word "same," in the act of 1836, refers to the town and not to the land. (*People* v. *Eggleston*, 13 How. 123.)

It is held that the commissioners may alter or discontinue a road of their own motion and without any application, so that proceedings based upon the application of a person not authorized to apply are not irregular. (*Gould* v. *Glass*, 19 Barb. 179; *Marble* v. *Whitney*, 28 N. Y. R. 297; *People* v. *Supervisors of Richmond*, 20 id. 252.)

Where a person desires to secure the alteration or discontinuance of a road, he should file a written application with the commissioners. (See forms Nos. 33, 34.)

The application to discontinue an old road and to lay out a new one may be in one form. (*People* v. *Robertson*, 17 How. 74.)

*Survey.*—Whenever the commissioners of highways shall lay out, alter or discontinue any road, either upon application to them or otherwise, they shall cause a survey to be made of such road, and shall incorporate such survey in an order, to be signed by them, and to be filed and recorded in the office of the town clerk, who shall note the time of recording the same. (1 R. S. 513, § 55.) (See form No. 26.)

The law applicable to the survey on laying out a highway, as given in the preceding chapter, is equally applicable on altering or discontinuing a highway.

*Order to be posted.*—It shall be the duty of the town clerk, whenever any order of the commissioners for laying out, altering or discontinuing a road shall be received by him, to post a copy of such order on the door of the house where the town meeting is usually held, and the time hereafter limited for appealing from such order shall be computed from the time of recording the same. (1 R. S. 513, § 56.)

*Jury, when necessary.*—The commissioners have power to alter a road without the intervention of a jury (*Garretson* v. *Clark*, Lalor Sup. 162), but to discontinue a road a jury is necessary. The statute says:

Whenever application shall be made for the discontinuance of an old road, on the ground that it has become useless and unnecessary, the commissioners of highways, to whom such application shall be made, shall summon twelve disinterested freeholders of the town, to meet on a day certain, to consider such application. Such freeholders when met shall be sworn well and truly to examine and certify in regard to the propriety of such discontinuance. (1 R. S. 517, § 81.)

The statute provides that the *commissioners shall summon*, and it appears that they have no authority to delegate this authority by issuing process to a constable or other person. (See *People* v. *Commissioners of Greenbush*, 24 Wend. 367.) They are not required to issue or have any process to procure the jury, but will sufficiently comply with the statute if they request the freeholders to act. (Id.) The better course, however, is to serve a summons on the persons required. (See form No. 35.)

The term "freeholder," is sufficiently described in the preceding chapter. Any one of the commissioners may administer the oath to the jury. (Laws of 1845, ch. 180.)

*Proceeding of jury.*—They shall then proceed to view such road, and if they shall be of opinion that the same is useless and unnecessary, they shall make and subscribe a certificate in writing to that effect, which shall be delivered to the commissioners of highways, who shall thereupon proceed to decide upon such application. (1 R. S. 518, § 82.) (See form No. 36.)

*Jury not to be paid.*—No compensation shall be allowed any juror for examining and certifying in regard to the propriety of any highway being discontinued, nor for appearing to make such examination. (Laws of 1845, ch. 180, § 14.)

*Order altering or discontinuing.*—Should the commissioners decide to alter or discontinue a road they should make an order in writing, to be signed by them or a majority of them, including therein the survey of the road, and should file such order with the town clerk. Where only two of the commissioners sign the order, it should appear upon the face of the order itself either that all the commissioners were present and deliberated upon the subject of the order, or that all the commissioners were duly notified of the intended meeting of the commissioners and of the subject upon which it was proposed to deliberate. Unless these facts are set forth in the order itself, the order will be invalid. (1 R. S. 525; *People* v. *Williams*, 36 N. Y. R. 441; *People* v. *Hynds*, 30 id. 470.) (See form No. 37.)

*Papers to be filed.*—All applications, certificates and other papers relating to the discontinuing of any road shall be filed by the commissioners, as soon as they shall have decided thereon, in the office of the town clerk of the town. (1 R. S. 518, § 83.)

*Altering roads between towns.*—When the commissioners of highways of any town shall disagree with the commissioners of any other town in the same county, relating to the laying out of a new road, or the alteration of an old road, extending into both towns, or when the commissioners of a town in one county shall disagree with the commissioners of a town in another county, relative to laying out a new road, or altering an old road, which shall extend into both counties, the commissioners of both towns shall meet together at the request of either disagreeing commissioners, and make their determination upon such subject of disagreement. (1 R. S. 516, § 72.)

*Description of road abandoned.*—Whenever any public highway or any part thereof, by reason of alterations made therein, or by the opening of a new road, or in any other way, shall be abandoned by the public, and is no longer used as a public road, the commissioners or commissioner of highways shall file in the town clerk's office of the town a description, in writing, signed by them or him, of the road so abandoned, and the same shall thereupon be discontinued. (Laws of 1853, ch. 174, § 15.) (See form No. 40.)

The abandonment of a highway cannot be predicated upon an obstruction interposed by the person upon whose property the easement is a burden. It can only be upon the acts of those entitled to the easement. (*Anesley* v. *Hinds*. 46 Barb. 622.)

*Ownership of discontinued highway.* — When any person shall be the owner of any land over which any highway shall run, and such highway shall be discontinued in whole or in part, by reason of some other road to be established and laid out through the lands of the same person, the person who shall assess the damages shall take into calculation the value of the road so discontinued, and the benefit resulting to such person by reason of such discontinuance, and shall deduct the same from the damages assessed for the opening and laying out such new road; and thereupon the owner of the land may inclose so much of the highway so discontinued as shall belong to him. (1 R. S. 516, § 71.)

In order to justify such deduction, the road abandoned must be on the land of the person owning the land taken for the new road. When the fee in the old road belongs to one person and that in the new road to another, the latter cannot take the old road as compensation for his land. (*Jackson* v. *Hathaway*, 15 Johns. 453.)

When a highway is discontinued or abandoned, the full and entire enjoyment of the land reverts to the owner of the fee. (Id.) And where the owner of adjoining lands is limited in his boundaries so as to extend only to the side or fence of a highway; the land of the highway reverts to the original owner having the fee. (Id.)

## CHAPTER VIII.

### APPEALS FROM ORDERS LAYING OUT, ALTERING OR DISCONTINUING HIGHWAYS.

*Right of appeal.* — Any person who shall conceive himself aggrieved by any determination of the commissioners of highways, either in laying out, altering or discontinuing any road, or in refusing to lay out, alter or discontinue any road, may, at any time within sixty days after such determination shall have been filed in the office of the town clerk, appeal to the county judge of the county in the same manner as appeals were heretofore allowed to be brought to three judges under title first, article fourth, chapter sixteenth, part first of the Revised Statutes; and when any appeal shall be brought under this section, the said judge, or in case of his residence in the town, or of his interest in the lands through which the road shall be laid out, or in case he is of kin to any of the persons interested in said lands, or in case of his disability for any cause, then one of the justices of the sessions, shall, after the expiration of the said sixty days, appoint, in writing, three disinterested freeholders who shall not have been named by the parties interested in the appeal, and who shall be residents of the county but not of the town wherein the road shall be located, as referees to hear and determine all the appeals that may have been brought within the said sixty days, and shall notify them of their appointment, and deliver to them all papers pertaining to the matters referred to them. Upon receiving notice of appointment the said referees shall possess all the powers and discharge all the duties heretofore possessed and discharged by the three judges, and give the same notices heretofore required to be given under title first, article four, chapter six, part one aforesaid, and before proceeding to hear the appeal or appeals they shall be sworn, by some officer authorized to take affidavits to be read in courts of record, faithfully to hear and determine the matters referred to them. (Laws of 1847, ch. 455, § 8.) (For forms see No. 41.)

Any person considering himself aggrieved may take the appeal, whether he is in fact aggrieved or not, or whether or not the road is laid through his lands. (*People* v. *Campion*, 16 Johns. 61.) Nor is one person concluded by the appeal of another. (*Clark* v. *Phelps*, 4 Cow. 190.)

The right to appeal from an order made by commissioners of highways laying out a public highway is not restricted to those persons over whose lands the road is proposed to be laid, but may be exercised by every person who is a resident tax payer of the town, and as such liable to assessment therein for highway labor. (*People* v. *Cortelyou*, 36 Barb. 164.)

So persons owning land in the town, though not residents thereof, may appeal in like manner as resident tax payers. (See 1 R. S. 513, § 54, as amended 1836, ch. 122.) A corporation comes under the denomination of "person," within the meaning of this statute, and enjoys the same right to appeal as individuals. (*People* v. *May*, 27 Barb. 238.)

*When appeal does not lie.*—An order of the highway commissioners, ascertaining and recording an old highway, is not appealable. (*People* v. *Judges of Cortland*, 24 Wend. 491.) So an appeal does not lie from a determination which is void for want of jurisdiction. (*People* v. *Judges of Suffolk*, 24 Wend. 249.)

Where the commissioners of highways of two adjoining towns in different counties assemble together in joint board, and unite in an order laying out or refusing to lay out, altering or discontinuing, or refusing to alter or discontinue, a road or highway, their judgment and determination cannot be reviewed by appeal to a county judge of one of the counties. The statute makes no provision for an appeal in such case. (*People* v. *County Judges of Dutchess*, 26 How. 346.)

It seems, that in the absence of any provision of the statute for review in such a case, the determination of the joint board of commissioners must be considered final and equivalent in all respects to an order of one board of commissioners affirmed by three referees on appeal. (Id.)

*Appeal, how brought.*—Every such appeal shall be in writing, addressed to the county judge of the county, and signed by the party appealing. It shall briefly state the ground upon which it is made, and whether it is brought to reverse entirely the determination of the commissioners, or only to reverse a part thereof; and in the latter case it shall specify what part. (1 R. S. 518, § 86, as modified by Laws of 1847, ch. 455, § 8.) (See form No. 42.)

The appeal must be taken within sixty days from the filing of the order or determination appealed from.

The appeal may be taken either to the county judge, as provided in the above act, or to the county court, under the eleventh subdivision of section 30 of the Code. By the Code concurrent jurisdiction has been extended to the county court, but without changing the statutory form of appeal from the order of the commissioners, or divesting the county judge of authority to direct a reference. (*People* v. *Van Alstyne*, 3 Keyes, 35.)

An appeal cannot be made to a judge who was one of the freeholders and signed the certificate on laying out the road, but, if this objection is not urged on the hearing of the appeal, it is not such an error as will justify a reversal of the proceedings on *certiorari*. (*Commissioners* v. *Judges of* Putnam, 7 Wend. 264.)

It has been held that a notice of appeal, stating as a ground that the order of the commissioners was illegal, was good. (*Commissioners* v. *Meserole*, 10 Wend. 122.) So a notice simply stating the appeal, without setting forth the grounds, was sustained. (*Commissioners* v. *Judges of Putnam*, 7 Wend. 264.) But the section above cited requires the grounds of the appeal to be briefly stated, and the appellant should in every case comply.

*Appointment of referees.*—Where several persons separately appeal, there should be but one set of referees, one hearing and one order. (*Disosway* v. *Winant*, 34 Barb. 578.)

If the provision of the above section, directing the judge to suspend proceedings upon the appeal to him until the expiration of sixty days from the determination of the commissioners of highways, is not merely directory, his neglect to do so is only erroneous, for which the remedy is by *certiorari*. It does not render his proceedings and decision void. (*Harrington* v. *People*, 6 Barb. 607.)

The referees are to be three disinterested freeholders, residents of the county but not of the town in which the highway is located. They are not to be named by the parties, nor are they to be kin to any such parties, as in such case they would acquire no jurisdiction and their proceedings would be void. (*People* v. *Flake*, 14 How. 527.)

*Order to be filed.* — All orders for the appointment of the referees shall be filed and recorded in the office of the town clerk of the town in which the road shall be located. (Laws of 1847, ch. 455, § 21.)

*Notice to referees.* — The county judge or justice appointing the referees is to notify them of their appointment and to deliver to them all papers pertaining to the matter referred to them. (Laws of 1847, ch. 455, § 8.)

*Referees to give notice.* — The referees are required to give the same notices required to be given by the provisions of the Revised Statutes. (Id.) The provision as modified by the act of 1847 is as follows:

It shall be the duty of the referees to proceed thereon as soon as may be convenient. Where the determination appealed from was against an application for laying out, altering or discontinuing a road, the referees shall give notice to the commissioners by whom such determination was made. Where the appeal is from a determination in favor of an application for laying out, altering or discontinuing a road, the notice shall be given to the commissioners, and to one or more of the applicants for such road. In all cases the notice shall specify the time and place at which the referees will convene to hear the appeal. (1 R. S. 518, § 87.) (See form No. 43.)

Every such notice shall be served at least eight days before the time mentioned therein, by delivering the same to one of the commissioners whose determination is appealed from, or by leaving the same at his dwelling-house. If the notice be also directed to an applicant, it shall be served in the same manner. (1 R. S. 518, § 88.)

The notice must be in writing. (*Gittrel* v. *Columbia Turnpike Co.*, 1 Johns. Cases, 107.) The referees are the persons whose duty it is to give the notices, and their neglect cannot be regarded as laches on the part of the appellant.

The referees have no jurisdiction to proceed on the appeal until the necessary notices have been given. (*People* v. *Judges of Herkimer*, 20 Wend. 186.) Should they proceed without giving such notice, their proceedings will be reversed by certiorari. (*People* v. *Tallman*, 36 Barb. 222; *Commissioners* v. *Claw*, 15 Johns. 537; *Bradhurst* v. *President and Directors*, 16 id. 8.) The attendance of one of the commissioners is not a waiver of notice. (*People* v. *Osborne*, 20 Wend. 186.)

Upon an appeal from an order of commissioners of highways, refusing to lay out a highway, the referees appointed by the county judge to hear and determine the same must give three days' notice, in writing, to the occupant of land through which the road is contemplated, of the time and place at which they will meet to determine the appeal. Unless such a notice is given, an order made by the referees reversing the decision of the commissioners will be void, and will furnish no justification for entry upon the land by a person claiming that the same is a public highway duly laid out by the referees. The 8th section of the act of 1847, cited above, virtually revives section 91 of 1 Revised Statutes, 519, which had been repealed by the Laws of 1845, ch. 180, and places the referees in the same position the judges were in under that provision. (*Terpening* v. *Smith*, 46 Barb. 208.)

The fact that the occupant was present and sworn as a witness is no waiver. (*People* v. *Judges of Herkimer*, 20 Wend. 186.) And where the occupants of the land waive notice of the proceedings of the referees, but afterward, and before any action was had on such waiver, withdraw it, the referees cannot proceed without giving the required notice. (*People* v. *Crozier*, 12 Abb. 445.) (See form No. 44.)

*Proceedings of the referees.*—It shall be the duty of the referees to convene at the time and place mentioned in the notice, and to hear the proofs and allegations of the parties. They shall have power to issue process to compel the attendance of witnesses, and may adjourn from time to time, as may be necessary. Their decision, or that of any two of them, shall be conclusive in the premises, and every such decision shall be reduced to writing, be signed by the referees making it, and be filed by them in the office of the town clerk of the town, who shall record the same. (1 R. S. 519, § 89, as modified by act of 1847.)

If the judges do not or will not proceed they may be compelled by *mandamus* to hear and decide the appeal. (*Lansing* v. *Caswell*, 4 Paige, 519.)

Having met, the first duty of the referees is to be sworn by a judge of a court of record, a justice of the peace, commissioner of deeds or clerk of a court of record. The taking of the oath is a preliminary essential to give the referees jurisdiction. Neither the commissioners of the town nor the parties appealing can waive the taking of the oath, since the whole town have an interest in the proceeding. (*People* v. *Connor*, 46 Barb. 333.)

The parties to an appeal have a right to presume that the referees have taken the oath, and cannot be charged with implied notice of a neglect of it. (Id.)

The referees may issue process to compel the attendance of witnesses, on the application of either party. (See form No. 45.)

They may also adjourn from time to time, as may be necessary. The only limit to the power of adjournment is, that such adjournments be *necessary*, of which the referees are to judge. After the hearing has terminated they may adjourn to enable them to make their decision. (*People* v. *Ferris*, 41 Barb. 124.) But when once the decision has been made and they have adjourned without day, they cannot again meet and proceed in the matter. (*Rogers* v. *Runyon*, 9 How. 248.)

Where referees have heard both parties and duly closed the hearing, and have entered upon the task of forming a determination, they have no power to entertain a motion of third persons to open the cause for a further hearing, and for the reception of evidence impeaching the original testimony and adding to the weight of the original evidence. (*People* v. *Ferris*, 18 Abb. Pr. 64; 27 How. Pr. 193; 41 Barb. 121.)

Such referees are like other inferior and subordinate officers and tribunals that are creatures of statute to be confined to powers expressly conferred, or such as are necessarily incident to express powers. (Id.)

In a case where they have power to open the hearing, the same notice should be given as upon the first hearing. (Id.)

The referees appointed, upon appeal from the determination of the commissioners of highways in refusing to lay out, alter or discontinue a road, possess all the powers and are required to discharge all the duties formerly possessed by the three judges under 1 R. S. 518, § 85. (*People* v. *Barber*, 12 Barb. 193;

*People* v. *Commissioners of Cherry Valley*, 8 N. Y. R. 476.)

Their authority on the appeal is confined to a hearing on the merits. They cannot entertain a question as to the regularity of the proceedings before the commissioners. (*Commissioners of Warwick* v. *Judges of Orange*, 13 Wend. 432; *Lawton* v. *Commissioners of Cambridge*, 2 Cai. 179.)

If the proceedings anterior to the commissioners' order are regular upon their face, the jurisdiction of the referees is limited to the consideration of the case upon its merits. They cannot receive extrinsic evidence to impeach the freeholders' certificate of the necessity of the road. (*People* v. *Van Alstyne*, 3 Keyes, 35.)

Evidence that the certificate of freeholders, as to its necessity, was obtained by fraudulent representations, is not admissible. This objection does not go to the jurisdiction of the commissioners. It should be raised by a direct proceeding to review the decision, and not by proof before the referees on an appeal. (*People* v. *Kniskern*, 50 Barb. 87.)

It is the duty of the referees to hear the proofs and allegations of the parties, and make a determination reversing or affirming the order of the commissioners. They have no power to dismiss the appeal. But, if they dismiss, the remedy is not by a common-law certiorari, but, it seems, by a mandamus. (*People* v. *Cortelyou*, 36 Barb. 164.)

The referees may hear and decide the appeal as well on facts existing at the time of the hearing before them as upon the facts existing at the time of the original application, and, on reversing the decision, they may make such order as they judge the commissioners should have made. (*People* v. *Albright*, 14 Abb. 305; 23 How. 306.)

Where the commissioners of highways made an order refusing to lay out a road through cultivated and inclosed lands because the applicant had not given notice of a meeting of freeholders to examine and certify as to its necessity, etc., and because a certificate of twelve freeholders had not been obtained, on appeal the referees reversed the order of the com missioners and laid out the road, it was held that the proceeding of the referees was void, and that the commissioners would be trespassers if they opened the road. (*People* v. *Eggleston*, 13 How. 123.)

The referees are to decide upon the unfitness or fitness of laying out, altering or discontinuing the road. They are substituted in place of the commissioners, and all the considerations which are proper for the one are also proper for the other. (*Commissioners of Bushwick* v. *Meserole*, 10 Wend. 126.)

*Decision of the referees.*—Since the act of 1847 (ch. 455), the referees may reverse the decision of the commissioners in part and confirm in part. (*People* v. *Commissioner of Cherry Valley*, 8 N. Y. R. 482; *People* v. *Baker*, 19 Barb. 240.) The case of *The Commissioners of Sherburne* v. *Judges of Chenango* (25 Wend. 453) was decided prior to that act.

Section eight of the act of 1847, above cited, gives to the referees all the powers and requires them to discharge all the duties heretofore possessed or discharged by the three judges, and therefore, where an appeal shall have been made from a determination of commissioners refusing to lay out or alter a road, and the referees shall reverse such determination, such referees shall lay out or alter the road applied for; and in doing so shall proceed in the same manner in which the commissioners of highways are directed to proceed in the like cases. Such road shall be opened by the commissioners of the town, in the same manner as if laid out by themselves. (1 R. S. 519, § 91.)

On reversing the order of the commissioners, the referees must make such order as the commissioners should have made. (*People* v. *Albright*, 14 Abb. 305; 23 How. 306.)

The referees cannot lay out the road, except as it was submitted to the commissioners. (*Ex parte Commissioners of Danube*, 1 Cow. 142.)

The referee, on reversing the determination of the commissioners, may order the commissioners to lay out the road, and an order to lay it out "as applied for," is sufficiently explicit. (*People* v. *Commissioners of Salem*, 1 Cow. 23.)

A mere reversal of an order refusing to lay out a road is not an order to be carried out by laying out the road. (*People* v. *Commissioners of Watertown*, 7 How. 28.)

The commissioners have no power to lay out or alter a road upon the mere reversal, on appeal, of their former refusal to lay out. They have no power to do any act in the premises except to carry out the order made by the referees. (Id.)

Where the referees simply reverse an order refusing to lay out a highway, without giving further directions, the commissioners are not bound to lay out the highway, and a mandamus will not be granted to compel them to proceed and do it. (*People* v. *Commissioners of Cherry Valley*, 8 N. Y. R. 476.)

Should the referees conclude their proceedings by simply reversing the order of the commissioners refusing to lay out a highway, without making an order for laying it out, a mandamus will be granted to compel the referees to lay out the road. (*People* v. *Barker*, 12 Barb. 193.)

An order by the referees to lay out as applied for, is sufficiently explicit. (*People* v. *Commissioners of Salem*, 1 Cow. 23.)

Upon an appeal from a decision refusing to lay out a road, the judges may lay it out with reference to the written application for it, giving the termini and general route proposed; and it is of no consequence what particular route the jury or the commissioners had examined. (*People* v. *Judges of Dutchess*, 23 Wend. 360.)

*Determination, how made.*—The decision of the referees, or of any two of them, must be reduced to writing, be signed by the referees making it, and be filed in the office of the town clerk of the town, who shall record the same. (1 R. S. 519, § 89.) (See form No. 46.)

In making the decision the referees must all meet and confer together on the subject-matter, although a majority of them may decide. (2 R. S. 255, § 27; *Downing* v. *Rugar*, 21 Wend. 178; *Crooker* v. *Crane*, id. 211; *Lee* v. *Parry*, 4 Denio, 125; *Keeler* v. *Frost*, 22 Barb. 400; *Ex parte Rogers*, 7 Cow. 526.)

An appeal from the commissioners of highways was heard by the referees, who then separated, intending to meet again; but they did not, and an order on the appeal was drawn by the attorney of the appellant, and signed by the referees at their several residences. Held, that this was ground of reversal. (*Harris* v. *Whitney*, 6 How. Pr. 175.)

After the decision has been made, the referees have no power to review or alter such decision; but where errors have occurred in the order or certificate filed by them, as in the description of the road, they may file an amended order or certificate correcting such errors. In making up the certificate they act ministerially. (*Woolsey* v. *Tompkins*, 23 Wend. 324; *Rogers* v. *Runyan*, 9 How. 248.)

When the referees have duly closed the hearing and entered upon the task of forming a determination, they have no power to entertain the motion of third persons to open the cause for a further hearing, and for the reception of evidence impeaching the testimony and adding to the weight of the original evidence. (*People* v. *Ferris*, 18 Abb. 64; 27 How. 193; 41 Barb. 121.)

*Notice of decision.* — Where referees appointed on an appeal from the decision of commissioners give timely notice to the owners and occupants of the land that they will meet on a specified day to decide upon the application to lay out the highway, it is not necessary, upon their subsequently determining to lay out such highway, that they should serve an additional notice on the owners and occupants. Their first notice, although it precedes the taking of the testimony, and the reversing of the order of the commissioners appealed from, satisfies the statute. (*People* v. *Kniskern*, 50 Barb. 87.)

*Commissioners to carry out determination.* — Whenever there shall have been any final determination upon any appeal or appeals provided for as aforesaid, making it necessary that any road or highway shall be laid out, altered, opened or discontinued, it shall be the duty of the commissioner or commissioners of highways of the town where the same is to be done, to carry out such determination the same as if the decision of such commissioner or commissioners had been in favor thereof, and there had been no appeal." (Laws of 1845, ch. 180, § 13.)

When the commissioners refuse to open the road laid out by the judges on reversing the commissioners' decision, a mandamus lies to compel them to open it. (*People* v. *Champion*, 16 Johns. 61.)

Such writ is to be directed to "the commissioners." It is only in case of disobedience that the commissioners are to be proceeded against personally. The "final determination" intended by § 13 of Laws of 1845, making it the commissioner's duty to carry out such determination, was a laying out or altering a road. A mere reversal is not an order to be carried out by laying out a road. (*People* v. *Commissioners of Watertown*, 7 How. Pr. 28.)

*Decision to remain unaltered for four years.*—The decision of the referees, laying out, altering or discontinuing any road, in whole or in part, shall remain unaltered for the term of four years from the time the same shall have been filed in the office of the town clerk. (Laws of 1847, ch. 455, § 9.) The affirmance of the decision of the commissioners laying out a road is making a decision laying out a road within the meaning of the statute. The policy of the provision is to prevent litigation for the period specified in regard to the road, after a decision on appeal. (*People* v. *Pike*, 18 How. 70.)

*Decision conclusive.*—The decision of the referees or of any two of them is conclusive in the premises. (1 R. S. 519, § 89.)

The provision that the decision of the referees shall be conclusive in the premises means only that it shall be conclusive on the merits as to the particular case in which the appeal is taken, and does not prevent or affect a new application for the same road. (*Bruyn* v. *Graham*, 1 Wend. 370.)

The decision of the referees is only conclusive on the merits. They can only entertain, examine and decide the appeal on its merits. But, if any irregularity occur in their proceedings, or in the proceedings of the commissioners in making the order appealed from, such irregularity may be corrected by the supreme court on *certiorari*. (*Commissioners of Warwick* v. *Judges of Orange*, 13 Wend. 432.)

*Appeal stays proceedings.*—When an appeal is taken from the determination of the commissioners, their power over the matter is suspended until the decision of the appeal, and where several appeals are taken, a decision of one cannot give the commissioners power to open the road through the lands of the other appellants. (*Clark* v. *Phelps*, 4 Cow. 190.) But though an appeal operates as a stay of proceedings, it operates only from the time it is taken, and cannot undo or render illegal what has lawfully been done under the order appealed from. (*Drake* v. *Rogers*, 3 Hill, 604.)

*Removal of fences.*—Whenever the commissioners of highways shall have laid out any public highway through any inclosed, cultivated or improved lands, in conformity to the provisions of this title, and their determination shall not have been appealed from, they shall give the owner or occupant of the land through which such road shall have been laid, sixty days' notice, in writing, to remove his fences. If such owner shall not remove his fences within the sixty days, the commissioners shall cause such fences to be removed, and shall direct the road to be opened and worked. (1 R. S. 520, § 96.)

If the determination of the commissioners shall have been appealed from, then the sixty days' notice shall be given after the decision of the judges upon such appeal shall have been filed in the office of the town clerk of the town. (1 R. S. 520, § 97.)

Sixty days' notice must be given before proceeding to open the road, as well where it has been established by an alteration made by referees after the same has been laid out by them on appeal, as when a road is originally laid out by commissioners. Actual notice must be shown, as it will not be presumed. (*Case* v. *Thompson*, 6 Wend. 634.)

Though a road has been laid out, the owner is entitled to sixty days' notice to remove his fences, and the overseer has no right to abate or remove them without such notice. (*Kelley* v. *Horton*, 2 Cow. 424.) (See form No. 47.)

*Referees' fees.*—Every referee appointed as above provided shall be entitled to receive two dollars for every day employed in the hearing and decision of such appeal or appeals, to be paid by the party appealing, where the determination of the commissioners shall be confirmed, but where it is reversed, to be a charge upon the county. (Laws of 1847, ch. 455, § 9.)

Where the determination of the commissioners is reversed in part and affirmed in part, the county would probably be required to pay the costs, although no provision is made therefor by statute. Where several appeals are taken, the referees are entitled to the costs of one appeal only. (*Disosway* v. *Winant*, 34 Barb. 578; 13 Abb. 216.) The liability of the appellants in such case, provided they are unsuccessful, is joint and several, and the referees may recover their entire fees from any one. (Id.) The one compelled to pay could, however, recover the proportionate parts from the other appellants.

The fact that a writ of certiorari has been served out to remove the proceedings of the referees into the supreme court does not suspend their right to their fees. (*Disosway* v. *Winant*, 34 Barb. 578; 13 Abb. 216.)

*Certiorari of proceedings.* — Either party may sue out a writ of *certiorari* to the supreme court to review the proceedings of the referees. (*Commissioners of Kinderhook* v. *Claw*, 15 Johns. 537; *People* v. *Van Alstyne*, 32 Barb. 131; Aff'd, 3 Keyes, 35.)

The application is to be made to the court at special term, and is to be founded on affidavits showing that there is reasonable ground to apprehend that a wrong has been done, of a nature that the court can correct. (*Gardner* v. *Commissioners of Warren*, 10 How. 181; 12 Barb. 219.) (See form No. 48.)

Notice of the certiorari must be given to the other party, and of the time and place of the hearing. (*Commissioners of Kinderhook* v. *Claw*, 15 Johns. 537; *People* v. *Commissioners of Brookfield*, 2 Code R. 54.)

The court may either allow the writ at once or grant an order to show cause. (*Matter of Bruni*, 1 Barb. 187.) When the writ is granted it should be in the name of the people, should recite the names of the appellants and the cause of complaint, and should be directed to the referees by name, and give their title as referees appointed by the county judge, etc., commanding them to certify and return the appeal, together with the testimony given or offered on the hearing, with their decision, and all things touching the same. (*People* v. *Salem*, 1 Cow. 23.) The writ should be made returnable at a general term of the district in which the proceedings sought to be reviewed were had. (*People* v. *Kelly*, 35 Barb. 444.)

It should be tested, signed and sealed. (2 Bur. Pr. 195.) An indorsement is to be made thereon, signed by the clerk, showing that the writ was issued by order of the court. (*Mott* v. *Commissioners of Rush*, 19 Wend. 640.) (See form No. 49.)

The writ stays the proceedings, and the commissioners cannot proceed to open the road until a decision is rendered. (*Patchin* v. *Mayor of Brooklyn*, 13 Wend. 664; *Disosway* v. *Winant*, 33 How. 460.)

The referees, prior to the return day mentioned in the writ, must certify and return to the supreme court at general term the appeal, together with the testimony given and offered to be given on the hearing thereof, with their decision thereon, with all things touching and concerning the same. The return must show affirmatively that the referees had authority to act; and where their authority and jurisdiction depends upon a fact to be proved before them, and such fact is disputed, they must certify the proofs given in relation to it for the purpose of enabling the higher court to determine whether the fact be established. (*People* v. *Goodwin*, 5 N. Y. R. 568; *People* v *Van Alstyne*, 32 Barb. 132.) (See form No. 50.)

But on the return of the referees to the *certiorari*, no other question can be raised than those relating to the jurisdiction of the referees and the regularity of their proceedings. (*Birdsall* v. *Phillips*, 17 Wend. 464; *Prindle* v. *Anderson*, 19 id. 391; *People* v. *Goodwin*, 5 N. Y. R. 572; *People* v. *Van Alstyne*, 32 Barb. 131.) The court, on such *certiorari*, cannot examine into the *merits* of the appeal, or of the decision; the determination of the referees thereon is final and conclusive, but it may examine into the regularity of their proceedings, and into all questions, whether of law or fact, on which the referees' jurisdiction depends. (*People* v. *Goodwin, supra; Commissioners of Warwick* v. *Judges of Orange*, 13 Wend. 432.) Among the questions of jurisdiction thus subject to review, is the question whether the owner of the inclosed, improved or cultivated lands, through which a highway is laid, has given his consent thereto (*People* v. *Goodwin*, 5 N. Y. R. 568); also the question whether the persons making the certificate of its necessity were freeholders (*People* v. *Commissioners of Seward*, 27 Barb. 94); also the question whether they were twelve in number (*Town of Gallatin* v. *Loucks*, 21 Barb. 578); also the question whether the highway was laid out through the yard or garden of the owner without his consent (*Ex parte Clapper*, 3 Hill, 458), or through an orchard. (*People* v. *Commissioners of Dutchess*, 23 Wend. 360; see also *People* v. *Van Alstyne*, 32 Barb. 131.)

Where the proceedings of the referees are removed into the supreme court, the prevailing party is not entitled to costs. (*People* v. *Heath*, 20 How. 304.)

## CHAPTER IX.

### DAMAGES ON LAYING OUT HIGHWAY.

*May be ascertained by agreement.*—The damages sustained by reason of the laying out and opening such road may be ascertained by the agreement of the owner and the commissioners of highways, provided such damages do not exceed one hundred dollars; and unless such agreement be made, or the owner of the land shall, in writing, release all claim to damages, the same shall be assessed in the manner prescribed by law, before such road shall be opened or worked or used. Every such agreement or release shall be filed in the town clerk's office, and shall forever preclude such owner from all further claim for such damages. (1 R. S. 515, § 64.)

The commissioners can only agree with the owner of the land, as no provision is made for recognizing the claims of occupants and tenants. The agreement or release must be in writing, and is to be filed by the commissioners.

Where the damages cannot be agreed upon the commissioners must proceed to have them assessed. Should they attempt to enter upon the lands and open the road before causing such assessment, they would be trespassers. (*Peckham* v. *Henderson*, 27 Barb. 207.)

Although the commissioners must have the damages legally assessed before entry upon the land to open the road, it is not necessary that such damages be paid before the road is opened. (*Bloodgood* v. *Mohawk R. R. Co.*, 14 Wend. 51.)

*Damages, how to be assessed.*—Wherever any damages are now allowed to be assessed by law when any road or highway shall be laid out, altered or discontinued in whole or in part, such damages shall be assessed by not less than three commissioners, to be appointed by the county court of the county in which such road or highway shall be, on the application of the commissioner or commissioners of the town; and the commissioners so appointed shall take the oath of office prescribed by the constitution, and shall proceed, on receiving at least six days' notice of the time and place, to meet the highway commissioners and take a view of the premises, hear the parties and such witnesses as may be offered before them; and they shall all meet and act, and shall assess all damages which may be required to be assessed on the same highway, and shall be authorized to administer oaths to witnesses which may be produced before them under this section; and when they shall all have met and acted, the assessment agreed to by a majority of them shall be valid, and when so made shall be delivered to a commissioner of highways of the town, who, within ten days after receiving it, shall file it in the town clerk's office. (Laws of 1845, ch. 180, as amended, 1847, ch. 455, § 2.) (See Form No. 50.)

If any commissioner appointed should refuse or be unable to serve, another may be appointed in his place by the county court.

The number of commissioners to assess is not limited to three, though it cannot be less. If more than three are appointed, an odd number should be chosen, to prevent the contingency of a tie vote.

The application is to be made to, and the appointment by, the county court, and not the judge; and the owner of the land should receive notice of the application. The commissioners should not be of kin to any of the parties interested.

The commissioners are first to take the oath prescribed. (See Form No. 3.) As the people of the town are interested in the proceeding, the immediate parties cannot consent to an omission of the commissioners to take the oath; and such an omission will prevent the latter from acquiring jurisdiction. (See *People* v. *Connor*, 46 Barb. 333.)

At least six days' notice of the meeting of the commissioners should be served upon them by the commissioners of highways, and like notice should also be given to the land owners, though not required by the statute.

The commissioners are to meet at the appointed time and place, view the premises, hear the parties, and such witnesses as may be offered before them. In making up their judgment as to the value of the land taken, the commissioners may cause estimates to be made, and receive the opinions of others; and when they act upon such estimates and opinions without exercising their own judgment, they should require the same to be verified by oath; but, where they ultimately exercise their own judgment, they may make inquiries and obtain information from others without putting them under oath. (*In re William and Anthony streets*, 19 Wend. 678.)

The measure of damage is the difference between the market value of the land before the improvements are made, and its value after such improvements are made. (*Matter of Furman street*, 17 Wend. 649; *Troy and Boston R. R. Co.* v. *Lee*, 13 Barb. 164.)

While the commissioners cannot take into consideration any remote, contingent or speculative damages, they are not confined, in making their appraisal, to the actual value of the land to be taken, but may consider how the laying out and opening of the road will affect the residue of the owner's land. Will it leave that residue in an inconvenient and unmarketable shape? If so, that fact may properly be taken into account in determining the compensation. (See *Albany Northern R. R. Co.* v. *Lansing*, 16 Barb. 68.)

Where any person shall be the owner of any land over which any highway shall run, and such highway shall be discontinued, in whole or in part, by reason of some other road to be established and laid out through the lands of the same person, the persons who shall assess the damages shall take into calculation the value of the road so discontinued and the benefit resulting to such person by reason of such discontinuance, and shall deduct the same from the damages assessed for the opening and laying out of such new road; and thereupon the owner of the land may inclose so much of the highway so discontinued as shall belong to him. (1 R. S. 516, § 71.)

Where a highway shall hereafter be laid out through uninclosed, unimproved and uncultivated lands, the damages shall be assessed in the same manner as if the same were laid out through inclosed, improved and cultivated lands. (Laws of 1857, ch. 491, as amended 1858, ch. 51.)

When the commissioners, or a majority of them, have agreed upon their assessment, they are to make their award in writing, which is to be delivered to the commissioners of highways, who are required to file it in the town clerk's office within ten days thereafter. (See Form No. 51.)

*Provision in case persons conceive themselves aggrieved.* — Any person conceiving himself aggrieved, or the commissioner or commissioners on the part of the town, feeling dissatisfied with any such assessment, may, within twenty days after the filing thereof, as aforesaid, signify the same by notice in writing, and serving the same on the town clerk and on the opposite party, that is, the persons for whom the assessments were made, or the commissioner or commissioners of highways, as the case may be, asking for a jury to re-assess the damages, and specifying a time, not less than ten nor more than twenty days from the time of filing said assessment, when such jury will be drawn at the clerk's office of an adjoining town of the same county by the town clerk thereof; which notice shall be served upon said opposite party within three days after service upon the town clerk as aforesaid, and may be served personally or by being left at the dwelling-house of the party with some person in charge thereof, or, if there be no such person, or the house be closed, then by fixing the same upon the outer door of said dwelling-house. (Laws of 1847, ch. 455, § 3.) (See Forms Nos. 51, 52.)

Wherever there are more than one commissioner of highways in a town, notice of appeal from an assessment of damages under the highway act must be served on each and all of the commissioners. If there are three commissioners, service upon one alone is not sufficient. (*The People ex rel. Mitchell* v. *Lawrence*, 54 Barb. 589.)

This notice and service is a condition precedent to jurisdiction. Without it, no authority exists for drawing and summoning a panel of jurors, and the justice has no authority in the premises; nor have the jurors summoned and drawn any jurisdiction of the subject-matter. (Id.)

Where application shall be made by two or more persons for the re-assessment of damages by a jury, such jury shall be obtained in conformity with the terms of the notice first served upon the clerk of the town in which the damages are to be assessed. (Laws of 1847, ch. 455, § 7.)

The party dissatisfied has not, in reality, twenty days from the filing of the assessment to give notice of his dissatisfaction, since he must specify a time, *not less than ten nor more than twenty days from such filing*, for the drawing of the jury. Notice of the drawing must also be served on the town clerk of the adjoining town at least three days prior to the drawing.

*Names of jurors to be put in box and drawn.* — At the time and place mentioned in the preceding section, the town clerk of such adjoining town, having received three days' previous notice that such jury is to be drawn, from the person or party asking a re-assessment, shall deposit in a box the names of all such persons, then residents of his town, whose names are on the last list filed in said town clerk's office of those selected and returned as jurors, pursuant to article second, title four, chapter seven, part third of the Revised Statutes, who are not interested in the lands through which such road shall be located, nor of kin to either or any of the parties, and shall draw therefrom the names of twelve persons, and shall make a certificate of such names and the purposes for which they were drawn, and shall deliver the same to the party first asking for the re-assessment. (Laws of 1847, ch. 455, § 4.) (See Form No. 53.)

*Jury, when to be summoned.*—The party receiving such certificate shall, within twenty-four hours thereafter, deliver the same to a justice of the peace of the town wherein the damages are to be assessed; and it shall be the duty of such justice forthwith to issue a summons to one of the constables of his town, directing him to summon the persons named in said certificate, and shall specify a time and place in said summons at which the persons to be summoned shall meet; but no meeting of such persons shall be had within twenty days from the time of filing the assessment of damages in the town clerk's office by the commissioner or commissioners of highways. (Id. § 5.) (See Form No. 54.)

The certificate is to be delivered to a "justice of the peace of the town wherein the damages are to be assessed;" that is, of the town in which the highway is to be laid out. The justice is to specify a place in his own town for the meeting of the jury. The party receiving the certificate may select any justice in the town.

*Jurors to be drawn to re-assess damages.*—Upon such persons appearing at the time and place mentioned in the summons, the justice who issued the summons shall draw by lot six of the persons attending to serve as a jury, and the first six persons drawn, who shall be free from all legal exceptions, shall be the jury to re-assess all the damages required to be re-assessed upon the same highway; and the said jury shall be sworn by the said justice well and truly to determine and re-assess such damages as shall be submitted to their consideration, and shall take a view of the premises, hear the parties and such witnesses as may be offered by the parties and sworn by said justice before them, and shall render their verdict in writing under their hands, which shall be certified by said justice, and be delivered to the commissioners of highways of the town, and the same shall be final. (Id. § 6.) (See Form No. 55.)

The person whose land is taken for a highway is entitled to notice of the time and place of the impanneling of the jury, and of the subsequent proceedings before the jury in making such assessment. The jurors selected are to be free from all legal exceptions; that is, are not to be of kin to the parties within the ninth degree, nor interested in the subject-matter, and are to have the amount of property sufficient to enable them to sit as jurors in a court of justice. It is not essential to the validity of the proceedings that the same justice who summons and impannels the jury should certify their verdict. If that justice refuses to certify, it may be done by any other justice of the town who was present. (*People* v. *Supervisors of Ulster*, 34 N. Y. R. 268.) The jury are to proceed in the same manner as the commissioners.

The justice having charge of the proceedings should keep the jury together until they agree upon their verdict. Should they fail to agree, however, after a reasonable time, he may discharge them, and a new jury may be summoned and impanneled. (*People* v. *Lewis*, 26 How. 378.)

After a delay of eleven months to call a new jury after the first has failed to agree, the party applying for such re-assessment will be deemed to have abandoned the same. (Id.)

The award of the commissioners appointed to assess the damages is, in effect, a judgment in favor of the owner against the town, and is conclusive until reversed on *certiorari* or vacated by a re-assessment actually made. (Id.)

*Costs, and by whom to be paid.*—In all cases of assessments of damages, under the provisions of this act, by commissioners appointed by a county court, the costs thereof shall be paid by the town in which the damages shall be assessed, and in cases of re-assessments of damages by a jury on the application of the commissioners of highways of any town, and the first assessment shall be reduced thereby, the costs of such assessment shall be paid by the party claiming the damages, otherwise by the town; and in case a re-assessment of damages shall be had on the application of the party for whom the damages were assessed, and such party shall fail to increase the same, he shall pay the costs thereof, but when such damages shall be increased by the jury the costs shall be paid by the town; and when applications shall be made by two or more persons for the re-assessment of damages by a jury, such jury shall be obtained in conformity with the terms of the notice first served upon the clerk of the town in which the damages are to be assessed; and all persons who may be liable for costs under this section shall be liable in proportion to the amount of damages respectively assessed to them by the first assessment, and may be recovered in an action of assumpsit at the suit of any person or persons entitled to the same before a justice of the peace. (Laws of 1847, ch. 455, § 7.)

Town clerks shall be allowed the sum of fifty cents for drawing and certifying a jury as provided by this act, and a constable for summoning such jury shall be allowed two dollars, except when the jury shall be taken from the same town wherein the road is located, in which case he shall be allowed only one dollar. And jurors who shall be summoned from an adjoining town, and shall attend but not serve, shall be entitled each to fifty cents, and if they shall serve, then one dollar; if from the same town and shall attend and not serve, twenty-five cents; if they shall serve, then fifty cents each. (Id. § 19.)

*Vacancies, how filled.*—If, for any cause, any commissioner or referee appointed under the above provision shall be prevented from serving, or shall refuse to serve, the court or officer who appointed him shall have power to appoint another to supply his place. (Laws of 1847, ch. 455, § 20.)

*Orders to be filed.*—All orders for the appointment of commissioners or referees, under the above provisions, shall be filed and recorded in the office of the town clerk of the town in which the road shall be located. (Id. § 21.)

*Damages assessed to be audited by board of supervisors.*—All damages which may be finally assessed or agreed upon by commissioners of highways for the laying out of any road except private roads, shall be laid before the board of supervisors by the supervisor of the town, to be audited with the charges of the commissioners, justices, surveyors or other persons or officers employed in making the assessment and for whose services the town shall be liable, and the amount shall be levied and collected in the town in which the road is located, and the money so collected shall be paid to the commissioners of such town, who shall pay to the owner the sum assessed to him, and appropriate the residue to satisfy the charges aforesaid. (Id. § 23.)

The supervisors have nothing to do with the merits of the appraisal. The statute declares that *the amount shall be levied and collected.* The award of the commissioners, they having jurisdiction, is conclusive upon the board as to the amount. (*Ex parte Caldwell*, 5 Cow. 292.)

And should they refuse to proceed and audit the damages a mandamus will be issued to compel them to do so. (*People* v. *Supervisors of Ulster*, 3 Barb. 332; *People* v. *Supervisors of Westchester*, 11 id. 446.)

If the supervisors allow their session to expire without taking any action on the claim, it will be regarded as rejected so far as to permit a mandamus to compel its allowance. (*People* v. *Supervisors of Richmond*, 20 N. Y. R. 252.)

*Damages and expenses, how collected.*—Where the plaintiff's damages on laying out a highway had been assessed by three commissioners appointed by the county judge, and had afterward been re-assessed by a jury, the defendant, who was supervisor of the town, laid before the board of supervisors the award of the commissioners but refused to present the award of the jury. The amount assessed by the commissioners was audited by the board of supervisors and was tendered to the plaintiff and refused, and an action brought against the supervisor to recover the amount assessed by the jury, it was held that the defendant was liable for the whole amount assessed by the jury. (*Clark* v. *Miller*, 42 Barb. 255; 47 id. 38.)

*Certiorari.*—The proceedings for assessment or re-assessment may be reviewed by the supreme court on certiorari. (*People* v. *Lewis*, 26 How. 381; *People* v. *Talman*, 36 Barb. 222.)

## CHAPTER X.

### BRIDGES.

A bridge has been defined to be a building of brick, stone, wood or iron, erected across a river, ditch or other stream, in order to facilitate the passage over the same. (Whart. Lex. 114; 1 Bouv. Law Dic. 224.)

Public bridges may be divided into three classes; first, those built at the public expense and over which all persons have a right to pass free; second, those built by private individuals or corporations, and over which all persons may pass on payment of a prescribed toll; third, those built by private individuals and which have been surrendered or dedicated to the public.

A public bridge is a highway, and is governed by the same principles of the common law as highways; yet from a difference in the nature of the respective objects of their operation the reduction of these principles to practice in the one case varies from that of the other. (Wellbeloved on Highways, 324; 2 Lord Raym. 1174; Woolrych on Ways, 195.)

The principle circumstance necessary to constitute a public bridge is that the people at large have a free and uninterrupted use of it, not upon sufferance, but as a matter of right. (Woolrych on Ways, 196.)

Yet a bridge may be common to all people without becoming a public bridge, so as to impose upon the town the responsibility of repairing it. Thus, where a man digs a channel across a road for his own private use or convenience, although the public have a right to use the bridge yet the public is not charged with keeping it in repair. (*Dygert* v. *Schenck*, 23 Wend. 446.) If, in such case, an injury happen to another in consequence of the bridge being out of repair, the party building it is responsible. (*Heacock* v. *Sherman*, 14 Wend. 58.) The public to become chargeable must derive some benefit from a bridge constructed by a private individual, which they do not when the road was as good before the erection of the bridge as after it. (*Rex* v. *Kerrigan*, 3 M. and S. 526.) But where an individual erects a bridge over a *natural stream* for his own benefit, and it is of public utility, and is used by the public, the public is bound to keep it in repair; for, in such case, although the bridge is of advantage to the individual, he cannot be said to have created the necessity for it. (*Heacock* v. *Sherman*, 14 Wend. 58; *Dygert* v. *Schenck*, 23 id. 446.) As where a man builds a bridge across a stream that intersects a highway, which is of great public utility, the public is bound to keep it in repair. (*King* v. *Glamorganshire*, 2 East, 356, *note.*)

*What bridges Commissioners to repair.* — At common law the duty of repairing public bridges rested upon the county at large, where it was not shown that others were bound to repair a particular bridge. But in this state this obligation is imposed by statute upon the towns. (*Hill* v. *Supervisors of Livingston*,

12 N. Y. R. 52; *Morey* v. *Town of Newfane*, 8 Barb. 645.)

The commissioners of highways of a town are bound to keep in repair all such public bridges in the town as are chargeable to the public under the rules above laid down, unless such bridge is made by statute a county charge. The duty of keeping bridges in repair is imposed by statute upon the commissioners and not upon the overseers. (*Bartlett* v. *Crozier*, 17 Johns. 439.)

The commissioners, however, are not bound to repair or rebuild a bridge unless they have the requisite funds for that purpose. (*Garlinghouse* v. *Jacobs*, 29 N. Y. R. 303; *People* v. *Commissioners of Hudson*, 7 Wend. 474.) Their liability in this respect is the same as in case of highways. (See *ante*, p. 34.)

When the commissioners have funds and neglect to repair bridges, a mandamus will be issued to compel them to proceed to repair, but not so if they have not funds sufficient. (*People* v. *Commissioners of Hudson*, 7 Wend. 474.)

The commissioners may erect new bridges where none have before existed, but only over streams intersecting an existing highway. (*Mather* v. *Crawford*, 36 Barb. 564.)

Whenever a corporation owning a toll bridge shall become dissolved, such bridge shall be left without waste or damage and shall be a public highway. (Laws of 1838, ch. 262, § 3.)

In such case the commissioners are to keep it in repair and may be compelled so to do.

*When supervisors may build or repair at expense of county.*—Whenever it shall appear to the board of supervisors of any county, that any one of the towns in such county would be unreasonably burthened, by erecting or repairing any necessary bridge or bridges in such town, such board of supervisors shall cause such sum of money to be raised and levied upon the county as will be sufficient to defray the expenses of erecting or repairing such bridge or bridges, or such part of such expenses as they may deem proper; and such moneys, when collected, shall be paid to the commissioners of highways of the town in which the same are to be expended. (1 R. S. 524, § 119.)

No board of supervisors shall, under the last preceding section, cause any sum exceeding one thousand dollars, to be levied and raised on any county in any one year. (Id. § 120.)

In case the commissioners of highways of any town shall be dissatisfied with the determination of the board of supervisors of their county, touching an allowance for any such bridges, such determination shall, on the application of the commissioners, be reviewed by the court of sessions of the same county, whose order in the premises shall be observed by every such board of supervisors. (Id. § 121.)

Notice of the application should be served upon the chairman of the board, or, in his absence, on the clerk.

Where a bridge is a county charge the board may raise over $1,000 per year for its repairs. (*People* v. *Supervisors of Dutchess*, 1 Hill, 50.)

By section 1 of chapter 314 of the act of 1838, it is provided that the board of supervisors of each county in this state shall, in addition to the powers now conferred upon them by law, have power, at their annual meeting, or when lawfully convened at any other meeting,

1. To cause to be levied, collected and paid to the treasurer of the county, such sum of money as may

be necessary to construct and repair bridges therein, and to prescribe upon what plan and in what manner the moneys so to be raised, shall be expended.

2. To apportion the tax so to be raised, among the several towns and wards of their county, as shall seem to them to be equitable and just.

The third section of the same act provides that all persons intending to apply to any board of supervisors for the imposing any tax pursnant to the first section of the above act, shall cause a notice of such application to be published once in each week for four successive weeks immediately preceding the meeting of the board of supervisors at which such application shall be made, in a newspaper printed in such county; but if no newspaper be printed in the county, then such notice shall be published in like manner in some public newspaper printed nearest thereto.

It is thought that this provision did not relate exclusively to bridges which are a charge upon the whole county, but that the only limitation of the subject in respect to which the power is to be exercised, is that the bridge be in the county. (*Hill* v. *Supervisors of Livingston*, 12 N. Y. R. 52; See *People* v. *Supervisors of Dutchess*, 1 Hill, 50.)

*Repair of bridges between towns.*—Whenever any two or more towns shall be liable to make or maintain any bridge or bridges, the same shall be built and maintained at the joint expense of said towns, without reference to town lines. (Laws of 1841, ch. 225, § 1, as amended 1857, ch. 383, § 1.)

For the purpose of building and maintaining such bridges, it shall be lawful for the commissioners of said towns, or of commissioners of either one or more towns respectively, the other or others refusing to act, to enter into joint contracts, and such contracts may be enforced in law or equity, against such commissioners or their representative successors, jointly or severally, respectively; and the commissioners of said towns, so liable, may be proceeded against jointly, for any neglect of duty, in reference to such bridges. (Laws of 1841, ch. 225, § 1, as amended 1857, ch. 483, § 2.)

If the commissioners of highways of either of such towns, after notice, in writing, from the commissioners of highways of any other of such towns, shall not, within twenty days, give their consent, in writing, to build or repair any such bridge, and shall not, within a reasonable time thereafter, do the same, it shall be lawful for the commissioners so giving such notice, to make or repair such bridges, and then to maintain a suit at law in their official capacity against said commissioners so neglecting or refusing to join in such making or repairing; and in such suit the plaintiff or plaintiffs shall be entitled to recover so much from the defendant or defendants, respectively representing said other towns, as the town or towns would be liable to contribute to the same, together with costs of suit and interest, without proving any contract; and in an action in pursuance of the act hereby amended, to recover the expenses of building or repairs, it shall not be necessary to entitle such commissioner or commissioners to recover on the trial of the above action, to prove that the defendants, or their predecessors in office, were, at the time of the service of the notice above mentioned, in the possession of funds belonging to the town which he or they represent, sufficient to make such repairs; nor shall the want of funds be any defense to the said action; and it shall be the duty of the board of supervisors of the county in which such towns are located, to levy the amount of any judgment so obtained, with costs and interest, on the taxable property of any town, against the commissioner or commissioners of which such judgment has been so obtained, but the commissioner or commissioners of such town shall not be personally liable for such judgment. (Laws of 1841, ch. 225, § 1, as amended 1857, ch. 383, § 3.)

Any judgment recovered against the commissioners of highways in their official capacity under the provisions of this act shall be a charge on said town and collected in the same manner as other town charges, except in cases where the court before which the judgment shall be recovered shall certify that the neglect or refusal of said commissioners was willful and malicious, in which case said commissioners shall be personally liable for such judgment, and the same may be enforced against them in the same manner as against individuals. (Id. § 4.)

*Freeholders may petition for erection or repair of bridges between towns.*—Whenever any adjoining towns shall be liable to make or maintain any bridge over any stream dividing such towns, whether in the same or in different counties, it shall be lawful for three freeholders in either of such towns, by a petition in writing signed by them, to apply to the commissioners of highways in each of said towns, to build, rebuild or repair such bridge, and if such commissioners refuse to build or repair such bridge within a reasonable time, either for the want of funds or any other cause, the said freeholders, upon affidavit and notice of motion, a copy of which shall be served on each of said commissioners at least eight days before the hearing thereof, may apply to the supreme court at a special term thereof, to be held in a judicial district in which such bridge or any part thereof shall be located, or to a judge of said court at chambers, for a rule or order requiring such commissioners to build, rebuild or repair such bridge, and such court or judge upon such motion may, in doubtful cases, refer the matter to some disinterested person to ascertain the requisite facts in relation thereto, and to report the evidence thereof to said court or to such judge. Upon the coming in of such report, in case of such reference, or upon or after the hearing of the motion, in case no such reference shall be ordered, the court or judge shall make such order thereon as the justice of the case shall require. If such motion be granted in whole or in part, whereby funds shall be needed by the said commissioners to carry said order into effect, such court or judge shall specify the amount of money required for that purpose, and how mnch thereof shall be raised in each town. (Laws of 1857, ch. 639, § 1.)

In case a reference shall be ordered as specified in the first section of this act, the referee shall appoint a suitable time and place for taking the evidence, and shall notify one of said freeholders and the said commissioners thereof, or cause them to be notified; he shall have power to issue subpœnas for witnesses at the instance of either party, and may compel the attendance of such witnesses, or failing to appear in obedience to such subpœna by attachment, and may punish defaulting witnesses for contempt, by fine or imprisonment; he shall have power to adjourn such proceedings, from time to time, and to administer the requisite oath to witnesses before him. The referee shall report the evidence taken before him to the court or justice who made the order of reference, without unnecessary delay, and shall be entitled to three dollars a day for his services, to be paid, in the first instance, by the said freeholders. (Laws of 1857, ch. 639, § 2.)

*Commissioners of adjoining towns, how compelled to join in building bridge.*—The commissioners of highways of any such town are hereby authorized to institute and prosecute proceedings, under this act, to compel the commissioners of such adjoining towns to join in the building, rebuilding or repair of any such bridge, in like manner as the said freeholders are hereby authorized so to do. (Id. § 3.)

Upon the said order for building, rebuilding or repairing such bridge being made, and a copy thereof being served on the commissioners of highways of such adjoining towns respectively, the commissioners of highways of said two towns shall forthwith meet and fix on the plan of such bridge, or the manner of repairing such bridge, and shall cause such bridge to be built, rebuilt or repaired, out of any funds in their or either of their hands, applicable thereto; and in case no funds, or an inadequate amount thereof, are on hand, then they shall cause the same to be built, rebuilt or repaired upon credit, or in part for cash, and in part upon credit, according to the exigency of the case; and the commissioners are authorized to enter into a contract, with any contractor, for building, rebuilding or repairing such bridge, pledging the credit of each town for the payment of its appropriate share, so far as the same shall be done upon credit. (Id. § 4.)

The commissioners of highways in each town shall make a full report of their proceedings in the premises, to the auditors of town accounts, at the time of making their annual report. The said commissioners, for each town, shall attach to the copy of the said order granted by the supreme court, or a judge thereof, an accurate account, under oath, of what has been done in the premises, and deliver the same to the supervisors of each town. The board of supervisors, at their annual meeting, shall levy a tax upon each of such towns, when in the same county, and upon the appropriate town when in different counties, its share of the cost of building, rebuilding or repairing such bridge, after deducting all payments actually made by said commissioners thereon; which tax, including prior payments, shall, in no case, exceed the amount specified in said order. (Laws of 1857, ch. 639, § 5.)

Either party considering himself aggrieved by the granting or refusal to grant such order by the court at special term, or by a judge of such court, may appeal from such decision to the supreme court at general term, for the review of such decision. The supreme court, at the general term, shall have power to alter, modify or reverse such order, with or without costs. (Id. § 6.)

The supreme court at special term, or a judge at chambers, shall have power to grant or refuse costs as upon a motion, including also witnesses' fees, referees' fees and disbursements. The appeal provided for in the last section shall conform to the practice of the supreme court in case of appeals from the decision of a motion at a special term, to the general term of the supreme court. (Id. § 7.)

*Proceedings where such bridge has been repaired by individuals.*—Whenever any such bridge shall have been or shall be so out of repair as to render it unsafe for travelers to pass over the same, or whenever such bridge shall have fallen down, or been swept away by a freshet or otherwise, if the commissioners of highways of such adjoining towns, after reasonable notice of such condition of such bridge, have neglected or refused, or shall neglect or refuse to repair or rebuild such bridge, then, and in such case, whatever funds have been or shall be necessarily or reasonably laid out or expended in repairing such bridge, or in rebuilding the same, by any person or persons, or by any corporation, shall be a charge upon such adjoining towns, each being liable for its just proportion; and the person or persons, or corporation, who has made such expenditure, or shall make the same, may apply to the supreme court at a special term, or to a judge at chambers, for an order requiring such towns severally to reimburse such expenditures, which application shall be made upon serving papers for such application upon the commissioners of highways in each of such towns, at least eight days before such application shall be made, and such court or judge is authorized to grant an order requiring each of such adjoining towns to pay its just proportion of such expenditure, specifying the same; and in case such order shall be granted, it shall be the duty of the commissioners of highways, in each of such towns, forthwith to serve a copy of such order upon the supervisor of each of such towns, who shall present the same to the board of supervisors at their next annual meeting. The board of supervisors shall raise the amount justly chargeable upon each town, and cause the same to be collected and paid to such person or persons, or corporation, as incurred such expenditure. The right of appeal is given to such party under this section, provided for under the sixth section of this act. (Laws of 1857, ch. 639, § 8.)

*Money for repair of bridges, how raised.*—The money for the repair of bridges is to be raised in the same manner as for the repair of roads, for which see *ante*, chapter 2, section 3.

*Commissioners may put up notice.*—The commissioners of highways of each town may put up and maintain, in conspicuous places, at each end of any bridge in such town, maintained at the public charge, and the length of whose chord is not less than twenty-five feet, a notice with the following words in large characters: "one dollar fine for riding or driving on this bridge faster than a walk." (1 R. S. 525, § 122.)

*Penalty.*—Whoever shall ride or drive faster than on a walk, over any bridge upon which such notices shall have been placed, and shall then be, shall forfeit, for every offense, the sum of one dollar. (Id. § 123.)

*Injury to bridge.*—Whoever shall injure any bridge maintained at the public charge shall, for every offense, forfeit treble damages. (Id. § 124.)

*Bridges over canals.*—In all cases where a new road or public highway shall be laid out by legal authority, in such direction as to cross the line of any canal, and in such manner as to require the erection of a new bridge over the canal, for the accommodation of the road, such bridge shall be so constructed and forever maintained, at the expense of the town in which it shall be situated. (1 R. S. 247, § 174.)

No bridge shall be constructed across any canal without first obtaining for the model and location thereof, the consent, in writing, of one of the canal commissioners, or of a superintendent of repairs, on that line of the canal which is intersected by the road. (Id. § 175.)

Every person who shall undertake to construct or to locate such bridge without such consent, and shall proceed therein so far as to place any materials for that purpose on either bank of the canal, or on the bottom thereof, shall forfeit the sum of fifty dollars; and each of the commissioners, superintendents or engineers shall be authorized to remove all such materials, as soon as they are discovered, wholly without the banks of the canal. (1 R. S. 247, § 176.)

*Toll bridges.*—A toll bridge is a highway over which the public have the right to pass on the payment of a certain toll. The public, on payment of the toll, have the same rights and privileges on a toll bridge as on an ordinary public bridge. (*Thompson* v. *Matthews*, 2 Edw. 212.)

An injunction will not be granted to prevent a person's taking heavy loads across a toll bridge. If persons take improper loads, and the bridge has been properly constructed, then the owners of it have a remedy by a special action on the case, or in trespass for damage done; while on the other hand, if passengers and their property should sustain an injury by a breaking from ordinary loads, the owners must respond in damages. (Id.)

Bridge companies who take toll are bound to keep their bridge in repair and will be liable for any injuries received through their neglect so to do. (*Townsend* v. *Susquehanna Turnpike Co.*, 6 Johns. 90; *Kane* v. *People*, 3 Wend. 363.)

The obligation of the company, however, only extends to the exercise of ordinary care and prudence. (Id.) When the bridge of a company is dangerous they must cease to take toll, to relieve themselves from liability. A notice that it is dangerous is not enough. (*Randall* v. *Cheshire Turnpike Co.*, 6 N. H. 147.)

*Bridge company must rebuild bridge destroyed.*—If a bridge be carried away by a sudden flood, the company must rebuild it within a reasonable time, regard being had to the importance of the road, the magnitude of the work, the opportunity for procuring materials, and other circumstances connected with its reconstruction. (*People* v. *Hillsdale, etc., Turnpike Co.*, 23 Wend. 254.) Should the bridge remain impassable, and the business of the company be thereby stopped for the period of one year, it will amount at common law to a forfeiture of their charter; but a legal course of proceeding must be instituted to obtain judgment of ouster. (Id.) And where a toll bridge is out of repair, the public are not limited to the remedy of having the gates thrown open, but may proceed by information. (Id.) Under the act of 1848, hereafter cited, the bridge must be rebuilt within three years, or the company shall cease to be a body corporate.

*Injuring or passing gate.*—It is provided that every person who shall willfully break, throw down, or injure any gate erected on any bridge, erected or constructed by virtue of the act of 1848 (hereafter cited), or forcibly or fraudulently pass any such gate thereon, without having first paid the legal toll for crossing said bridge, shall, for each offense, forfeit to the corporation injured the sum of twenty-five dollars, in addition to the damages resulting from such wrongful act. (Laws of 1854, ch. 120.)

*Notice on toll bridge.*—It shall be lawful for any corporation or individual owning a toll bridge to put up at each end thereof, in a conspicuous place, a notice in the following words: "One dollar fine for riding or driving faster than a walk on this bridge;" and during the continuance of such notice any person who shall ride or drive faster than a walk on such bridge, shall forfeit the sum of one dollar, to be sued for in the name of the corporation or person or persons owning such bridge, and to be recovered with costs of suit. (Laws of 1838, ch. 262, § 2.)

*Bridges to become highways.*—Whenever a corporation owning a toll bridge shall become dissolved, such bridge shall be left without waste or damage, and shall be a public highway. (Id. § 3.)

*Incorporation of bridge companies; corporation may be formed.*—Any number of persons, not less than five, may be formed into a corporation, for the purpose of constructing and owning a bridge across any stream of water, as hereinafter provided, upon complying with the following requirements:

*Articles of association.*—1. They shall severally subscribe articles of association, in which shall be set forth the name of the corporation, the number of years the same is to continue, which shall not exceed fifty years; the amount of the capital stock of the corporation, which shall be divided into shares of twenty-five dollars each, the number of directors and their names, who shall manage the concerns of the corporation for the first year, and until others are elected; the location of such bridge, and the plan thereof.

2. Each subscriber to such articles of association shall subscribe thereto his name and place of residence, and the number of shares of stock taken by him in such corporation.

3. Whenever one-fourth part of the amount of the capital stock, specified in the articles of association, shall have been subscribed, and on complying with the provisions of the next section, such articles may be filed in the office of the state engineer and surveyor, and clerk of the county or counties in which the bridge is built; and thereupon the persons who have subscribed the articles of association, as aforesaid, and such other persons as shall become stockholders in such company, and their successors, shall be a body corporate, by the name specified in such articles of association, and shall possess the powers and privileges, and be subject to the provisions, of titles three and four of chapter eighteen of the first part of the Revised Statutes, so far as those provisions are consistent with the provisions of this act. (Laws of 1848, ch. 259, § 1.)

All the stockholders of every company incorporated under this act, shall be severally and individually liable, to an amount equal to the amount of the capital stock held by them respectively, to the creditors of such company, for all the debts contracted by the directors or agents of such company for its use, until the whole amount of the capital stock fixed and limited by such company is paid in, and a certificate thereof filed in the offices aforesaid, and the whole capital stock paid in, shall be one-half thereof within one year, and the other half thereof within two years from the time of the incorporation of such company, and if not so paid in, such corporation shall be dissolved. If the directors of any corporation formed under this act shall contract debts for the company, exceeding in the aggregate the amount of the capital stock, they shall be personally liable for all the debts of the corporation. (Id. § 2.)

Such articles of association shall not be filed as aforesaid, until five per cent on one-fourth of the amount of the stock of such company, fixed as aforesaid, shall have been actually paid in, in good faith, to the directors named in such articles of association, in cash, nor until there shall be indorsed thereon, or annexed thereto, an affidavit made by at least three of the directors named in such articles of association, that the amount of stock required by the first section of this act to be subscribed has been subscribed, and that five per cent on the amount has been actually paid in as aforesaid. (Laws of 1848, ch. 259, § 3.)

A copy of such articles of association filed in pursuance of this act, with a copy of such affidavit indorsed thereon or annexed thereto, and certified to be a copy by the proper officer, shall, in all courts and places, be presumptive evidence of the facts therein contained. (Id. § 4.)

The business and property of every such corporation shall be managed and conducted by a board of directors, consisting of not less than five nor more than nine, who shall be chosen, except those for the first year, at such place within a county in which the bridge of such corporation or some part thereof shall be located, as shall be prescribed by the by-laws thereof. The directors shall give notice of every such election, previous to the holding thereof, by publishing the same once in each week, for four successive weeks, in a public newspaper, published in each county in which such bridge or any part thereof shall be located, and if in any such county no such paper shall be published, such notice shall be published in some county adjoining such last-mentioned county. All elections of directors shall be by ballot and by a majority of all votes given thereat; and every stockholder being a citizen of the United States and attending in person or by proxy shall be entitled to one vote for each share of stock which he shall have owned absolutely, or as executor, administrator or guardian, for thirty days previous to such election. No person shall be a director unless he shall be a stockholder, owning at least four shares of stock, absolutely in his own right or as executor, administrator or guardian, and entitled to vote at the election at which he shall be chosen, nor unless he shall be a citizen of this state; and a majority of the directors shall, at the time of their election, be residents of the county or counties in which such bridge shall be located. Whenever any vacancy shall happen in the board of directors, it shall be supplied until the next election by the remaining directors. The directors of every such company shall be elected in the same month in each and every year, and such election, after the first, shall be held on the first Tuesday of such month, and the directors chosen at any election shall hold their offices to and including the Tuesday next after that appointed by law for holding the election next succeeding that at which they were chosen. If an election of directors shall not be held on the day prescribed by this act for holding the same, the directors in office on that day shall hold their offices until their successors shall be elected, but, after the expiration of their regular term of office as prescribed by this section, they shall be incapable of doing any act, as such directors, except such as may be necessary to give effect to an election of directors. The provisions of the second article of the second title of the eighteenth chapter of the first part of the Revised Statutes shall apply to every corporation formed under this act, so far as such provisions shall be consistent with the provisions of this act. (Laws of 1848, ch. 259, § 5.)

When any bridge corporation shall be desirous of constructing a bridge, or any part thereof, in any county, it shall apply to the board of supervisors of such county, at the annual or any special meeting thereof, for authority to construct such bridge; of which application such corporation shall give notice, by publishing the same in at least one public newspaper in such county, or if no newspaper is published therein, then in an adjoining county, once in each week for six weeks successively, previous to the time of presenting such application to such board, specifying such time and the location of such proposed bridge. If the place of the location of such bridge shall be situated in more than one county, such application shall be made to the board of supervisors of every such county. Such application shall also specify the length and breadth of such bridge; and the notice of such application shall set forth all the particulars required to be specified in such application. Upon the hearing of the said application, all persons residing in such county, or interested in such application, may appear and be heard in respect thereto. Such board may take testimony in respect to such application, or may authorize it to be taken by a county judge or justice of the peace of such county; and it may adjourn the hearing from time to time. A copy of the articles of association of such corporation, certified by the state engineer and surveyor, or by the clerk, where such articles are filed, shall be attached to and filed with such application. No such corporation shall be authorized to bridge any stream, in any manner that will prevent or endanger the passage of any raft of forty-five feet in width, or any ark, where the same is navigated by rafts or arks. (Laws of 1848, ch. 259, § 6.)

Where the notice is given before the incorporation of the company, but the company is duly incorporated at the time of the application, the proceeding will be valid. (Laws of 1852, ch. 372.)

Where the stream is navigable, or the bed of it belongs to the state, application must be made to the legislature. (*Fort Plain Bridge Co.* v. *Smith*, 30 N. Y. R. 44.)

If, after hearing such application, such board shall be of opinion that the public interests will be promoted by the construction of such bridge on the proposed site, it may, if a majority of all the members elected to such board shall assent thereto, by an order to be entered in its minutes, authorize such company to construct such bridge, as shall have been specified in the application which shall be particularly described in such order. Such corporation shall cause a copy of such order, certified by the clerk of such board, with such application, to be recorded in the clerk's office of such county, before it shall proceed to do any act by virtue thereof; and such board shall cause such application, when it shall have finally acted on the same, to be filed at the expense of the corporation, with all the other papers relating thereto, or to the proceedings of said board thereon, in the office of the clerk of the county in which it shall have been made. Any corporation formed under this act may use, in such manner as such board shall prescribe, so much of any public highway on either side of any stream as may be necessary for the construction and maintenance of such bridge and toll houses. (Laws of 1848, ch. 259, § 7.)

In case any bridge shall be constructed, under the provisions of this act, over any stream navigable by rafts, it shall be the duty of the corporations constructing such bridge, at all times, to keep the channel of said stream, both above and below said bridge, free and clear from all deposits, in any wise prejudicial to the navigation thereof, which may be formed or occasioned by the erection of such bridge. (Laws of 1848, ch. 259, § 8.)

Any corporation organized under the provisions of this act, which shall construct a bridge over any stream, navigable by rafts as hereinbefore provided, shall be liable to pay all persons who may be unnecessarily or unreasonably hindered or delayed in passing such bridge, all damages which they shall sustain thereby, to be recovered, with costs of suit. (Id. § 9.)

Every bridge constructed by virtue of this act shall be built with a good and substantial railing or siding, at least four and a half feet high. Whenever such bridge shall be completed, and a certificate signed by the county judge of the county in which such bridge is situated, or if such bridge shall be located in more than one county, by the county judge of each of such counties, and such certificate filed in the office of the clerk of such county, or of each of said counties, if such bridge shall be located in more than one county, that such bridge is constructed and completed in a manner safe and convenient for the public use, the directors may erect a toll gate at such bridge, and demand and receive such sum as shall be, from time to time, prescribed by the supervisors of the county or counties where the bridge is located. (Id. § 10.)

No toll shall be collected for crossing any bridge constructed by any corporation formed under this act, from any person going to or from public worship, or to or from a funeral, or to or from school, or to or from a town meeting or election, at which he is entitled to vote, for the purpose of giving such vote, and returning therefrom; or to or from a military parade which he is, by law, required to attend, or to or from any court which he shall be required to attend, as a juror or witness, or to or from his legally required work upon any public highway. (Laws of 1848, ch. 259, § 11.)

The directors of any incorporation, formed under this act, may require payment from the stockholders of the sums subscribed to the capital stock, at such times and in such proportions, and on such conditions as they shall see fit, under the penalty of the forfeiture of their stock, and all previous payments thereon; and they shall give notice of the payments thus required, and of the place and time when and where the same are to be made, at least thirty days previous to the time fixed for the payment of the same, for the time and in the manner herein prescribed for giving notice of the election of directors, and by sending such notice to such stockholder, by mail, directed to him at his usual place of residence. (Id. § 12.)

The shares of any corporation, formed under this act, shall be deemed personal property, and may be transferred in such manner as shall be prescribed by the by-laws of such corporation; and the directors of every such corporation may, at any time, with the consent of a majority in amount of the stockholders in such corporation, provide for such increase of the capital stock thereof, as may be necessary for the completion or reconstruction of such bridge, and the certificate of the amount of any such increase, within thirty days thereafter, shall be filed in the offices of the state engineer and surveyor, and theclerk or clerks of the county or counties in which such bridge is located, which certificate shall be authenticated by the signatures and oaths of a majority of said directors. (Id. § 13.)

So much of any such bridge or toll houses, constructed by virtue of this act, as shall be within any town, city or village, shall be liable to taxation in such town, city or village, as real estate. (Laws of 1848, ch. 259, § 14.)

Every company incorporated under this act shall cease to be a body corporate:

1. If, within two years from the filing of their articles of association, they shall not have commenced the construction of their bridge, and actually expended thereon at least ten per cent of the capital stock of such company; or,

2. If within five years from the filing of such articles of association such bridge shall not be completed according to the provisions of this act; or,

3. If, in case the bridge of such company shall be destroyed, it shall not be reconstructed within three years thereafter. (Id. § 15.)

It shall be the duty of the president and secretary of every corporation formed under this act, to report annually to the state engineer and surveyor, and the county clerk where the papers are filed, under oath, the cost of their bridge, the amount of all money expended, the amount of their capital stock, and how much paid in, and how much actually expended; amount received during the year for tolls, and from all other sources, stating each separately; the amount of dividends made, and the amount of indebtedness of such company, specifying the object for which the indebtedness accrued, and such other particulars in respect to the business affairs of such corporation, as the said state engineer and surveyor, or the legislature, or either branch thereof, require to be so reported. (Id. § 16.)

When any bridge may be in process of construction by private subscriptions at the time of the passage of this act, the subscribers may organize into a corporation pursuant to the provisions of this act, with the same power and privileges as if such bridge had not been so commenced. (Laws of 1848, ch. 259, § 17.)

All companies formed under this act shall, at all times, be subject to visitation and examination by an officer or agent, in pursuance of law, or by the legislature, or by a committee appointed by either house thereof; and the courts of this state shall have the same jurisdiction over such corporations and their officers as over those created by special acts. (Id. § 18.)

Every report required to be made by the 16th section of this act shall be made in the month of January in each year, and shall show, in respect to the particulars required therein to be set forth, the affairs and business of the corporation, making the same at the close of the year ending on the thirty-first day of December next preceding the time of making the same, and shall be published in the nearest newspaper four weeks, and every corporation formed under this act, which shall neglect to make such report as thereby required, shall forfeit to the people of this state for every such neglect the sum of two hundred dollars, and for every week such corporation shall neglect to make such report after the expiration of the time within which it is required as aforesaid to make the same, it shall forfeit, as aforesaid, the further sum of fifty dollars. The state engineer and surveyor shall report to the attorney-general every such forfeiture, by whom the same shall be sued for and recovered, with costs, in the name of the people; and the certificate of the said state engineer and surveyor of any such neglect shall be presumptive evidence thereof, and if any such river, water course or lake, now so navigable, shall hereafter be rendered navigable up stream by vessels or steamboats, power to require such bridge to be altered or removed is reserved to the legislature. (Laws of 1848, ch. 259, § 19.)

Nothing in this act shall be construed so as to authorize the bridging of any river or water course where the tide ebbs and flows, or any water used for a harbor, any lake, river or water, which is navigable by sail vessels or steamboats, nor the construction of any bridge within the limits prescribed by any existing law for the erection or maintenance of any other bridge. (Id. § 20.)

Any existing corporation, having for its object the construction and maintenance of any bridge, whose charter shall expire may be continued as such corporation by complying with the provisions of this act, so far as the same are applicable to them, with the consent of the supervisors of the county or counties in which their bridge is located, to be obtained on application to them as hereinbefore provided. (Id. § 21.)

## CHAPTER XI.

### SIDEWALKS.

While commissioners of highways are not under obligations to work the whole space between the boundaries of a road, it is their duty to keep the entire space free from unusual obstructions. The citizens are entitled to travel over the whole width of the road as laid out, without being subjected to other or greater dangers than may be presented by natural obstacles or those occasioned by making and repairing the traveled path. In country towns the circumstances do not usually require, nor the ordinary means permit, the commissioners to devote much attention to the construction and care of sidewalks. Yet, where this is practicable, it should be done.

The act of 1860 (ch. 61), for the construction and protection of sidewalks, provides as follows:

*Sidewalks to be constructed.*—It shall be lawful for any person owning or occupying lands adjoining a highway or road to construct a sidewalk within said highway or road, along the line of such land, and when a sidewalk shall be or has been so constructed, every person who shall ride or drive a horse or team upon it, except for legitimately crossing the same, shall forfeit not less than two nor more than five dollars for each offense, in the discretion of the court, one-half to the use of the owner or occupant and the other half to the path-master of the road district, to be expended in the improvement of sidewalks therein, to be recovered in any court having cognizance thereof, with costs of suit. (Laws of 1860, ch. 61, § 1.)

*Neglect to prosecute for penalty.*— Whenever any owner or occupant of any such land shall refuse or neglect to prosecute for the forfeiture incurred by such trespass, it shall be lawful for any other party or person owning or occupying lands adjoining any continued portion of said sidewalk, wherein such trespass was committed, and interested as a user thereof, to prosecute, in his own name, the person or persons so incurring such forfeiture, the proceeds of which shall go, one-half to the prosecutor, for his trouble and expense, and the other half for the improvement of sidewalks as in section first. (Id. § 2.)

*Authority of commissioners of highways.*—This act shall not be so construed as to diminish in any way, or interfere with the authority of commissioners or overseers of highways, or any other authority legally exercised over highways or roads; but the said commissioners of highways of the several towns in this state are hereby authorized to expend a part of the highway tax levied in their road districts, upon the sidewalks therein, and in planting shade trees upon the public greens or squares in said towns, provided the roads are always kept in good repair. (Laws of 1860, ch. 61, § 3.)

A further act was passed in 1863, which provides as follows:

All persons owning lands fronting upon any highway (except in cities and incorporated villages) may make and have sidewalks along such land in the highway, and plant and have shade trees along the roadside of such sidewalks; such sidewalks with shade trees shall not extend more than six feet in width from the outward line of such highway; provided such highway is not over three rods wide, with the right to add one additional foot in width to such sidewalk for every additional rod in width of said highway where such sidewalks may or shall be built or shade trees planted, and for the protection of such walks or trees may also construct a railing upon the roadside adjacent and within two and a half feet of such trees or walks, of not more than one bar in height with posts, and also protectives at the ends in such way or manner as not to prevent foot passengers from using such walks, but so built as may and shall prevent cattle from going thereon.

Where trees are set out along a highway they are to be set at least fifty feet apart, except elms, which are to be at least seventy feet apart, and locusts, which may be set at least thirty feet apart. (Laws of 1870, ch. 595.)

*Sidewalks in cities and villages.*—In cities and incorporated villages, sidewalks are parts of the public streets, and are to be kept in a safe and convenient state of repair for public use through their whole width. (*Wallace* v. *Mayor, etc., of N. Y.* 2 Hilt. 440.) Though the corporation may impose upon the owners of lots abutting upon a street the burden of paving and keeping the sidewalks in repair, they do not relieve themselves thereby of the duty of altering, amending and keeping in repair the streets and sidewalks within the city. (Id.)

And this obligation is not varied or discharged by the exercise of the right of an adjoining owner of land, to use the street or sidewalk for some private purpose, not inconsistent with the right of the public. Thus, the owner of adjoining land may build thereon and construct his cellar in such a way that the doors, windows and passage ways communicate with the street, through apertures opening in the sidewalks; but it is, nevertheless, the duty of the city to guard against the danger which might result therefrom.

And the fact that similar apertures have existed for a long time, and to a great extent in the same city, would not authorize the jury to find them, not such defects as would charge the city, if they in reality cause the sidewalks to be *dangerous*, though it might be admissible as evidence tending to prove that they were not unsafe nor inconvenient. (Angell on Highways, 239; *Davenport* v. *Ruckman*, 37 N. Y. R. 568.)

In the case of *Bacon* v. *The City of Boston* (3 Cush. 174), where there was an aperture thirty-seven inches long and fourteen inches in width, for a cellar window, made in a sidewalk six and a half feet wide, which the plaintiff stepped into and injured his ankle, the court said: "It is true that when a road of suitable width is made and kept in a proper state of repair, and guarded with proper barriers, to protect travelers using the same, if a traveler voluntarily leaves the made road or usually traveled path, and thereby encounters pitfalls or obstructions, endangering his person or his property, he can have no remedy against the town for an injury thus received without the limits of the traveled way. But the case supposed is not one of city travel. The law as to the extent of repair and what will constitute obstructions, rendering a public way unsafe or inconvenient for the traveler, must depend in a good degree upon the locality of the road. In the present case, the entire sidewalk was only six and a half feet in width. A sidewalk of this width in the city of Boston should be for its whole extent so constructed and fitted for use as to be safe for all persons passing over it."

It is the duty of corporations to see that the sidewalks are kept in a safe condition, and when excavations, openings, etc., are made therein, by their permission, they are responsible for injuries necessarily resulting therefrom. (*Davenport* v. *Ruckman*, *supra.*) Negligence, however, on the part of the corporation, must be shown, in actions for injuries from defects in sidewalks. (*McGinity* v. *Mayor, etc.*, 5 Duer, 674.) The corporation must, in some way, be connected with the defect, either as having directly caused it, or as having assented to its creation by another, or as having, with a knowledge of its existence, suffered it to remain. (*Hutson* v. *Mayor, etc.*, 9 N. Y. R. 163; *Mayor, etc.* v. *Furze*, 3 Hill, 612; *Hart* v. *Brooklyn*, 36 Barb. 226; *Storrs* v. *Utica*, 17 N. Y. R. 104; *Grant* v. *Brooklyn*, 41 Barb. 381.)

Where the dangerous condition of a sidewalk is of recent occurrence, it is probable that notice of the defect would be required to charge the corporation, but where the want of reparation or defect has continued for a long time, express notice is not required. (*Davenport* v. *Ruckman*, 37 N. Y. R. 568; 16 Abb. 341; see, however, *McGinity* v. *Mayor, etc.*, 5 Duer, 674.)

The streets and sidewalks are for the benefit of all conditions of people, and all have the right, in using them, to assume that they are in good condition, and to regulate their conduct upon that assumption. A person may walk in the darkness of the night, relying upon the belief that the corporation has performed its duty and that the walks are in a safe condition. He walks by a faith justified by law, and if his faith is unfounded and he suffers an injury, the party in fault must respond in damages, per Hunt, Ch. J., in *Davenport* v. *Ruckman*, (37 N. Y. R. 573.)

*Snow and ice on sidewalks.*—Municipal corporations are also required to keep their streets and highways safe and convenient as to defects and obstructions from snow and ice. The leading case on the subject of obstruction of streets from snow and ice is that of *The City of Providence* v. *Clapp* (17 How. [U. S.] 161), decided in the supreme court of the United States.

In that case the obstruction consisted of a ridge of hard-trodden snow and ice on the center of the sidewalk, along which the plaintiff was passing in the night-time, and by means of which he fell across the ridge, breaking his thigh bone in an oblique direction. In addition to the usual obligation imposed, the statute, under which the action was brought, specially directed, that when the highways were blocked up or incumbered with snow, so much thereof should be removed or trodden down, as would render the road passable. In view of this provision it was contended that the towns and cities were bound only to keep their highways and streets open, in case of falls of snow, so as to be passable for travelers, and not to keep them from being slippery from ice or trodden down snow. But the court were of the opinion that the liability of the city was not modified by this special provision; that when a fall of snow took place, it was the duty of the city to use ordinary care and diligence to restore it to a reasonably safe and convenient state; that the law did not prescribe how this should be done, whether by treading down or removing the snow; and that it was for the jury to find, as matter of fact, whether the sidewalk, at the time in question, was in a reasonably safe and convenient state, having reference to its uses. And it was also held, that in determining this question the jury might take into consideration the ordinances of the city, not as prescribing a binding rule, but as evidence that a removal, and not a treading down of the snow, was reasonably necessary.

"The powers of the towns and of the city," said Mr. Justice Nelson, in delivering the opinion of the court, "are as ample for the purpose of removing obstructions from the highways, streets and sidewalks, arising from falls of snow and accumulation of ice, as those arising from any other cause; and the reason for the removal, so that they may be safe and convenient for travelers, is the same in the one case as in the others. The 13th section of the act which gives the personal remedy makes no distinction in the two cases; and, in the absence of some plain distinction pointed out by the statute, it would be exceedingly difficult, if not impossible, to state one. It is conceded, that an obstruction from falls of snow or accumulations of ice must be removed by the towns and cities, so as to make the highways and streets passable, and that this is a duty expressly enjoined upon them. The question is, what sort of removal will satisfy the requirements of the statutes? It is admitted, that, as it respects every other species of obstruction, the repairs must be such that the highways and streets may be safe and convenient for travelers; and that this is a question of fact to be determined by the jury. Is an obstruction by snow or ice to be determined by any other rule or by any other tribunal? The counsel for the defendant suggests, that as it respects such safety and convenience for travelers, in case of falls of snow, the statute should be construed as meaning merely, that the snow should be trodden down or removed, so that the highways and streets should not be so blocked up and incumbered as not to be safely and conveniently open and passable. But it is quite clear that this would be a very indefinite and uncertain rule to guide either the officers, whose duty it is to remove these obstructions, or the jury in the passing upon them when the subject of legal proceedings. The suggestion may be very well as an argument to the jury, for the purpose of satisfying them that the repairs in the manner mentioned were such as to fulfill the requirements of the statute, but to lay it down as a rule of law, in the terms stated, might, in many cases, and under the circumstances, fall far short of it.

"The treading down of snow when it falls in great depth, or in case of drifts, so that the highway or street shall not be blocked up or incumbered, may, in some sense, and for the time being, have the effect to remove the obstructions; but as it respects the sidewalks and their uses, this remedy would be, at best, temporary, and, in case of rains or extreme changes of weather, would have the effect to increase rather than remove it. It is but common observation and knowledge of those familiar with the climate of our northern latitudes, that not unfrequently the most serious obstructions arise from the great depth of snow and changes in the temperature of the weather; and that simply treading down the snow, and leaving it in that condition without further attention, would have the effect to render the highways and sidewalks utterly impassable. In the case also of obstruction from snow, the sidewalks may frequently require its removal so as to make a safe and convenient passage for the pedestrian, when, at the same time, the treading of it down in the street would answer the purpose for the traveler with his team. The nature and extent of the repairs must necessarily depend upon their location and uses; those thronged with travelers may require much greater attention than others less frequented. The just rule of responsibility, and the one, we think, prescribed by the statute, whether the obstruction be by snow or by any other material, is the removal or abatement, so as to render the highway, street or sidewalk, at all times, safe and convenient, regard being had to its locality and uses."

A municipal corporation is liable for damages caused by a fall upon ice lying upon a sidewalk, of which the city government had, or might have had, timely notice, and which might have been removed by it in the exercise of due care, before the accident happened. And it is no defense that city ordinances require the adjoining owners to remove the ice. (*Baltimore* v. *Marriott*, 9 Md. 160; see *Wallace* v. *Mayor, etc.*, 2 Hilt. 440.) In *Stanton* v. *Springfield* (12

Allen [Mass.], 566), the plaintiff, using due care, fell upon a piece of smooth ice which extended across the sidewalk upon which she was walking, the court held the defendant not liable. Bigelow, J., in *Johnson* v. *City of Lowell* (12 Allen [Mass.], 272), said: "If the sole cause of the accident was the slipperiness of the ice, and the walk was properly constructed for ordinary travel, so that it would not cause ice and snow to accumulate thereon, and continue there, and there was, at the time, no such accumulation, creating an obstruction, but the snow was trodden down level and even, such a condition of sidewalk would not be a defect for which the city would be liable." (See, also, *Luther* v. *Worcester*, 97 Mass. 268.)

## CHAPTER XII.

### ENCROACHMENTS ON HIGHWAYS.

*By fences.* — In every case where a highway shall have been laid out or ascertained, described and entered of record in the town clerk's office, and the same has been or shall be encroached upon by fences erected by any occupant of the land through or by which such highway runs, the commissioners of highways of the town shall, if in their opinion it be deemed necessary, order such fences to be removed, so that such highway may be of the breadth originally intended. The commissioners making the order shall cause the same to be reduced to writing and signed. Thay shall also give notice in writing to the occupant of the land to remove fences within sixty days. Every such order and notice shall specify the breadth of the road originally intended, the extent of the encroachment, and the place or places in which the same shall be. (1 R. S. 521, § 103, as amended, Laws of 1870, ch. 125.)

No person shall be required to remove any fence under the preceding provisions of this article, except between the first day of April and the first day of November in any year. (1 R. S. 522, § 109.)

This section, authorizing commissioners to order the removal of fences, by the erection of which highways have been encroached upon, does not abrogate the common-law remedy of abatement of nuisance by the mere act of individuals, or abolish the remedy by indictment; the remedy given by this section is cumulative. (*Wetmore* v. *Tracy*, 14 Wend. 250.)

Some doubt was expressed before the amendment of section 103, whether that section would apply in case the highway had not been laid out. (*Doughty* v. *Brill*, 36 Barb. 488.) The amendment, however, has put the matter at rest by inserting in the second line the words, *or ascertained, described and entered of record in the town clerk's office.*

An order for a removal of fences, to be effective, must be made upon a meeting and deliberation of all the commissioners, or at least all the commissioners should be notified to attend a meeting for the purpose of deliberating thereon, and the order should show the fact. (*Spicer* v. *Slade*, 9 Johns. 359; *Fitch* v. *Commissioners of Kirkland*, 22 Wend. 132.) (See form No. 59.)

The order must specify with precision, "the breadth of the road originally intended; the extent of the encroachment, and the place or places in which the same shall be." An omission of any of these details will render the order null. (*Mott* v. *Commissioners of Rush*, 2 Hill, 472.)

*How width to be ascertained.*—The commissioners are to ascertain the width of the road originally intended from the order on file in the town clerk's office laying out the road, or ascertaining, describing and entering it of record. The jury called to determine a disputed question of encroachment have no power to determine the question of the width intended. (*Talmage* v. *Hunnting*, 29 N. Y. R. 447.)

*On plank and turnpike roads.*—Where a highway is used as a plank or turnpike road the commissioners of highways have still authority, and it is their duty, to take proceedings to remove all encroachments thereon. (*Walker* v. *Caywood*, 31 N. Y. R. 51.)

*Penalty for not removing.*—If such removal shall not be made within sixty days after the service of such notice, the occupant to whom the notice shall be given shall forfeit the sum of fifty cents for every day, after the expiration of that time, for which such fences shall continue unremoved, and the commissioners of highways may remove, or cause to be removed, such encroachment, and the occupant of the premises shall pay to the commissioners of highways all reasonable charges therefor, to be collected in the manner provided in the forty-fifth section of said title. (1 R. S. 522, § 104, as amended, Laws of 1840, ch. 300.)

The "45th section" does not provide for collecting penalties. The latter part of the section is probably directory; if so, the penalty may be collected by an ordinary action. The commissioners can only proceed to remove the encroachment where such encroachment is not denied within the time specified in the next section.

The commissioners of highways of two towns cannot unite as plaintiff, and bring an action to recover a penalty or forfeiture for an encroachment upon a highway running on a line between such towns. (*Bradley* v. *Blair*, 17 Barb. 480.)

A road laid out between two towns is to be divided into districts and allotted, and when thus allotted each district is to be considered as belonging wholly to the town to which it shall be allotted. (Id.)

*Proceedings if encroachment be denied.*—If the occupant to whom notice is given shall, within five days, deny such encroachment, the commissioners, or some one of them, shall apply to any justice of the peace of the county for a precept, directed to any constable of the town, to summon twelve freeholders thereof, to meet at a certain day and place, to be specified in such precept, and not less than four days after the issuing thereof, to inquire into the premises. The constable to whom such precept shall be directed shall give at least three days' notice to the commissioners of highways of the town, and to the occupant of the land, of the time and place at which such freeholders are to meet. (1 R. S. 522, § 105.)

The denial of the encroachment by the occupant must be in writing. (*Lane* v. *Cary*, 19 Barb. 537.) Where the encroachment is denied and the fact is to be inquired into by a jury, the commissioners act as informers merely, and one commissioner may make complaint.

The justice should not annex to the precept the list of jurors to be summoned. If he should do so, however, the objection should be made at the time, or it will be deemed to have been waived. (*Mott* v. *Commissioners of Rush*, 2 Hill, 473.) (See form No. 62.)

*Hearing before jury.*—On the day specified in the precept, the jury so summoned shall be sworn, by such justice, well and truly to inquire whether any such encroachment has been made, and by whom. Such witnesses as may be produced by either party shall also be sworn by such justice; and the jury shall hear the proofs and allegations which may be produced and submitted. (1 R. S. 522, § 106.)

Upon the hearing before a jury, as provided in section one hundred and six of article fifth, title first, chapter sixteenth and part first of the Revised Statutes, the justice who has issued the precept to such party shall preside at the trial, in the same manner as upon the trial of an issue joined in a civil action commenced before him; six of the jurors summoned shall be drawn and impanneled in the same manner as upon trial by jury in civil action before him, and he shall have the power and it shall be his duty to decide as to the competency of jurors, the competency and admissibility of evidence, and all other questions which may arise before him, in the same manner and with the like effect as upon a jury trial in civil actions before him; and such justice shall adjust and determine the costs of such inquiry, and in case the jury shall find an encroachment, he shall render and docket a judgment to that effect, and for such costs against the person or persons who shall have denied such encroachment; in case the jury find no encroachment, he shall render and docket a judgment to that effect against the commissioner or commissioners prosecuting the proceedings, and also for such costs, together with the damages, if any, which may have been fixed by the jury, and payment thereof shall be enforced by such justice, as in other cases of judgments rendered by him. (Laws of 1862, ch. 243, § 1.)

Should the jury disagree it may be discharged and a new jury impanneled. (*People* v. *Cortelyou*, 36 Barb. 164.)

If the jury find that any encroachment has been made, they shall make and subscribe a certificate in writing, stating the particulars of such encroachment, and by whom made; which shall be filed in the office of the town clerk. The occupant of the land, whether such encroachment shall have been made by him, or by any former occupant, shall remove his fences within sixty days after the filing of such certificate, under the penalty provided in the one hundred and fourth section of this title. He shall also pay the costs of such inquiry; and if the same shall not be paid within ten days, the justice shall issue a warwant for the collection thereof, in the manner provided in the forty-third section of this title. (1 R. S. 522, § 107.)

The act of 1862, cited above, provides a different manner for collecting the costs, and is to be followed. The certificate of the jury finding that an encroachment has been made, must state the particulars of the encroachment so as to guide the party in removing it. (*Fitch* v. *Commissioners of Kirkland*, 22 Wend. 132.)

If the jury find that no encroachment has been made, they shall so certify, and shall also ascertain and certify the damages which the then occupant shall have sustained by such proceeding; which, together with the costs thereof, shall be paid by the commissioners, and shall be a charge in their favor against the town by which they shall have been elected. (1 R. S. 522, § 108.)

Under the act of 1862, cited above, the justice is to adjust the costs.

*Appeal in encroachment proceedings.*—The person or party against whom such judgment shall be rendered, may, within sixty days after filing the certificate of the jury, appeal from the finding and judgment to the county court of the same county; such appeal shall be made by the service, within twenty days after the docketing of said judgment, of notice of appeal upon the justice and upon the successful party or parties, or one of them, stating the grounds of such appeal. It shall be the duty of such justice, in his return to such appeal, to embrace copies of all the papers made and served in the proceeding prior to issuing the precept for such jury, and all the evidence and proceedings before him, together with the finding of the jury and judgment entered thereon. All the provisions of title eleven, chapters third and fifth of the Code of Procedure are hereby extended to such appeals, so far as the same are applicable thereto. (Laws of 1862, ch. 243, § 2.)

In case the decision of the jury finding an encroachment shall be affirmed by the appellate court, such court, in addition to the costs now allowed by law, may, in its discretion, order judgment against the appellant for the penalties provided by section one hundred and four of article one, title one, chapter sixteen, part first of the Revised Statutes aforesaid, for such period as shall intervene between the time fixed for the removal of fences, as provided by section one hundred and seven of the said article, title and chapter, and the decision of such appeal; and in case of the continued neglect or refusal of the occupant, after judgment, to make such removal, the court rendering judgment may, by order from time to time, enforce the additional penalties incurred, or may provide for the removal of such fences at the expense of the occupant, payment of such expense to be enforced by order. Such applications to be made according to the usual practice of the court. (Laws of 1862, ch. 243, § 3.)

## CHAPTER XIII.

### OBSTRUCTIONS IN HIGHWAYS.

The public have a right to a free and uninterrupted use of a highway along its entire width, and any thing which abridges this right is an obstruction. (*Hart* v. *Mayor of Albany*, 9 Wend. 584.)

It has been held, where the highway has been laid out and established of a certain width by statute, to be no justification, on an indictment for this offense, that the obstruction is placed in a part of the highway which has not been prepared, and cannot be used for travel, by reason of ledges of rocks and stones, and that said obstruction does not obstruct or hinder the travel thereon. The court distinguished between the right of the public or town, as against the individual, for an obstruction, and the right of the individual, by private action, under the statutes, as against the town for a defect or want of repair. The latter, it is said, "only requires a road of proper width, and kept in good repair. But the town, on the other hand, to enable itself to discharge its obligation to the public, requires the full and entire width of the whole located highway. The space between the made road and the exterior limits of the located highway, may be required for various purposes; as for making and keeping in repair the traveled path; for making sluices and water courses; for furnishing earth to raise the road, and, not unfrequently, from the location of the road, and from its exposure to be obstructed by snow, the entire width of the located road is required to be kept open, to guard against accumulations of snow that might otherwise wholly obstruct the public travel at such seasons. For these and other uses, in aid of what is the leading object, the keeping in good repair the made or traveled road, the general easement in the public, acquired by the location of a highway, is coextensive with the exterior limits of the located highway; and the question of nuisance or no nuisance does not depend upon the fact, whether that part of the highway, which is alleged to have been unlawfully entered upon and obstructed by the defendant, was a portion of the highway capable of being used by the traveler. (*Commonwealth* v. *King*, 13 Met. [Mass.] 115; *People* v. *Cunningham*, 1 Denio, 524.)

In the latter case the defendants, being distillers in the city of Brooklyn, were in the habit of delivering their slops to those who came for them, by passing them through pipes to the public street opposite their distillery, where they were received into casks standing in wagons and carts; and the teams and carriages of the purchasers were accustomed to collect there in great numbers to receive and take away the article; and in consequence of their remaining there to await their turns, and of the strife among the drivers for priority, and of their disorderly conduct, the street was obstructed and rendered inconvenient to those passing thereon; on an indictment for nuisance they were held to be guilty. Jewett, J., who delivered the opinion of the court, said:

"The main points made by the defendants upon the merits in this case are, first, that the business which they pursued being lawful in itself, they had a right to use, in carrying it on, so much of the public highway, adjoining their premises on which their distillery was situate, as was necessary for the delivery of the slops manufactured at their establishment, however much such business, so conducted, might obstruct the passage of the citizens with their carriages in the street, provided they used *reasonable* diligence and dispatch in the delivery; and, second, that although the street was obstructed by carts and teams remaining therein for an unreasonable time waiting opportunities to obtain loading, the defendants, not being the owners of such carts and teams, and having no control over them, were not responsible.

"There can be no doubt but that the citizens in general have a right of passage in the street or highway, called Front street, in the city of Brooklyn, for themselves and their carriages, to its utmost extent, unobstructed by any impediments, subject, however, to such *temporary* partial obstruction as all public highways must suffer, in cases of plain, evident necessity. That the delivery of slops by the defendants to their customers in the manner appearing on the trial was a constant and serious obstruction to passing the street by the citizens generally, I think admits of no doubt; and I do not see that the defendants even make a grave question of it. They, however, insist that what they have done is lawful, because, from the position and extent of their establishment and business, and its peculiarity, it was necessary for them to do what they have done; and that their mode of delivery was decidedly preferable, as well for private as public convenience, to that which was formerly used or to any method which can be devised.

"I cannot better state the principle applicable to this question than to refer to the language of the court in *The Commonwealth* v. *Passmore* (1 Serg. and Rawle, 219). In that case the defendant had been indicted for a nuisance, in placing goods on the foot way and carriage way of one of the public streets in Philadelphia, and suffering them to remain for the purpose of being sold there at auction, so as to render the passage less convenient, although not entirely to obstruct it. Chief Justice Tilghman says, 'it is true that necessity justifies actions which would otherwise be nuisances. It is true, also, that this necessity need not be *absolute;* it is enough if it be *reasonable.* No man has a right to throw wood or stones into the street at his pleasure. But inasmuch as fuel is necessary, a man may throw wood into the street for the purpose of having it carried to his house, and it may lie there a reasonable time. So, because building is necessary, stones, bricks, lime, sand and other materials may be placed in the street, provided it be done in the most convenient manner. On the same principle a merchant may have his goods placed in the street for the purpose of removing them to his store in a reasonable time. But he has no right to keep them in the street for the purpose of selling them there, because there is no necessity for it.'

"The case of *The King* v. *Russell* (6 East, 427), seems to me very much in point, in determining upon the defendants' right to use the street for the delivery of the article referred to. The case was this: The defendant was found guilty upon an indictment for a nuisance, which stated that he, before and at the times after mentioned, was, and still is, proprietor of divers wagons for conveyance for hire of goods of others to and from Exeter, and as such proprietor, without any just cause or excuse, but wrongfully, etc., caused divers, viz., twenty, wagons to stand and remain for a long time, viz., ten hours on each day, before his warehouse, and divers cumbrous and other parcels, which had been conveyed, or were intended to be conveyed, in such wagons, to lie during such time scattered about such public street, to the great hindrance, etc., of his majesty's subjects passing and repassing such street. The second count charged that the defendant permitted divers wagons to stand in the said public street and highway, and there to remain before his warehouse for a long and unreasonable time, by which the king's subjects were, during that time, much impeded and obstructed. It appeared at the trial, that one or two, and sometimes three, large wagons of the defendant were for several hours, both day and night, standing in the street before his warehouse, and usually occupied one-half of the street, so that no carriage could pass on that side next the warehouse; though two carriages might pass on the opposite side, the gutter being in the middle of the street; that the wagons were loaded and unloaded in the street, and the packages thrown down on the same side of the street, so as frequently, with the wagons, to obstruct even foot passengers and oblige them to cross the gutter to the other side. It was then contended by the defendant, that it was not every public inconvenience which was a nuisance; that partial obstructions of that kind, which arose out of the necessary means of carrying on a trade and business in a populous city having narrow streets, and the access to houses necessarily confined, did not constitute a nuisance, the public passage not being impeded, though narrowed, by such partial obstructions; that the same thing happened, though in a less degree, in the necessary carriage of goods to and from every tradesman's shop in a street, and it was sufficient if no unreasonable time were consumed in the loading or unloading of the goods; that scaffoldings erected in the street before houses under repair stood upon the same plea of necessity, though the passage was thereby greatly obstructed for the time. And the same reasoning applied to carriages stopping before the doors of inns and other places. The defendant being brought up for judgment, the court said that it should be fully understood that the defendant could not legally carry on any part of his business in the public street, to the annoyance of the public; that the primary object of the street was for the free passage of the public, and any thing which impeded that free passage, without necessity, was a nuisance; that if the nature of the defendant's business were such as to require the loading and unloading of so many more wagons than could conveniently be contained within his own private premises, *he must either enlarge his premises or remove his business to some more convenient spot.*

So in the case of *Rex* v. *Carlile* (6 Carr. and Payne, 636), Park, J., said, "no doubt, if a man does an act which injures a particular neighbor, he is not liable to be indicted if no one else but that neighbor be injured; but if a place is situate near a highway, and the defendant do that which causes the persons passing to be prevented from passing as they ought to do, and besides this, people are annoyed in the occupation of their houses; this is a nuisance for which the party is indictable." And, again, "there is no doubt that a tradesman may expose his wares for sale; but he must do it in such a way as not, by so doing, to cause obstruction to the public street."

In *Rex* v. *Jones* (3 Campb. 230), the defendant, a timber merchant, occupied a small yard close to the street, and from the smallness of his premises was obliged to deposit the long pieces of timber in the street, and to have them sawed up there before they could be carried into the yard. It was argued that this was necessary for his trade, and that it occasioned no more inconvenience than draymen letting down hogsheads of beer into the cellar of a publican. But Lord Ellenborough said, "If an unreasonable time is occupied in the operation of delivering beer from a brewer's dray into the cellar of a publican, this is certainly a nuisance. A cart or wagon may be unloaded at a gateway, but this must be done with promptness. So, as to the repairing of a house; the public must submit to the inconvenience occasioned necessarily in repairing the house; but if this inconvenience be prolonged for an unreasonable time, the public have a right to complain, and the party may be indicted for a nuisance. The defendant is not to *eke out the inconvenience of his own premises by taking the public highway into his timber yard;* and if the street be narrow he must remove to a more commodious situation for carrying on his business."

The fact that the defendants' business was lawful does not afford them a justification in annoying the public in transacting it: it gives them no right to occupy the public highway so as to impede the free passage of it by the citizens generally.

The obstruction complained of is not of the temporary character which may be excused within the necessary qualifications referred to in the cases cited, but results from a systematic course of carrying on the defendants' business. It is said that this business cannot be carried on in any other manner at that place, so advantageously either to individuals or the public. The answer to this is to be found in the observation of the court in Russell's Case. "They must either enlarge their premises or remove their business to some more convenient spot." Private interest must be made subservient to the general interest of the community.

The facts proved on the trial of this case showed clearly an unjustifiable obstruction of the highway, not one of a partial and temporary character which the law from necessity tolerates, but an obstruction almost total in effect, and as permanent in duration as the defendants' business.

A ditch dug on a public highway is a nuisance, and who ever sustains injury thereby without fault on his part, may recover from the author of it. (*Harlow* v. *Humiston*, 6 Cow. 189.)

Where the owner of lands, over which a highway passes, digs a raceway across the road to conduct water to his mill, he must restore the road to as good and safe condition as it was before the race was built, by building and maintaining a bridge over it, or otherwise; and if an injury occurs by reason thereof, though he use the utmost care to prevent it, he is, in the absence of gross negligence on the part of the party injured, liable for damages, and the raceway will be adjudged a nuisance. (*Dygert* v. *Schenck*, 23 Wend. 446.) So a ditch dug in a public highway which, from the local circumstances of the country, is seldom or never used but by one or more families, is still a public nuisance, not because any considerable portion of the public is actually affected by it, but because it obstructs a passage which all have a right to use. (*Lansing* v. *Smith*, 8 Cowen, 152.)

So one who under a license excavates a street, is bound to restore it to a safe condition, and neglect to do so, is no less culpable because of having received permission of the public authorities. (*McCamus* v. *Citizens' Gaslight Co.*, 40 Barb. 380.)

The legislature, being entirely competent to declare the uses to which highways may be appropriated, may legalize that which would otherwise be a nuisance, and that which the legislature has constitutionally authorized is not, in judgment of law, a nuisance. (*Leigh* v. *Westervelt*, 2 Duer, 618; *Harris* v. *Thompson*, 9 Barb. 350.) If, however, there is an excess or irregularity in the exercise of the power conferred, it becomes a public nuisance *pro tanto*. (*Renwick* v. *Morris*, 3 Hill, 621; S. C., 7 id. 575.)

An opening in the sidewalk in a public street, communicating with a cellar or vault underneath, made without proper authority is a public nuisance, and the party making or using it is bound at his peril to keep it in a safe condition. (*Irvin* v. *Wood*, 4 Rob. 138; see same case, 5 Rob. 482.)

Not every encroachment upon a highway is such a nuisance that it may be summarily abated. It is the essence of a nuisance that it annoy the public. If an encroachment by fences upon a highway is of such a nature that no one using the highway is incommoded, then it is not a nuisance. (*Griffith* v. *McCullum*, 46 Barb. 561.)

One who has occasion to leave a load upon a highway must remove it within a reasonable time or it may be removed as a nuisance. (*Northrop* v. *Burrows*, 10 Abb. 365.)

*Fallen Trees to be Removed.*—If any tree shall fall, or be fallen, by any person, from any inclosed land into any highway, any person may give notice to the occupant of the land from which such tree shall have fallen, to remove the same within two days. If such tree shall not be removed within that time, but shall continue in such highway, the occupant of the land shall forfeit the sum of fifty cents for every day thereafter, until such tree shall be removed. (1 R. S. 523, § 110.)

*Penalty for falling trees.*—In case any person shall cut down any tree on land not occupied by him, so that it shall fall into any highway, river or stream, unless by order and consent of the occupant, the person so offending shall forfeit, to such occupant, the sum of one dollar for every tree so fallen, and the like sum for every day the same shall remain in such highway, river or stream. (1 R. S. 523, § 111.)

*Removing trees from streams.* — Whoever shall cut, or cause to be cut down, any tree, so that the same shall fall into any river or stream which now is, or hereafter shall be, declared a public highway, and shall not remove the same out of such river or stream, within twenty-four hours thereafter, shall forfeit five dollars for every tree so cut down and left remaining. (Id. § 112.)

*Swinging Gates in Highway.* — No swinging or other gates shall be allowed on any public highway, laid out by virtue of this title, or which has heretofore been laid out, other than such public highways as run through lands liable to be overflowed by the waters of the adjacent rivers or streams, in such a manner as to remove the fences thereon. (Id. § 113.)

*How erected and preserved.*—Such gate shall be erected and kept in good repair by the overseers of highways of the town, at the proper costs and charges of the occupants of the land, for whose benefit the same shall be erected. (Id. § 114.)

*Expenses, by whom paid.*—If more than one gate shall be erected, and the intermediate land between the gates at the extremities of such lands shall be in the occupation of more than one person benefited by such gates, the whole charge of erecting and keeping the same in repair shall be borne by all the occupants benefited thereby, in proportion to the extent of land each occupies adjoining the highway, between the gates and the extremities aforesaid. (1 R S. 523, § 115.)

The overseer of every road district in which such gates shall be, shall, on or before the first day of November, in every year, make out and file with the town clerk a statement of the charges incurred in the erection or repairing of such gates, with the name of the person bound to defray the same, which account shall be verified by the oath of such overseer. If more than one person is liable to defray such charges, the statement shall also contain an apportionment thereof between such persons, stating the amount to be paid by each. (Id. § 116.)

The overseer shall, within ten days after filing the statement, demand of every person bound to pay such charges, or to contribute thereto the sum due from him according to such statement, and if any person shall refuse or neglect to pay such moneys within six days after demand, it shall be the duty of the overseer to make complaint to a justice of the peace of the town, and the like proceeding shall be had for the recovery of such money, as in the recovery of fines for refusing or neglecting to work on the highways. (1 R. S. 524, § 117.)

*Gates to be closed.* — The commissioners of highways shall file an account of such gates in the town clerk's office; and if any person shall open any such gate, and shall not, immediately after having passed the same, close it, or shall willfully or unnecessarily ride over any of the grounds adjoining the road on which such gates shall be permitted, he shall forfeit to the party injured treble damages. (Id. § 118.)

*Remedies for obstruction.*—Obstruction in highways may be remedied by an action for penalties under the statute by indictment, or by abatement.

*Penalties for obstruction under the statute.*—Whoever shall obstruct any highway, or shall fill up or place any obstruction in any ditch constructed for draining the water from any highway, shall forfeit for every such offense the sum of five dollars. (1 R. S. 521, § 102.)

Whoever shall injure any highway, by obstructing or diverting any creek, water-course or sluice, or by drawing logs or timber on the surface of any road or bridge, or by any other act, shall, for every such offense, forfeit treble damages. (1 R. S. 526, § 130.)

The penalty of five dollars and that of triple damages are not limited to obstructions of laid out highways. After a road has become a public highway by user, as such, for twenty years or more, a person obstructing it incurs a penalty for so doing, although the commissioners have not caused the road to be ascertained, described and entered of record. The commissioners can maintain an action to recover the penalty of five dollars for such obstruction. (*Devenpeck* v. *Lambert*, 44 Barb. 596.)

The remedy for obstructions given above is merely cumulative, and has not taken away or abridged the common law remedies by abatement or indictment. (*Wetmore* v. *Tracey*, 14 Wend. 250; *Dygert* v. *Schenck*, 23 id. 451.)

The penalty given above is recoverable only by the commissioners. They cannot maintain an action on the case for damages done the road; their remedy is by indictment, summary abatement, or action for the penalty; private remedies are confined to the owner of the soil, or persons who have sustained a particular injury. (*Cornell* v. *Butternuts, etc. Turnpike Co.* 25 Wend. 368.)

*Remedy by abatement.* — Where the obstruction of a highway is of such a nature as to interfere with its use, such obstruction may be abated or removed. (*Griffith* v. *McCullum*, 46 Barb. 561; *Hart* v. *Mayor of Albany*, 3 Paige, 213; *Harrower* v. *Ritson*, 37 Barb. 301.) Where the public use of the road is incommoded, the proper remedy is by indictment, and not abatement. (*Griffith* v. *McCullum*, *supra.*)

A passenger on a highway, or a private individual, may remove so much of an obstruction as prevents his use of the road; but he must do no unnecessary injury. (Id.)

*Remedy by indictment.* — Indictment is the proper remedy, both against individuals for positive obstructions, and against town officers for want of repair; and the indictable nature of the obstruction does not depend upon the question as to whether it incommodes the public in their use of the road. The public is entitled to the free use of a highway to its full extent; and whoever puts an obstruction within its limits may be indicted. (*Harrower* v. *Ritson*, 37 Barb. 301.)

Every continuance of a nuisance is, in judgment of law, a fresh nuisance; so that, though the person indicted did not create the obstruction, yet, if he continued it, he is liable. (*Brown* v. *Cayuga, etc., R. R. Co.*, 12 N. Y. R. 486; *Vedder* v. *Vedder*, 1 Denio, 257.

Nor is it any defense that the teams and carts that obstruct the highway are not owned by the defendant, nor under his control, provided the gathering of the teams and carts at the place is caused by the manner in which the defendants conduct their business. (*People* v. *Cunningham*, 1 Denio, 524.)

*Action for special damages.*—Where a person has obstructed a highway, and another has received some special injury therefrom not sustained by the rest of the public, the latter may maintain an action for special damages against the former. (*Pierce* v. *Dart*, 7 Cow. 609; *Dygert* v. *Schenck*, 23 Wend. 447; *Lansing* v. *Smith*, 8 Cow. 153; *Irvin* v. *Fowler*, 5 Rob. 482.)

There must, however, be some special injury to the plaintiff, not suffered by the rest of the community, to enable him to recover. (*Fort Plain Bridge Co.* v. *Smith*, 30 N. Y. R. 44–47.)

An individual who receives a bodily hurt, or suffers a damage to his horse or carriage, in consequence of a direct collision with an obstruction in the highway, is specially damnified, and may maintain an action against the author of the obstruction.

It has been held, that the being put to the necessity of going a circuitous route, or the being delayed on a journey by which some important affair is neglected, is not sufficient of itself to warrant the action. (*Pierce* v. *Dart*, 7 Cow. 609, and cases there cited.) So when the nuisance consists in maintaining a pile of wood on the street, constituting the bulk-head in front of the plaintiff's storehouse, injury to the rental of the storehouse, by reason of such nuisance, is an injury common to all other property in the neighborhood, and will not sustain a private action. (*Dougherty* v. *Bunting*, 1 Sandf. 1.)

Trifling injuries are sufficient to sustain the action, if they be special. (*Pierce* v. *Dart*, *supra.*)

## CHAPTER XIV.

### OF THE LAW OF THE ROAD.

*Carriages meeting.*—Whenever any persons traveling with any carriages shall meet on any turnpike road or public highway in the State, the persons so meeting shall seasonably turn their carriages to the right of the center of the road, so as to permit such carriages to pass without interference or interruption, under the penalty of five dollars, for every neglect or offense, to be recovered by the party injured. (1 R. S. 695, § 1.)

The persons meeting "shall seasonably turn," that is, shall turn in time not to retard the progress of the other. (*Brooks* v. *Hart*, 14 N. H. 307.)

The fact that a person riding or driving on a highway was on the wrong side of the road at the time of a collision is *prima facie* evidence of negligence on his part, but may be explained and justified. (*Burdick* v. *Worrall*, 4 Barb. 596; *Earing* v. *Lansingh*, 7 Wend. 185.) Thus he may excuse himself by showing that he was drawing up to his stopping place, or to water his horse, or to turn out of the road. (See *Burdick* v. *Worrall*, 4 Barb. 596). The roughness of the road on the right side is no excuse for not taking it unless so great as to present a serious obstacle to its use. (*Earing* v. *Lansingh*, 7 Wend. 185.) The person on the wrong side of the road assumes the risk of all experiments, and is bound to use greater care than if on the right side. (*Brooks* v. *Hart*, 14 N. H. 307.)

*Center of road.*—The "center of the road" means the center of the worked part of the road, not of the *smooth* or most traveled part, although the whole of the most traveled part be on one side. (*Earing* v. *Lan-*

*sing*, 7 Wend. 185.) In this case, which was an action for the penalty, Sutherland, J., who delivered the opinion of the court, said:

"The court charged the jury that the true construction of the act was, that parties were to keep to the right of the center of the worked part of the road, and that unless the defendant was to the right of that center when the plaintiff's wagon came in contact with his, the penalty had attached, and that the situation of the road, as being rough and rutty on the defendant's side, or the want of design on his part to run against the plaintiff, would be no defense unless the road on his side was such as to render it impracticable for him to turn out; and that the case was not affected by the circumstance that the plaintiff was driving fast and the defendant slow. This is the sound construction of the act; it was designed to settle and establish the rights of travelers in such a manner, that there could be no mistake about them; each party is to keep to the right of the center of the worked part of the road; although it may be more difficult for one party to turn out than the other, that is no answer to the action. The act establishes upon consideration of public policy, a broad general rule, which must be enforced, although sometimes it may operate inconveniently upon parties. It is not the center of the smooth or most traveled part of the road which is the dividing line, but the *center of the worked part*, although the whole of the smooth or most traveled path may be upon one side of that center, unless the situation of the road is such that it is impracticable or extremely difficult for the party to turn out. No such difficulty existed in this case. The road on the defendant's side was rough from having been rutted and frozen, but not so much so as to present any serious obstacle to his riding or driving over it. The questions of fact were properly left to the jury, and their verdict is warranted by the evidence."

The rule, however, requiring persons meeting each other on a public highway to keep their vehicles to the right of the center of the worked part of the road, does not apply in the winter season, when the depth of snow renders it impossible or difficult to ascertain the center of the worked part of the road. It is a reasonable construction of the statute, to define the center of the road, when obscured by snow, to be the center of the beaten or traveled track, without reference to the worked part. (*Smith* v. *Dygert*, 12 Barb. 613.)

*When the rule does not apply.* — The "law of the road" requiring parties to turn to the right does not apply to the meeting of vehicles on a railroad with vehicles of a different kind. The latter may turn to that side which appears, under the circumstances, to be safest. (*Hegan* v. *Eighth Avenue R. R. Co.*, 15 N. Y. R. 380.) Nor does the rule apply to persons traveling on horseback or on foot. (*Dudley* v. *Bolles*, 24 Wend. 465; *Grant* v. *City of Brooklyn*, 41 Barb. 384.) Nor does the rule apply to travelers passing in the same direction.

*Contributory fault.* — An injured party cannot maintain an action when his own negligence contributed to the injury (*Welling* v. *Judge*, 40 Barb. 193), even when the defendant was on the wrong side of the road. (*Kennard* v. *Burton*, 25 Maine, 39; *Parker* v. *Adams*, 12 Met. 415.) It is not contributory negligence for a foot passenger on a country road to walk in the wagon way though there be a sidewalk, but he is bound to use due care, and he is entitled to the exercise of reasonable care from persons driving on the road. (*Coombs* v. *Parrington*, 42 Maine, 332.)

*Negligence in management of horse — breaking of harness, etc.* — The rider or driver of a horse must use ordinary care in its management, and is liable for any accident occasioned by his carelessness. (*Claflin* v. *Wilcox*, 18 Verm. 605; *Center* v. *Finney*, 17 Barb. 94; 2 Seld. notes, 44.) Reckless and noisy driving, which so frightens a horse on or near the highway that he runs away, to the injury of the plaintiffs' property, is a good cause of action, though no collision happen. (*Burnham* v. *Butler*, 31 N. Y. R. 480.) But if a horse run away through no negligence of the driver, out of mere viciousness, of which the driver had no notice, the latter is not liable for injury thereby caused. (*Hammack* v. *White*, 11 C. B. [N. S.] 588; *Sullivan* v. *Scripture*, 3 Allen, 564.)

A traveler upon a highway is bound to have his harness and carriage in a good road-worthy condition, and is liable for any damages occasioned by insufficiency in this particular. Thus, where, in going down hill, the defendant's cart broke and his horse became frightened thereby and ran away, the defendant was held liable. (*Welsh* v. *Lawrence*, 2 Chitty, 262; *Smith* v. *Smith*, 2 Pick. 621.)

*Drivers addicted to drunkenness, not to be employed.* — No person owning any carriage running or traveling upon any road in this state, for the conveyance of passengers, shall employ, or continue in employment, any person to drive such carriage, who is addicted to drunkenness, or to the excessive use of spirituous liquor; and if any such owner shall violate the provisions of this section, he shall forfeit at the rate of five dollars per day, for all the time during which he shall have kept any such driver in his employment, to be sued for by the district attorney of the county in which such owner shall reside. The penalty, when recovered, shall be for the use of the poor of such county, except that the court in which the recovery shall be had may allow a portion of said penalty, not exceeding twenty-five dollars, to be retained by such district attorney, as a compensation for his services and expenses, beyond the taxable costs. (1 R. S. 695, §. 2.)

If any driver, while actually employed in driving any such carriage, shall be guilty of intoxication, to such a degree as to endanger the safety of the passengers in the carriage, it shall be the duty of the owner of such carriage, on receiving written notice of the fact, signed by any one of said passengers, and certified by him on oath, forthwith to discharge such driver from his employment; and every such owner who shall retain or have in his service, within six months after the receipt of such notice, any driver who shall have been so intoxicated, shall forfeit at the rate of five dollars per day, for all the time during which he shall keep any such driver in his employment after receiving such notice, to be sued for and applied as directed in the last preceding section. (Id. § 3.)

*Running horses in any carriage, prohibited.* — No person driving any carriage upon any turnpike road or public highway within this state, with or without passengers therein, shall run his horses, or cause or permit the same to run, upon any occasion or for any purpose whatever; and every person who shall offend against the provisions of this section, shall be deemed guilty of a misdemeanor, and, on conviction thereof, shall be fined not exceeding one hundred dollars, or imprisoned not exceeding sixty days, at the discretion of the court. (1 R. S. 695, § 4.)

*Leaving horses without being tied, etc.*—It shall not be lawful for the driver of any carriage used for the purpose of conveying passengers for hire, to leave the horses attached thereto, while passengers remain in the same, without first making such horses fast with a sufficient halter, rope or chain, or by placing the lines in the hands of some other person, so as to prevent their running; and if any such driver shall offend against the provisions of this section, he shall forfeit, for the use of the poor, the sum of twenty dollars, to be recovered by action to be commenced within six months. And unless the amount of such recovery be paid forthwith, an execution shall be immediately issued therefor. (Id. § 5.)

*Owners of certain carriages liable for acts of drivers.*—The owners of every carriage running or traveling upon any turnpike road or public highway, for the conveyance of passengers, shall be liable, jointly and severally, to the party injured, in all cases, for all injuries and damages done by any person in the employment of such owner or owners, as a driver, while driving such carriage, to any person, or to the property of any person; and that whether the act occasioning such injury or damage be willful or negligent, or otherwise, in the same manner as such driver would be liable. (Id. § 6.)

*Term "carriages" defined.*—The term "carriage," as used in this title, shall be construed to include stage-coaches, wagons, carts, sleighs, sleds, and every other carriage or vehicle used for the transportation of persons and goods, or of either of them. (Id. § 7.)

*Hackney coaches.* — Nothing contained in this title shall interfere with or affect any law concerning hackney-coaches or carriages in any of the cities of this state, nor interfere with nor affect the laws or ordinances of any such city for the licensing or regulating such coaches or carriages. (1 R. S. 695, § 8.)

## CHAPTER XV.

### ANIMALS IN HIGHWAYS.

*Cattle not to run at large.* — It shall not be lawful for any cattle, horses, sheep, swine or goats, to run at large, or to be herded or pastured in any public street, park, place or highway in this state. (Laws of 1862, ch. 452, as amended Laws of 1869, ch. 424, § 1.)

*Duty of overseer.* — And it shall be the duty of every overseer of highways within his district, and of every street commissioner in any incorporated village, to seize and take into his possession, and keep till disposed of according to law, any animal so found running at large or being herded or pastured. (Id.)

*Penalty for suffering cattle to run in highway.* — And any person suffering or permitting any animal to so run at large or be herded or pastured, in violation of this section, shall forfeit a penalty of five dollars for every horse, swine or cattle, and one dollar for every sheep or goat so found, to be recovered by civil action, by any inhabitant of the town, in his own name, or in the name of the overseers of the poor of the town, or by the proceedings hereinafter provided. (Id.)

*Seizure of cattle running at large.* — It shall be lawful for any person to seize and take into his custody, and retain till disposed of as required by law, any animal which may be in any public highway, and opposite to land owned or occupied by him, contrary to the provisions of the foregoing section, or of any animal which may be trespassing upon the premises owned or occupied by him. (Laws of 1862, ch. 452, as amended Laws of 1867, ch. 814, § 2.)

*Proceedings after seizure.* — Whenever any such person or any officer shall seize and take into his possession any animal, under the authority of the preceding sections, it shall be the duty of such person or officer to make immediate complaint in writing, under oath, stating the facts, to a justice of the peace of the town in which such seizure occurred. (Id. § 3.) (See form No. 70.)

So far as applied to cases of animals at large in public highways this act is clearly constitutional. (*Campbell* v. *Evans*, 54 Barb. 566.) When animals are found running at large in highways and are seized by the overseer, and thereupon complaint is made in writing by him, stating the facts, to a justice of the town, it is not necessary that the complaint should state that the animals were running at large "by the sufferance or permission of the owner, (Id.) That question is not a jurisdictional fact. (Id.) The first section makes it the duty of seizing animals running at large in the highway, and this is the only fact necessary to be shown to justify the officers in making the seizure. If the complaint show this the justice has jurisdiction. (Id.)

*Summons.* — And such justice shall thereupon have jurisdiction to hear and determine such matter, and shall thereupon proceed in the same manner as in civil actions, except as specially changed in this act, and shall forthwith issue a summons under his hand, stating the fact of such seizure and complaint, and requiring the owner of such animal, or any party having an interest in the same, to show cause before such justice, at a time and place to be specified in said summons, why said animal should not be sold and the proceeds applied as directed by this act; such time shall not be less than ten nor more than twenty days from the issuing of such summons. (Laws of 1862, ch. 452, as amended, Laws of 1867, ch. 814, § 3.) (For form of summons, see Appendix No. 71.)

*Service of summons.* — The said summons may be served by any constable of the said town, or by any elector thereof authorized so to do by the said justice, in writing thereon; such service shall be made by posting the same in at least six public and conspicuous places in said town, and one of said places shall be the nearest district school-house, unless the said seizure shall have been made within the bounds of an incorporated village, having the schools in charge of a board of education, and in such case one of such notices shall be posted in one of the buildings in which such schools are taught. (Id.)

Personal notice should be given to the owner where he is known and resides near.

It was remarked by Porter, J., in *Rockwell* v. *Nearing* (35 N. Y. R. 312), "That the defendant knew that the property he seized belonged to the plaintiff, who resided within a mile of him in the same town. Ordinary good faith required him to notify the owner that the lost cow was in his stable; and, though the act of 1862 is silent in respect to such notice, it may well be questioned, under the authorities, whether the obligation to give it is not implied in a case where the owner is known." An affidavit made by the person serving a summons under this act, and indorsed thereon, stating that he has served the same, together with proof that such person is a constable, is sufficient to authorize the justice to proceed with the case, although it does not appear by the return that the person making it was a constable. (*Campbell* v. *Evans*, 54 Barb. 566.)

By the "nearest district school-house" in the above section is meant the district school-house *nearest* the place where the seizure was made, not nearest to the justice's office. (Id.)

*Hearing of complaint.* — At the time and place appointed for the return of said summons, the complainant aforesaid may appear, and any party or person owning or having an interest in said animal, or his agent duly authorized, shall be allowed, by the said justice, to appear in the said proceedings; and on his filing with said justice an answer, under oath, subscribed by him or his agent aforesaid, denying any or all the facts alleged in said complaint, an issue shall be deemed joined in the said proceedings, and the subsequent proceedings shall be as in civil actions, so far as they can be, unless otherwise provided in this act. (Laws of 1862, ch. 452, as amended, Laws of 1867, ch. 414.)

*When and how sale made.* — If no one shall appear to show cause, and the said summons shall be returned by a constable duly served, or by proof showing that fact, if served by any person other than a constable, or if the jury or the justice shall find, after a trial, that no sufficient cause is shown why such sale should not be made as directed by this act, then the said justice shall issue his warrant, under his hand, directed to any constable of the said town, commanding him to sell the said animal at public auction, for the best price he can obtain therefor, and make return thereof to the said justice, at a time and place therein specified, not less than ten nor more than twenty days thereafter. (Laws of 1862, ch. 452, as amended, Laws of 1867, ch. 814.) (See form No. 72.)

*Notice of sale.*—The said sale shall be made on the like notice as on constables' sale on civil process; and the said constable shall make return as required by the said warrant, and pay the proceeds of said sale to said justice. (Id.) (See form No. 73.)

*Costs and expenses.*—The said justice shall thereupon adjudge the costs of said proceedings, the same amounts being allowed as in civil actions; and, in addition, he shall allow to the party or officer making such seizure, for every horse or colt, one dollar; for every cow, calf, or other cattle, each fifty cents, and for every goat, sheep, or swine, twenty-five cents, together with the actual damages sustained by such party, by reason of the trespass or breaking of such animal into his premises, and a reasonable compensation to such person or officer, to be estimated by such justice, for the care and keeping of such animals, from the time of the seizure thereof to the sale; and the said justice shall be allowed the sum of one dollar for each animal so sold, and the constable the same fees as for service of a summons and execution in civil actions. (Id.)

*To whom penalty to be paid.*—And the penalty in the foregoing sections prescribed shall be paid to the overseers of the poor, or the officers and board having the support of the poor in charge. (Id.)

*To whom surplus to be paid.*—If, after paying the sums aforesaid, there shall be any surplus of the proceeds of said sale, the said justice shall pay the same to the owner or party establishing before him, on the return of said summons, or at such other time as he shall appoint, the right to the same. (Laws of 1862, ch. 452, as amended, Laws of 1867, ch. 814.)

*Where surplus is not claimed.*—If no person shall claim said surplus within one year after such seizure, the said justices shall pay the same to the overseers of the poor of such town, or the officer or board aforesaid, for the benefit of the poor thereof. (Id.)

*When surplus to be demanded.*—If such owner or party interested shall not appear and demand such surplus within said year, he shall be forever precluded from recovering any part of such moneys, and the receipt of the overseers of the poor of said town, or officer or board aforesaid, given at any time after the expiration of said year, shall be a full discharge to said justice for the same. (Id.)

*When owner may obtain animals before hearing.*—Any owner of any animal which shall have been seized under and pursuant to the foregoing provisions may, at any time before the justice aforesaid shall proceed to the hearing on the return of said summons, demand and shall be entitled to the possession of such animal, upon the payment to said justice of the several sums hereinbefore required to be paid to the said justice and constable, and to the person or officer by whom the seizure aforesaid shall have been made, and the penalty aforesaid, when such seizure is made by any officer, together with a reasonable compensation to the person or officer making such seizure, for the care and keeping of such animal, to be ascertained and fixed by such justice, and upon making to such justice satisfactory proof of ownership. (Laws of 1862, ch. 452, as amended, Laws of 1867, ch. 814, § 4.)

*When after hearing and before sale.*—And if such owner shall not have appeared upon said return day, and shall excuse such non-appearance to the satisfaction of said justice, and shall make such demand at least three days before the time appointed for such sale, he shall be entitled to the custody and possession of such animal, upon paying one half of the several sums above stated, together with the whole amount of penalty, compensation and damages which the said justice shall then adjust and award. (Id.)

*When animals set at large by third persons.* — In case the animal so seized under the foregoing provisions of this act shall have been so running at large or trespassing, or being herded or pastured, by the willful act of any other person than the owner, to effect that object, such owner shall be entitled to the possession of such animal, at any time before the actual hearing shall be commenced on the return of said summons, on making the demand therefor, and the proof required in the next preceding section, and on paying to such person or officer making such seizure the amount of compensation fixed by such justice for the care and keeping of such animal, and without paying any other charges. And the person committing such willful act shall be liable to a penalty of twenty dollars, to be recovered in an action at law at the suit of the owner of such animal, or the person or officer making such seizure. (Laws of 1862, ch. 452, as amended, Laws of 1869, ch. 424.)

*Appeals to county court.*—An appeal may be taken by either party who shall have appeared and contested in said proceeding before such justice, to the county court; and all laws relating to appeals from judgments of justices' courts, and the jurisdiction, powers and duties of county courts, to hear and determine such appeals and the proceedings therein, shall be applicable to said appeals, so far as the same can be applied, and are consistent with this act. (Laws of 1862, ch. 452, as amended, Laws of 1867, ch. 814.) (See form No. 74.)

*When and how appeal to be taken.*—Such appeals can only be taken from the finding or determination, that cause exists or does not exist, for the sale aforesaid, and must be taken within ten days after such finding or determination, and such appeal, when made by a claimant, shall not be effectual for any purpose unless the undertaking required on appeal to the county court contains a clause that, in case the finding or determination shall be affirmed, the claimant will pay all such sums as the said justice shall determine and adjudge for the costs, penalties and allowances so as aforesaid authorized to be made. (Id.)

*In case of affirmance.*—In case of an affirmance by the county court, said court shall appoint a time and place when said justice shall adjust the same, and such adjustment shall be made in the manner and for the sums hereinbefore specified. (Id.)

*Where undertaking is given.*—In case such undertaking is given and approved by the said justice he shall forthwith direct the said sale not to be had, and shall order the said animal to be delivered to the appellant, if it shall appear to him that he is the owner or entitled to the possession thereof. (Id.)

*When person seizing to pay costs, etc.*—In case any person making such seizure shall fail on said hearing to show causes sufficient to obtain such rule, the said justice shall render judgment against him for costs. (Laws of 1862, ch. 452, as amended, Laws 1867, ch. 814.)

*Where seizure was malicious.*—And if the jury or said justice shall find, from the evidence, that such seizure was malicious and without probable cause, the jury or the justice may assess the amount of damages sustained by the owner, by means of such seizure, and judgment shall, in such case, be given for double the amount assessed, with costs. (Id.)

Actions for any cause of action, arising out of any proceedings had or taken, or attempted to be had or taken, under the above act, can only be commenced within one year after the cause of action shall have accrued. (Laws of 1867, ch. 814, § 7.)

## CHAPTER XVI.

### HIGHWAYS BY DEDICATION.

Dedication is an appropriation of land to some public use, made by the owner of the fee, and accepted for such use by or on behalf of the public. A common public road, originating in such an appropriation and acceptance, is a highway by dedication. The interest which the public thus acquires is merely an easement, or right of passage over the soil; the original owner still retaining the fee, together with all rights of property not inconsistent with the public use. (Angell on Highways, 135; *Hunter* v. *Trustees, etc.*, 6 Hill, 407; *Kelsey* v. *King*, 33 How. 39.)

In the case of an ordinary highway, all which the public acquire by a dedication is the right of passing and repassing over the surface of the soil, and such privileges as are incident thereto. All else remains in the original owner or his assigns, subject only to such easement. Every right of use and ownership, and every right of action for an interference with either, which is not inconsistent with the free and common use of the highway, still belongs to the owner of the soil. If the highway is closed or the public rights are relinquished, the land at once revests in full and entire dominion. (Per Emott, J., in *People* v. *Kerr*, 27 N. Y. R. 196; see cases cited in *Kelsey* v. *King*, 33 How. 39.)

*The dedication.*—A dedication of lands to public uses can only be made by the owner of the fee. (*Post* v. *Pearsall*, 20 Wend. 111; *Ward* v. *Davis*, 3 Sandf. 502.) Dedication may be presumed against a married woman. (*Ward* v. *Davis*, *supra.*) Whether it can be made by or presumed against a person laboring under any of the common-law disabilities, such as idiocy, infancy, etc., does not appear to have been directly decided. But in *Devenpeck* v. *Lambert* (44 Barb. 599), it was thought that, under the statute declaring that "all roads, not recorded, which have been, or shall have been, used as public highways for twenty years or more, shall be deemed public highways" (1 R. S. 521, § 100), the intention of the owner of the land is not material, and that such a user of lands for that period makes it a public highway, under the statute, though the owner be a lunatic, an infant, or married woman, and has no knowledge thereof during the entire time.

*How made.*—No particular formality is required to constitute a dedication. It may be made either with or without writing, by any act which will indicate the intention of the owner to dedicate. Thus, the intention may appear by the owner's throwing open his land to the public travel; or platting it and selling lots bounded by streets designated in the plat;

or by an acquiescence in the use of the land for a highway; or by a declared assent to such use. It is for the jury to decide, from the evidence, whether there is sufficient indication of intention on the part of the owner to dedicate his land. (*Gould* v. *Glass*, 19 Barb. 195.)

The owner's acts and declarations must be deliberate, unequivocal, and decisive, manifesting a positive and unmistakable intention to permanently abandon his property to the specific public use; or else there must have been a user of such length of time by the public as will raise the presumption of acquiescence on the part of such owner in the free use and enjoyment of the way as a public road; and, in the absence of other evidence of a grant or dedication, such user must have been for the period of twenty years. (*McMannis* v. *Butler*, 51 Barb. 436; 3 Kent, 451; *Gould* v. *Glass*, 19 Barb. 195.)

A way may be dedicated as a public highway by an immediate act of dedication, and it will become a highway in fact and in law whenever it is laid out as such by the constituted authorities who are charged with the duty of laying out highways. (*Trustees of Jordan* v. *Otis*, 37 Barb. 51.) But where a road is opened by an individual, and is used by the public for less than twenty years, it is not a highway within the meaning of the highway act, unless it has been laid out by the commissioners. (Id.)

The law does not require any specific time to establish a dedication, and there may be such acts and declarations as would render a short time sufficient. (*Carpenter* v. *Gwynn*, 35 Barb. 395). But where there is no other evidence than lapse of time, twenty years must intervene before the presumption becomes conclusive. (*Gould* v. *Glass*, 19 Barb. 195.)

In *Colden* v. *Thurbur* (2 Johns. 424), twelve years'

use was held *prima facie* evidence that the road had been properly laid out. In *Denning* v. *Roome* (6 Wend. 651), where a street in the city of New York was widened from forty to sixty feet, and accordingly used by the public for nineteen years, although no legal measures had been taken to divest the title of the owner, it was held that the non-claim of the owner for such length of time, connected with his acts, such as the payment of an assessment for paving the street to the full width, and the recognition of the appropriation of the twenty feet, were sufficient to establish the right of the public to the use of the street to the full width of sixty feet.

A familiar way of evincing an intention to dedicate is by the owner making a plat or map of his lands with streets laid down between, and selling the lots according to the plat or map. But in order to make this an evidence of intent to dedicate, there must be a sale of the lots with reference to the streets. (*Bissell* v. *N. Y. Cent. R. R. Co.*, 23 N. Y. R. 61; *Matter of Twenty-ninth Street*, 1 Hill, 189; *Wyman* v. *Mayor*, 11 Wend. 486.) When the only evidence of dedication is an old map with the premises in question marked out thereon as a street, and there was no evidence that the maker of the map ever owned the premises or had authority to dedicate them, it was held not sufficient to show a dedication. (*McMannis* v. *Butler*, 49 Barb. 176.)

Where the owner of land has opened a passage thereon he may negative any presumption of dedication by placing at the entrance thereof any obstacle to public passage, or a notice that it is not for public use. (*Carpenter* v. *Gwynn*, 35 Barb. 395.)

*Dedication, how accepted.*—A dedication, to be effectual so far as the public is concerned, must be accepted by the public. (*Holdane* v. *Trustees*, 21 N. Y. R. 478 ; *Fonda* v. *Borst*, 3 Keyes, 48.) Such ac ceptance may be indicated by a user of sufficient length of time, or by a laying out of the road by the commissioners under the highway act. In order to make the town chargeable with the repairs of a way dedicated to the public, it must either have been laid out by the authorities or must have been used as a highway for twenty years. (*Oswego* v. *Oswego Canal Co.*, 6 N. Y. R. 257 ; *Bissell* v. *N. Y. Cent. R. R. Co.*, 26 Barb. 630 ; *Trustees of Jordan* v. *Otis*, 37 id. 50.) But when individuals have acquired right to a passage, as when they have purchased lots with reference to a plat or map in which the owner from whom they purchased has laid out streets adjoining the lots purchased, such individuals have a right to such passage without regard to an acceptance by the public.

Thus where the proprietors of lands in a village laid out the same by a plan, upon which an alley was laid down, and house-lots were conveyed bounded on the alley, — the court said : "As between the original proprietors and those to whom they conveyed, this act of the proprietors secured a right of way. But the alley thus designated, and in respect to which the purchasers had acquired an indefeasible right of way, did not thereby become a public highway. The dedication must be accepted. The highway must be laid out. Until that is done, the alley would remain the property of the original proprietors, subject to the right of way in those who had taken the deeds of lots bounded upon the alley." (*Clements* v. *West Troy*, 16 Barb. 251 ; see also *Child* v. *Chappell*, 9 N.Y. R. 257.)

The owner of lands may revoke a dedication thereof at any time before it has been rendered complete by the acceptance of the public (*Holdane* v. *Trustees*

21 N. Y. R. 478), except where individuals have acquired a vested right under the dedication, as when they have purchased lots bounded by land laid out as streets, but which have not been accepted.

## CHAPTER XVII.

### THE FEES IN HIGHWAYS.

A highway is nothing but an easement, comprehending merely the right of all the individuals in the community to pass and repass, with the incidental right of the public to do all acts necessary to keep it in repair. This easement does not comprehend any interest in the soil nor give the public the legal possession of it. The owner of the land over which a highway passes retains the fee and all rights of property not incompatible with the public enjoyment, and whenever the highway is abandoned, recovers his original unincumbered dominion. (Roll. Abr. 392; *Jackson* v. *Hathaway*, 15 Johns. 447; *Babcock* v. *Lamb*, 1 Cow. 238; *Carpenter* v. *Oswego, etc., R. R. Co.*, 24 N. Y. R. 655.)

The public have no need of the highway but to pass and repass. If it is used for any other purpose, not justified by law, the owners of the adjoining lands are remitted to the same rights they possessed before the highway was made. They can protect themselves against such annoyance, by treating the intruders as trespassers. (*Adams* v. *Rivers*, 11 Barb. 390.) The use of the highway by any person, for any purpose other than to pass and repass is a trespass upon the person who owns the fee. (Id.; *Babcock* v. *Lamb*, 1 Cow. 238; *Jackson* v. *Hathaway*, 15 Johns. 447.) The owner may sell the land subject to the easement; and a deed of a farm of land "reserving only the highway through the said farm," conveys the land subject only to the easement. (*Whitbeck* v. *Cook*, 15 Johns. 483; *Fairfield* v. *Williams*, 4 Mass. 427.) The owner of the fee may sink a drain or watercourse below the surface of his land covered with a way, if thereby he do not deprive the public of its easement. (*Percey* v. *Chandler*, 6 Mass. 454.) The herbage on a highway belongs exclusively to the owner of the fee, and he may maintain trespass against one who puts his cattle in the highway to graze. (*Dovaston* v. *Payne*, 2 H. Bl. 527; *Holaday* v. *Marsh*, 3 Wend. 142.) The owner still retains his exclusive right in all mines, quarries, springs of water, timber and earth not incompatible with the public right of way. (*Jackson* v. *Hathaway*, 15 Johns. 447.)

Therefore, the owner of the fee may maintain trespass against one who builds upon the highway (*Curtelyou* v. *Van Brundt*, 2 Johns. 357); or who digs up and removes the soil (*Gidney* v. *Earl*, 12 Wend. 98; *Willoughby* v. *Jenks*, 20 Wend. 96); or cuts down trees or timber growing thereon; and though an overseer may, as agent of the town, cut such trees other than those left for shade and ornament, to be used in the repair of the way, or in order to improve it, yet if he cut them for his own use he is a trespasser. (*Babcock* v. *Lamb*, 1 Cow. 238.)

So the owner may maintain trespass against one who comes upon the sidewalk and there remains using abusive language toward him and refusing to depart. (*Adams* v. *Rivers*, 11 Barb. 390.) In this case the court said: "The defendant committed a trespass while standing on the sidewalk by the plaintiff's lot where he lived and using toward him abusive language. While so engaged, he was not using the highway for the purpose for which it was designed, but was a trespasser. He stood there but about five minutes. It was not shown that he stopped on the sidewalk for a justifiable cause; on the contrary it was rendered probable that it was for a base and wicked purpose. It was therefore a trespass. Suppose a strolling musician stops in front of a gentleman's house and plays a tune or sings an obscene song under his window, can there be a doubt that he is liable in trespass? The tendency of the act is to disturb the peace, to draw together a crowd and to obstruct the street. It would be no justification that the act was done in a public street."

The owner may also maintain ejectment against any person appropriating the highway to private use or occupation. (*Goodtitle* v. *Alker*, 1 Burr. 133; *Perley* v. *Chandler*, 6 Mass. 454.)

The fee in plank and turnpike roads remains also in the owner of the land the same as highways. (*Hooker* v. *Utica, etc., Turnpike Co.*, 12 Wend. 371, and cases.)

The rule that the public have nothing but an easement of passage in highways, seems to be somewhat modified so far as relates to streets in cities. With regard to them it has been held, that the public have the additional right to construct sewers and to lay water and gas pipes. (*Milhau* v. *Sharp*, 15 Barb. 210; *People* v. *Kerr*, 27 N. Y. R. 202.) But a contrary doctrine was advocated in *Kelsey* v. *King*, 33 How. 39.

The owner of the fee of a highway may also remove and sell the soil if it be done without injury to the highway or to the ingress and egress of adjoining owners. (*Williams* v. *Keanney*, 14 Barb. 629.)

*Presumption from adjacent ownership.*—Where the lands on the opposite sides of a highway belong to the same person, the presumption is that he owns the fee of the entire highway; where it belongs to different persons, the presumption is that each owns to the center of the highway. (*Willoughby* v. *Jenks*, 20 Wend. 96; *Bissell* v. *New York Central R. R. Co.*, 23 N. Y. R. 61.) But this presumption may be rebutted by evidence, for one man may own the fee and another the adjoining lands. (*Bissell* v. *New York Central R. R. Co.*, 23 N. Y. R. 61; *Wager* v. *Troy Union R. R. Co.*, 25 id. 529.)

Where the adjoining owner on one side inclosed a portion of the highway which he cultivated, so inclosed, for twenty-eight years, it was held that the line of separation between the opposite owners continued to be the center of the original highway. (*Watrous* v. *Southworth*, 5 Conn. 305.)

*Boundaries by highways.* — "The established inference of law" says Chancellor Kent, "is that a conveyance of land bounded on a public highway carries with it the fee to the center of the road as part and parcel of the grant. The idea of an intention in a grantor to withhold his interest in a road to the middle of it, after parting with all his right and title to the adjoining land, is never to be presumed. It would be contrary to universal practice; and it was said in *Peck* v. *Smith*, that there was no instance where the fee of a highway, as distinct from the adjoining land, was ever retained by the vendor. It would require an express declaration, or something equivalent thereto, to sustain such an inference; and it may be considered as the general rule, that a grant of land bounded upon a highway or river carries the fee in the highway or river to the center of it, provided the grantor at the time owned to the center and there be no words or specific description to show a contrary intent. But it is competent for the owner of a farm or lot having one or more of its sides on a public highway to bound it by express terms on the side or edge of the highway, so as to rebut the presumption of law, and thereby reserve to himself his latent fee in the highway. He may convey the adjoining land without the soil under the highway, or the soil under the highway without the adjoining land. If the soil under the highway pass by a deed of the adjoining land it passes as parcel of the land and not as appurtenant." (3 Kent Comm. 433.)

Whether a conveyance of adjoining land carries the soil of the highway is purely a question of intention, to be ascertained in each particular case from the description contained in the deed, explained and illustrated by all the other parts of the conveyance, and by the localities and subject-matter to which it relates. (*Webber* v. *The Eastern R. R. Co.*, 2 Met. 151.)

A grant of land described as bounded generally "by," or "on," or "along" a highway, or "running to" a highway, is evidence of an intention to convey to the center of the highway. (*Jackson* v. *Hathaway*, 15 Johns. 447; *Child* v. *Starr*, 4 Hill, 369; *Hammond* v. *McLachlan*, 1 Sandf. 323; *Herring* v. *Fisher*, id. 344.) On the other hand, if the description is "by the side of," or "by the line of," or "by the margin of," or expressions equivalent thereto, the soil of the highway does not pass. (Id.; *Jones* v. *Cowman*, 2 Sandf. 234.)

Where the fee of the highway does not belong to the grantee, of course no words of description will carry to the center thereof; and a deed of lands described as bounded on a highway is satisfied by a title extending to the side of the road, where the title to the road-bed is not in the grantor. (*Dunham* v. *Williams*, 37 N. Y. R. 251.) So where a deed conveying a plat of ground, lying on the southerly side of Stewart street, described its boundaries as running along a certain road "to Stewart street, and thence along the southerly side of Stewart street," the deed was held to convey only to the side of the street. (*Anderson* v. *James*, 4 Rob. 35.)

A line not described as running on a street, but which in fact does, by courses and distance run along the side of a street, is to be held to convey the land to the center of the street, as if the line were described, in words, as running along the street. The road or street, though not mentioned, is in the nature of a monument, which controls the courses and distance. (*Sizer* v. *Devereux*, 16 Barb. 160.)

So a conveyance of land, with reference to a plat or map thereof, on which map such land is bounded by a street, conveys to the center of the street, although it was never adopted by the public authorities. (*Bissell* v. *N. Y. Central R. R. Co.*, 23 N. Y. R. 61; *Hammond* v. *McLachlan*, 1 Sandf. 323.)

There is a class of cases originating in the city of New York on appeals from assessments of damages for land appropriated as streets, in which it has been held that the owner of city land, which is platted into lots and intersected by streets, where he sells the lots, bounding them on the street, does not thereby part with the fee of the streets. (*Mercer street*, 4 Cow. 542; *Seventeenth street*, 1 Wend. 262; *Lewis street*, 2 id. 472; *Livingston* v. *Mayor, etc.*, 8 id. 85; *Wyman* v. *Mayor, etc.*, 11 id. 487; *Furman street*, 17 id. 650; *Twenty-ninth street*, 1 Hill, 189.) But in *Hammond* v. *McLachlan* (1 Sandf. 323, 342) the court entirely repudiated this doctrine, and refused to recognize any distinction between grants of land bounded by highways in the city and in the country. (See also *Bissell* v. *N. Y. Central R. R. Co.*, 23 N. Y. R. 61.)

# CHAPTER XVIII.

## WAYS AND PRIVATE ROADS.

A right of way is the privilege which one person, or a particular description of persons, may have of going over another man's ground. It is a right pertaining to the realty—a right which one has in another's land, termed in law an incorporeal hereditament. (Per NELSON, J., in *Gidney* v. *Earl*, 12 Wend. 98). Since a right of way is only an easement it follows that the person or persons having such right have no interest in the soil of the way, but that, as in case of a highway, every right and privilege remains in the owner of the land, which is not essential to the enjoyment of the way. (Id.) A right of way *ex vi termini* imports a right of passing in a particular line, and not a right to vary it at pleasure. (3 Kent Comm. 419.)

A right of way may arise, 1. By grant; 2. By prescription ; 3. From necessity ; 4. By proceedings under the statute.

*Ways by grant.*—A right of way may arise by grant, as where the owner of a piece of land grants to another the liberty of passing over his land in a particular direction. This right can be created by a reservation in a deed of land. A can purchase of B by deed a right to pass over his farm or through a particular field, or to go to a spring or creek, etc. The deed can be so limited in its terms as that A may have the right of passing or repassing when he pleases, or his family, or on horseback, or with carriages; or it may be limited to certain purposes, as to get water, go to mill, or to church. (*White* v.

*Crawford*, 10 Mass. 183.) A reservation in a deed will establish a right of way. (*Smiles* v. *Hastings*, 24 Barb. 44.)

It is a principle of law that nothing passes as incident to the grant of an easement but what is requisite to the enjoyment of the privilege. (*Lyman* v. *Arnold*, 5 Mason, 195.)

In giving his opinion in this case, Justice Story says, "In the construction of grants, that is doubtless to be adopted which gives entire and liberal effect to the intention of the parties. When the object is distinctly seen, the ordinary means by which it is to be attained are presumed to be within the purview of the parties. If the use of a thing is granted, whatever is necessary for the enjoyment of such use, or for the attainment of such use, is, by implication, granted also. But if it be not necessary, but may be a convenience only, it is not granted. So, too, grants are to be construed according to the subject-matter, and the natural presumptions arising from their terms, and thus to render them expositions of rational intentions. The mere fact that a person having a grant of a privilege, servitude, or easement, in the land of another, bestows his labor upon the soil, or separates it, and gives it value thereby, constitutes no sufficient ground to infer a change of property in the soil; for such labor is bestowed in order to enjoy such privilege, servitude, or easement."

A grant of an estate with "ways heretofore used," or "ways in use," or the like, passes all existing ways in actual use at the time, whether the same are used by the grantor over other parts of his own estate, and so are not properly appurtenant to such granted parcel, or are appurtenant to the same by having been in use over the land of another. But a mere reference in the deed to an intended way, without an express grant, will not pass such way. (Wash. on Ease. 225.)

Where a right of way is granted without any designation of the place in the deed, it becomes located by usage for a length of time; and being so located, it cannot be afterward changed by the grantor. But if changed, the grantee, by usage of the newly designated way for a length of time, will be deemed to have acquiesced in the change. (*Wynkoop* v. *Burger*, 12 Johns. 222.)

Where the defendant had a right of way over plaintiff's land, and the plaintiff fenced up the old one which had been used for many years, and opened a new one which defendant thereafter used, and less than twenty years after, the plaintiff forbade the defendant from passing, and took down a bridge which formed part of the new way, it was held, that, the change having been made by the plaintiff, the defendant's prescription acquired as to the old track became good as to the new one; and that he was not bound to pass by the old way which would require breaking inclosures. (*Hamilton* v. *White*, 5 N.Y.R. 9.)

The grantee of a private way which has become founderous and impassable, cannot, without being a trespasser, go on the adjoining close, and thus pass around the obstruction. The rule is the same where the owner of the close through which the private way passes caused the obstruction. It seems that the only remedy for the owner of the way is to remove the obstruction, and to prosecute for damages.

There is no distinction, with respect to the right of passing *extra viam,* between a private way by grant, and a private way by necessity, after the latter has once been selected or assigned. (*Williams* v.

*Safford*, 7 Barb. 309; *Bakeman* v. *Talbot*, 31 N. Y. R. 372.)

The grantee of a private way for his own accomodation must keep it in repair. (*Wynkoop* v. *Burger*, 12 Johns. 222; *Bakeman* v. *Talbot*, 31 N. Y. R. 372.)

*Ways by prescription.*—A right of way may be acquired by prescription. The nature of this claim is, that a person or certain persons have so long been accustomed to pass over the land of another, that the law will presume that there was originally a grant. An uninterrupted enjoyment of a way for twenty years, without evidence that it had been used by leave, favor or mistake, is sufficient to leave to the jury to presume a grant. It must be an uninterrupted use for twenty successive years. (*Miller* v. *Garlock*, 8 Barb. 153.) To be conclusive evidence of a right, the use must have been continuous, uninterrupted and exclusive; that is, under a claim of right with a knowledge and acquiesence of the owner. (Id.) The enjoyment is uninterrupted when it continues from ancestor to heir, or from seller to buyer. (*Corning* v. *Gould*, 16 Wend. 534.)

The enjoyment of a way for more than twenty years, by license of the owner, confers no right by prescription. (*Boyce* v. *Brown*, 7 Barb. 80.)

To establish a right of way by user or prescription, the user must be confined to one certain tract. (*Holmes* v. *Seeley*, 19 Wend. 507.)

*Ways by necessity.*—If a man sells land to another which is wholly surrounded by his own land, in this case the purchaser is entitled to a right of way over the land of the vendor, to pass and repass to his own premises. This is founded on the principle of law, that whatever is necessary to the enjoyment of the grant shall pass as incident to the grant; and without a passage to the land the grant would be useless. (*Holmes* v. *Seeley*, 19 Wend. 507.)

So if the land sold be not wholly surrounded by the land of the grantor, but partly by lands of a stranger, a way is presumed; for the grantee may not go over the stranger's land. (*Smyles* v. *Hastings*, 22 N. Y. R. 217.)

The grantor may, in the first instance, designate the way, but if he neglect to do so, the grantee may choose for himself; but he cannot claim the right to several ways, for the right cannot be carried beyond the necessity. (*Holmes* v. *Seeley*, 19 Wend. 507.)

A right of way from *necessity*, is to be construed strictly, and this right will cease with the necessity for it; as when the owner acquires the power of passing directly over his own land. It never exists where a man can get to his property through his own land. That the way through his own land is too steep or too narrow, does not alter the case. It is only where there is no way through his own land that the right of way over that of another can exist. (*Dodd* v. *Burchell*, 1 H. & Colt. 122.)

The right of way of necessity over the lands of the grantor, in a conveyance in favor of the grantee, and those subsequently claiming the dominant tenement under him, is not a perpetual right of way; but it continues only so long as the necessity exists. If the grantee obtains another convenient way, the way of necessity ceases. Not so, when a person has a right of way by prescription or express grant. (*N. Y. Life Ins. and Trust Co.* v. *Milnor*, 1 Barb. Ch. 354.)

If a man have several distinct parcels of inclosed land, and he sell all but one surrounded by the others, and to which he has no way or passage except over one of the lots sold, he is entitled to a right of way against his own deed, even where no right of way is reserved. (3 Kent Comm. 421.)

*Right of way, how lost or abandoned.*—A right of way acquired by deed can never be lost by non-user. (*Smyles* v. *Hastings*, 24 Barb. 44; 22 N. Y. R. 224.) But a right of way acquired by prescription, may be lost by a non-user for twenty years. (Id.) The non-user to work an abandonment must have been continuous for twenty years. (*Corning* v. *Gould*, 16 Wend. 531. See *Crain* v. *Fox*, 16 Barb. 184.)

*Ways or private roads by statute.*—An application for a private road shall be made in writing, specifying its width and location, courses and distances, and the names of the owners and occupants of the land through which the road is proposed to be laid out. (Laws of 1853, ch. 174, § 1.)

The application is to be made to the commissioners of highways. And it will be sufficient, if it states the width, location, courses and distances of the road, and the other matters specified by the section, in general terms, without more precision than is necessary to enable the owners of land to know what part of their property is intended to be taken, and to enable the jury to determine intelligently upon the necessity of the road, and assess the damages. (*People* v. *Taylor*, 34 Barb. 481.) (See form No. 75.)

*Jury to be called.*—The commissioner or commissioners, to whom such application shall be made, shall, thereupon, appoint as early a day as the convenience of the parties interested will allow, when, at his office, a jury will be selected for the purpose of determining upon the necessity of such road, and to assess the damages by reason of the opening thereof. (Laws of 1853, ch. 174, § 2.)

*Copy of application and notice to be delivered to applicant.* — Such commissioner or commissioners shall, thereupon, deliver to the applicant a copy of such application, to which shall be added a notice of the time and place appointed for the selection of such jury, addressed to the owners and occupants of such land. (Laws of 1853 ch. 174, § 3.) (See form No. 76.)

*Service of notice and application.* — The applicant, on receiving such copy and notice, shall, on the same day or the next day thereafter, cause such copy and notice to be served upon the persons to whom it is addressed, by delivering to each of them who resides in the same town a copy thereof, or, in case of his absence, by leaving the same at his dwelling-house, and, upon such as reside elsewhere, by depositing in the post-office a copy thereof to each, addressed to them respectively at their places of residence, and paying the postage thereon, or, in case of infant owners, by like services upon the their parent or guardian. (Id. § 4.)

One entitled to the notice of the meeting of the jury, waives the omission of it by appearing before the jury and contesting. (*Mohawk, etc.*, v. *Artcher*, 6 Paige, 83.)

*List of jurors.* — At such time and place, on due proof of the service of such notice, such commissioner, or, in a town where there are more than one, either of them, shall present a list of the names of eighteen persons, residents of said town, who are freeholders, and in no wise of kin to such applicant, owner or occupant, or either of them, and not interested in such lands. (Laws of 1853, ch. 174, § 5, as amended in 1860, ch. 468.)

The remainder of the above section as amended, providing for an appeal, is given hereafter.

Parties who agree upon the jurors cannot upon appeal object that it does not appear that such jurors were freeholders. (*People* v. *Taylor*, 34 Barb. 481.)

*Certain number may be struck from list.*—The owners or occupants of such lands may strike off from such list any number of names not exceeding six; the applicant may, in like manner, strike off six names or less, and the persons whose names are not stricken off, or, if more than six names are left upon the list, then the six persons whose names stand first upon the list shall be the jury for the purpose aforesaid. (Laws of 1853, ch. 174, § 6.)

*Place of meeting.*—The commissioner shall then appoint some convenient time and place for the jury to meet and be sworn in the premises, and shall summon them accordingly. (Id. § 7.)

*Jury to be sworn.*—If, at the time and place last mentioned, all the persons named as such jury shall meet, they shall be sworn well and truly to determine as to the necessity of said road, and to assess the damages by reason of the opening thereof; if one or more of such six persons shall not appear, the commisioner shall summon, of the bystanders or others, so many, free from all legal objections, as will be sufficient to make the number six, who shall be sworn as aforesaid. (Id. § 8.)

*Commissioners to swear jury.*—Such commissioner is hereby authorized to swear the jury, and to administer any oath necessary to carry this act into effect. (Id. § 9.)

*Proceeding of jury.*—The jury shall view the premises, and, after hearing the allegations of the parties and such witnesses as they may produce, shall proceed to deliberate and make up their verdict; and, if they shall determine that the proposed road is necessary, they shall assess the damages to the person or persons through whose land the same is to pass, and deliver their verdict, in writing, to the commissioners. (Laws of 1853, ch. 174, § 10.) (See form No. 77.)

In determining as to the necessity of the road, and in assessing damages, the jury should proceed in the same manner as in case of public highways. The proceedings in such cases have been, heretofore, given.

*Value of road discontinued.*—If the necessity of such private road has been occasioned by the alteration or discontinuance of a public highway running through the lands belonging to the same person or persons, through whose lands the private road is proposed to be opened, the jury shall take into calculation the value of the road so discontinued, and the benefit resulting to such person or persons by reason of such discontinuance, and shall deduct the same from the damages assessed for the opening and laying out of such private road. (Id. § 11.)

*Proceedings after verdict.*—The commissioner shall annex to such verdict the application mentioned in the first section of this act, and hand the same to the town clerk, who shall file the same, and the commissioner or commissioners shall lay out and make a record of said road, as described in the petition of the applicant. (Id. § 12.)

*Proceeding may be adjourned.*—In case any accident shall prevent any of the proceedings required by this act to be done on the day assigned, the proceedings may be adjourned to some other day, and the commissioner shall publicly announce such adjournment. (Laws of 1853, ch. 174, § 13.)

*Damages to be paid before opening road.*—The damages assessed by the jury shall be paid by the party for whose benefit the road is laid, before the said road shall be opened or used. But in case the assessors of said town shall certify that the necessity of such private road was occasioned by the alteration or discontinuance of a public highway, such damages shall be paid by said town and refunded to the applicant. (Id. § 14.)

*Description of road abandoned.*—Whenever any public highway, or any part thereof, by reason of alterations made therein, or by the opening of a new road, or in any other way, shall be abandoned by the public, and is no longer used as a public road, the commissioners or commissioner of highways shall file in the town clerk's office of the town a description in writing signed by them or him, of the road so abandoned, and the same shall thereupon be discontinued. (Id. § 15.)

*Roads along division lines.*—Whenever a public or private road shall be laid along the division line between the lands of two or more persons, and wholly upon one side of said line, and the lands upon both sides of said division line shall be cultivated or improved; then and in that case the person owning or occupying the lands joining said road shall be paid for building and maintaining such additional fence as he may be required to build or maintain by reason of the laying out and opening said road, which said damages shall be ascertained and determined in the same manner that other damages are now ascertained and determined in the laying highways or private roads. (Laws of 1853, ch. 174, § 16.)

*Appeals.*—And if any person shall consider himself aggrieved by the said decision of the freeholders, either in laying out or closing a road, he may, within sixty days after such determination shall have been filed in the office of the town clerk, appeal to the county judge of the county in the same manner as appeals were heretofore allowed to be made to those judges under title first, article fourth, chapter sixteenth, part first of the Revised Statutes. (Last clause of section 5, of act of 1853 as amended 1860, ch. 468.)

The county judge having acquired jurisdiction by the appeal, becomes vested with the same authority to dispose of such appeal in the manner provided in reference to public roads, which includes the appointment of referees. (*West* v. *McGurn*, 43 Barb. 198.) For the manner of proceeding on appeal, see heretofore the chapter on that subject.

*For what purpose road to be used.*—Every such private road, when so laid out, shall be for the use of such applicant, his heirs and assigns; but not to be converted to any other use or purpose than that of a road. Nor shall the occupant or owner of the land through which such road shall be laid out, be permitted to use the same as a road unless he shall have signified his intention of so making use of the same, to the jury or commissioners who ascertained the damages sustained by laying out such road, and before such damages were so ascertained. (1 R. S. 517, § 79.)

If the occupant of the land, at the time a private way is laid out, does not signify his intention to make use of it, so that the damages may be assessed accordingly, the person on whose application it is laid out has an exclusive right to use it, and may maintain trespass on the case against the former for injuries done by his using it. (*Lambert* v. *Hoke*, 14 Johns. 383.)

*Width of roads.*—All private roads to be laid out by the commissioner shall not be more than three rods wide. (1 R. S. 517, § 80.)

The owner of the lands must so build his fence as to leave the road the full width as laid out by the commissioners: he cannot build a Virginia or zig-zag fence, placing the center on the exterior lines of the road as laid out, with the angles projecting into the road. But a party will be deemed to have assented to such location of the fences, if he gave his consent to have the defendants' damages assessed with reference to such fence as was built, or if he permitted the fence to be thus built without objection. (*Herrick* v. *Stover*, 5 Wend. 580.)

*Extra viam.*—The owner of the private road has no right to go upon the adjoining lands when his road is obstructed or impassable, even where the road was so obstructed by the owners of such adjoining lands. (*Williams* v. *Safford*, 7 Barb. 309.)

# FORMS.

---

**No. 1.**

ORDER FILLING VACANCY; OFFICE OF COMMISSIONER.

See *ante*, *p.* 23.

COUNTY OF RENSSELAER, } *ss:*
*Town of Grafton.* }

Whereas a vacancy has occurred in the office of commissioner of highways of the town of *Grafton*, by reason of the death (*or*, *as the case may be*), of *John Doe*, heretofore elected to said office from said town;

Now, therefore, by virtue of the power vested in us by the statute, in such case made and provided, we the undersigned, three of the justices of the peace of said town, do hereby, in order to fill such vacancy, nominate and appoint *John Smith*, commissioner of highways of said town, to hold his said office until the next succeeding annual town meeting of said town, as by law provided.

In witness whereof we have hereto set our hands this second day of August, 1870.

Signatures.

---

**No. 2.**

COMMISSIONER'S BOND.

See *ante*, *p.* 24.

Know all men by these presents, that we, A. B., C. D., and E. F., of the town of ———, county of ———, and State of New York, are held and firmly bound unto ———, supervisor of said town, in the penal sum of one thousand dollars, to be paid to the said supervisor, or to his successor in office; for which payment, well and truly to be made, we bind ourselves, our heirs, executors, administrators and assigns, jointly and severally, firmly by these presents.

Sealed with our seals, and dated the 12th day of April, 1870.

Whereas, the above named bounden A. B. was, on the 5th day of April, 1870, duly elected commissioner of highways of the town of ———, in the county of ———,

Now, therefore, the condition of this bond is such, that if the said A. B. shall faithfully discharge his duties as such commissioner, and shall, within ten days after the expiration of his term of office, pay over to his successor all moneys remaining in his hands as such commissioner, and render to such successor a true account of all moneys received and paid out by him as such commissioner, without fraud or delay, then this obligation to be void, otherwise to be of full force and effect.

Signatures and Seals.

Witness, ———.

AFFIDAVIT OF JUSTIFICATION.

COUNTY OF ———, *ss:*

C. D. and E. F., the sureties named in the foregoing bond, being severally duly sworn, doth each for himself say, that he is a resident and freeholder (or householder) within this State, and worth one thousand dollars over and above all his debts and liabilities, and exclusive of property exempt from execution.

C. D.

Sworn, etc. E. F.

ACKNOWLEDGMENT.

COUNTY OF ———, *ss:*

On this 12th day of April, 1870, personally appeared before me C. D. and E. F., to me known to be the persons described in, and who executed the foregoing obligation, and severally acknowledged that they executed the same. R. A.,

*Justice of Peace.*

APPROVAL.

I approve of the within bond, and of the sufficiency of the sureties therein named. G. H.,

*Supervisor of the town of* ———.

Dated, etc.

---

**No. 3.**

OATH OF COMMISSIONER.

See *ante, p.* 26.

ALBANY COUNTY, *ss:*

I, J. B., of the town of Watervliet, in said county, having been elected commissioner of highways of said town, do solemnly swear (or affirm), that I will support the Constitution of the United States and the Constitution of the State of New York, and that I will faithfully discharge the duties of commissioner as aforesaid, according to the best of my ability.

Sworn, etc. J. B.

CERTIFICATE OF JUSTICE.

COUNTY OF ALBANY,<br>*Town of Watervliet,* } *ss:*

I, G. H., justice of the peace in and for the town of Watervliet, in said county (or town clerk of the town of Watervliet, in said county), do hereby certify, that on the 12th day of April, 1870, personally appeared before me J. B. of said town, who then and there duly took and subscribed the foregoing oath.

G. H.,
Dated, etc. *Justice of the Peace.*

---

**No. 4.**

ORDER ASCERTAINING AND DESCRIBING ROAD.

See *ante*, *p.* 30.

Whereas a road, used as a highway in the town of Portland, in the county of Chautauqua, leading from the Erie road, between the dwelling-houses of Elijah Fay and John R. Coney, to the old Erie road on the east line of Elisha Fay's farm, was laid out by the commissioners of highways of the said town, on the 10th day of June, 1860, but not sufficiently described: (or has been used as a public highway for twenty years last-past but not recorded).

Now, therefore, we, the undersigned commissioners of said town, having met at the house of John Adams, in said town, for the purpose of causing said road to be ascertained, described and entered of record in the town clerk's office, all the said commissioners being present, and having deliberated (*or* all the said commissioners having been duly notified to attend this meeting for the purpose of deliberating) on the subject embraced in this order, do hereby order that the said road be ascertained, described and entered of record. And the said commissioners, having caused a survey of the said road to be made, do further order that said road is hereby ascertained and described according to the said survey, being as follows: beginning at (*insert survey*). And it is further ordered that the line above described be the *center* line of the said road, and that the said road be of the width of *three* rods.

In witness whereof, the said commissioners have hereunto subscribed their names the first day of April, 1870.

A. B.,<br>E. F.,<br>C. D., } *Commissioners.*

---

## No. 5.

### ORDER DIVIDING TOWN INTO ROAD DISTRICTS.

See *ante, p.* 39.

The undersigned commissioners of highways of the town of Arkwright, in the county of Chautauqua, having met and deliberated on the subject embraced in this order; all said commissioners being present, and having deliberated thereon (*or* all said commissioners having been duly notified to attend here for the purpose of deliberating thereon), do hereby order that the said town be and the same is hereby divided into *ten* road districts, as follows, to wit:

District No. 1 shall comprise all that part of the said town lying north of the south line of the road leading from the dwelling-house of                    , to the east line of said town, and all the inhabitants residing in said district, and all those residing on the said road above mentioned, liable to work on highway, are hereby assigned to work in said district No. 1. (*If any out of said district be assigned to work therein, insert*) And the following inhabitants, residing out of said district, are hereby assigned and required to work therein, to wit: J. C., etc., and all persons residing with them on their farms, and liable to work on highways, are assigned the said district No. 1.

District No. 2, etc. (*proceed in like manner till all are described*).

In witness whereof, we have hereto subscribed our names this tenth day of April, 1870.

A. B., }
C. D., } *Commissioners.*
E. F., }

---

**No. 6.**

COMMISSIONERS' ANNUAL ACCOUNT.

See *ante*, *p.* 42.

The undersigned, commissioners of highways of the town of Auburn, in the county of Cayuga, hereby render to the board of auditors of said town their annual account for the year ending February 28th, 1870.

1. The highway labor assessed in said town for the year ending on the said twenty-eighth day of February was *eight hundred and ten* days, and the highway labor performed in said town during the said year was *seven hundred and eighty-nine days*, as appears by the accounts rendered us by the several overseers of highways in said town.

2. The said commissioners have received, during the said year, the following sums of money for fines and commutations under the statute relative to highways, to wit:

| Date. | From whom received. | On what account. | Amount. |
| --- | --- | --- | --- |

They have also received from other sources under said statute, etc.

3. The improvements which have been made on the roads and bridges in said town, during said year, are as follows: (*Specify improvements.*) And the roads and bridges in said town are (*give state of them, and specify whether they are in good repair or otherwise*).

4. The following improvements are necessary to be made on the roads and bridges in said town, to wit: (*Specify necessary improvements.*)

5. The probable expense of making such improvements, beyond what the labor to be assessed this year will accomplish, is by us estimated at $250.

Given under our hands this tenth day of March, 1870.

*Signatures*, Commissioners.

---

**No. 7.**

CERTIFICATE OF TOWN AUDITOR.

See *ante*, *p*. 43.

CAYUGA COUNTY, } *ss:*
*Town of Auburn.* }

We, the undersigned, composing the board of town auditors of said town, do hereby certify, that we have this day audited and allowed to E. F. (*commissioner of highways*), of said town, by whom the foregoing account has been presented to us, the sum of $50, as and for his services as such commissioner (*insert if necessary*), and the disbursements necessarily paid out by him in the execution of his duty, up to and including the 28th day of February, 1870, and that we find a balance of $23 to be due from said E. F. to the town of Auburn.

Dated, etc. Signatures.

## No. 8.

### STATEMENT AND ESTIMATE FOR SUPERVISOR.

See *ante, p.* 44.

*To the supervisor of the town of Watervliet, in the county of Albany:*

The commissioners of highways of said town do hereby report that the following improvements are necessary to be made on their roads and bridges in their said town, to wit: (*Specify improvements.*) That the probable expense of making such improvements is by us estimated at $250.

Given under our hands, etc.

---

## No. 9.

### NOTICE OF APPLICATION FOR ADDITIONAL APPROPRIATION.

See *ante, p.* 45.

Notice is hereby given to the electors of the town of Berlin, in the county of Rensselaer, that the commissioners of highways of said town are of opinion that the sum of two hundred and fifty dollars, as now allowed by law, will be insufficient to pay the expenses actually necessary for the improvement of roads and bridges in said town, and that the additional sum of two hundred and fifty dollars is necessary to make a bridge across the —— creek near ——, (or to repair the bridge, etc., or to improve the road at, etc.) And that we, the undersigned, commissioners of highways of said town, shall, at the next annual town meeting of said town, to be held at —— on the tenth day of March next, apply in open town meeting for a vote authorizing the said sum of two hundred and fifty dollars, to be raised for the purpose aforesaid.

Dated, etc. Signed.

## No. 10.

### DECISION OF FENCE VIEWERS.

See *ante*, *p*. 52.

COUNTY OF RENSSELAER, } *ss*:
*Town of Pittstown.* }

A dispute having arisen between John Doe and Richard Roe, owners of adjoining lands in said town, concerning the proportion or particular part of the division fence running (*describe the fence*) to be maintained by each, and the undersigned fence viewers of said town having been selected to settle such dispute, according to the statute in such case made and provided, and having examined the premises and heard the allegations of the said parties, we do hereby determine and decide, that the said John Doe shall maintain all that portion of said fence being between the highway on the north side of said adjoining lands and a point ten chains and three links south thereof on said boundary line; and that the said Richard Roe shall maintain all that portion of said fence between the last-mentioned point and the south boundary of said adjoining lands. And we do further determine and decide, that the said John Doe shall pay one-third of the costs and expense of this proceeding, to wit: the sum of three dollars, and that the said Richard Roe shall pay the remaining two-thirds of such costs and expense, to wit, the sum of six dollars.

In witness whereof we have hereto set our hands this tenth day of July, 1869.

Signatures.

**No. 11.**

SUBPŒNA OF FENCE VIEWERS.

See *ante, p.* 55.

*The People of the State of New York,*
*To ——:*

We, fence viewers of the town of Pittstown, in the county of Rensselaer, command you, that (all and singular, business and excuses being laid aside) you appear and attend before us, at the house of John Doe, in said town, on the tenth day of July, 1869, at ten o'clock in the forenoon, to be examined as a witness, there and then, touching (*insert object*); and for a failure to attend you will be deemed guilty of contempt, and will be proceeded against in the manner provided by law.

Dated. Signed.

---

**No. 12.**

CERTIFICATE OF SHEEP KILLED BY DOGS.

See *ante, p.* 61.

RENSSELAER COUNTY, *Town of Brunswick.* } *ss:*

William E. Smith, of said town, having applied to us, two fence viewers of said town, to appraise the value of certain sheep alleged to have been killed by dogs, and the amount of damage sustained by him, pursuant to the statute, and having this day inquired into the matter and viewed the sheep killed, and examined witnesses in relation thereto, we do hereby certify and find, that the said sheep were hurt and killed by dogs only, and in no other way, and that there were ten sheep killed, of the value of four dollars each, and that the owner, William E. Smith, has sustained damage to the amount of twenty-five dollars.

In witness whereof we have hereto set our hands the ninth day of October, 1869.

Signatures.

---

**No. 13.**

COMMISSIONERS, CONSENT FOR RAILROAD TO CROSS HIGHWAY.

See *ante*, *p.* 63.

COUNTY OF RENSSELAER, *Town of Pittstown.* } *ss:*

We, the undersigned commissioners of highways of said town, do hereby consent that the Troy and Boston Railroad company may construct a railroad across the public highway leading from (*describe highway*), provided the usefulness of said highway be not impaired.

Given under our hands this tenth day of June, 1850. Signed.

---

**No. 14.**

AGREEMENT TO USE HIGHWAY FOR PLANK ROAD, ETC.

See *ante*, *p.* 65.

This agreement made this —— day of ————, between A. B., supervisor of the town of ————, county of ————, and C. D. and E. F., commissioners of highways of said town, of the first part, and the ——— Turnpike company of the second part.

Witnesseth, That the said party of the first part, having first become satisfied that at least two-thirds of all the owners of land along the highway (*describe it*), and who actually reside thereon, have consented in writing to the construction of a turnpike by said party of the second part, on such highway, do for values received, hereby grant and convey to the said party of the second part the right to use and occupy the public highway above described for the purpose of a turnpike road, so long as the same shall be needed by said party of the second part.

In witness whereof, etc.

*Witness.*

---

## No. 15.

### COMPLAINT TO COMPEL DELIVERY OF BOOKS, ETC., TO SUCCESSOR.

See *ante*, *p.* 69.

STATE OF NEW YORK, } *ss:*
*County of* ——. }

To the Hon. C. R. INGALLS,
*Justice of the Supreme Court:*

A. B. of said county, being duly sworn, makes complaint against C. D., late commissioner of highway of the town of ——, in said county, and says: that the deponent was duly elected commissioner of highways of said town of ——, at an annual town meeting of such town, held on the 6th day of March, 1870, that he has taken and filed the oath prescribed by law, and has given the requisite bond.

That by virtue of such election he is successor to the said C. D., late commissioner as aforesaid. That he has required and demanded that the said C. D. deliver over to him, as such successor, all the records, books and papers in his possession or under his control, belonging or appertaining to the said office of commissioner of highways.

And this deponent further alleges that the said C. D. has refused and neglected so to deliver such records, books and papers, or any part thereof, and that, as this deponent is informed and believes, said C. D. has in his possession, or under his control, the following records, books and papers appertaining to the said office of commissioner of highways (*insert description if known, if not say so*), and that he unjustly and unlawfully withholds the same from this deponent. A. B.

Sworn to, etc.

#### ORDER THEREUPON GRANTED.

See *ante*, *p*. 70.

STATE OF NEW YORK, *County of* ———, } *ss:*

Complaint having been made to me, the undersigned, as follows, to wit: (*insert a copy of the complaint*), and being satisfied by the oath of the said complainant (*add* "and other testimony offered," *if any such was offered*), that the said books and papers (*or either*, *according to the fact*) are withheld as aforesaid, I, therefore, pursuant to the provisions of the statute in such case made and provided, do hereby order and direct the said C. D., the person so refusing, to show cause before me at my office in ———, in said county, on the tenth day of May instant, at 10 o'clock in the forenoon, why he should not be compelled to deliver the same books and papers (or either as the case may be). Signature.

Dated, etc.

#### AFFIDAVIT OF DELIVERY.

See *ante*, *p*. 70.

STATE OF NEW YORK, *County of* ———. } *ss:*

C. D., of said county, being duly sworn, says, that he is the person mentioned and described as late commissioner of highways of the town of ———, in said county, in a certain affidavit and complaint made by one A. B. before the Hon. C. R. Ingalls, Justice of the Supreme Court, on the tenth day of May, 1867, and that he has truly delivered over to his successor in said office of commissioner of highways all the books, records and papers in his custody or appertaining to his said office, within his knowledge.

Sworn, etc. C. D.

WARRANT TO COMMIT THE PERSON WITHHOLDING.

See *ante*, *p.* 70.

*The People of the State of New York, to the Sheriff of the County of Rensselaer:*

Complaint having been made to the undersigned, as follows, to wit: [*Insert a copy of the complaint.*] Whereupon, pursuant to the provisions of the statute, being satisfied by the oath of the said complainant (*add, and other testimony offered, if any such was offered*), that the said books and papers (*or either, according to the fact*) were withheld as aforesaid, the undersigned granted an order, directing the said C. D., the person so refusing, to show cause before the undersigned, at, etc. (*as in the order*), why he should not be compelled to deliver the same books and papers (*or either, as the case may be*) at which place and time so appointed (*or if at any other time, to which the matter was adjourned, so state*), upon due proof being made of the service of the said order, the undersigned proceeded to inquire into the circumstances, and the said C. D. having omitted to make the oath prescribed by the statute in such case made and provided, and it appearing to the undersigned that the said books and papers (*or either of them, to be described*) are withheld as aforesaid.*

Now, therefore, you are commanded that you take the said C. D., if he may be found in your bailiwick, and commit him to the jail of the said county of Rensselaer, there to remain until he shall deliver the said books and papers (or either or such of them as are withheld), or be otherwise discharged according to law.

Witness, C. R. I. justice of the Supreme Court, at the city of Troy, this tenth day of July, 1870.

Seal. Signature.

SEARCH WARRANT FOR SUCH BOOKS OR PAPERS WITHHELD.

See *ante*, *p.* 70.

*The People of the State of New York, to the Sheriff of the County of Rensselaer, or to any Constable of any Town in said County:*

[*As in the form above to.**] And the undersigned being required by the said complainant, A. B., to issue this warrant:

Now, therefore, you are commanded, in the daytime, to search C. D.'s house, situated (*insert a particular designation or description of the said house, and of any other place to be searched*), for the said books and papers (or either of them, as the case may be), so withheld, and all other such books and papers as belonged to the said C. D., as commissioner of highways as aforesaid, in his official capacity, and which appertained to the said office of commissioner of highways, and seize and bring them before the undersigned.

Witness, C. R. I., justice of the Supreme Court, at the city of Troy, this tenth day of July, 1867.

Signature and Seal.

### No. 16.

### ORDER APPOINTING OVERSEERS.

See *ante*, *p.* 81.

STATE OF NEW YORK, }
*County of* ———. } *ss:*

We the undersigned, commissioners of highways of the town of ———, in the county of ———, having met and deliberated on the subject of this order, being present, and all the commissioners having deliberated thereon (*or* all the commissioners, etc., having been duly notified to attend said meeting of the commissioners, for the purpose of deliberating thereon), do, hereby appoint the following named persons overseers of highways of and for the several road districts in said town, set opposite their respective names, to wit: District No. 1, John Doe; district No. 2, John Smith. Each of said overseers to hold his said office for and during the term of one year from the third day of March, 1870.

In witness whereof we have hereto placed our hands this third day of March, 1870.

Signed.

---

### No. 17.

### APPOINTMENT OF OVERSEER IN CASE OF VACANCY.

See *ante*, *p.* 81.

TOWN OF———, }
*County of*———. } *ss:*

Whereas, a vacancy has occurred in the office of overseer of highways for road district number *eight*, in said town, by reason of the refusal to serve (*or as the case may be*) of A. B. Now, therefore, by virtue of the power vested in us by the statute in such case made and provided, we, the undersigned, commissioners of highways of said town, having met and deliberated on the subject embraced in this warrant (*where only two sign, add* all the commissioners of highways of said town having met and deliberated, or all the commissioners, etc., having been duly notified to attend this meeting of the commissioners for the purpose of deliberating on the subject embodied in this warrant), do hereby, in order to fill said vacancy, appoint Peter Cook, overseer of highways, of and for said road district number *eight*, in said town.

In witness whereof, we have hereto placed our hands this tenth day of July, 1867.

Signed.

---

### No. 18.

### ASSESSMENT BY OVERSEER FOR SCRAPER OR PLOW.

See *ante*, *p*. 86.

Whereas, the commissioners of highways of the town of Ellicott, in the county of Chautauqua, on the 10th day of April, 1848, by writing under their hands, directed and empowered me, Henry Baker, overseer of highways of road district No. 5, in said town, to procure a good and sufficient iron [*or steel*] shod scraper and a plow, [*or either separately,*] for the use of my said road district, to be paid for by the moneys arising from commutations and fines within such district; and whereas, such moneys are insufficient for the purpose, by the amount of $8.50.

Now, therefor, I, the said overseer, according to the form of the statute in such case made and provided, do hereby assess the deficiency of eight dollars and fifty cents aforesaid, upon the inhabitants of the said district, in the proportion they are respectively assessed on the assessment roll of said town, which said assessment is as follows, viz.:

| Names of Inhabitants. | Town Assessment. | Overseer's Assessment. |
|---|---|---|
| John Johnson, ................ | $9 00 | $0 90 |
| James Smith, ................. | 12 00 | 1 20 |

A. B.,
*Overseer of Dist. No.* 3.

Dated *April* 6, 1870.

---

### No. 19.

#### OVERSEER'S LIST OF PERSONS LIABLE TO DO HIGHWAY LABOR.

See *ante, p.* 86, 91.

I, John Doe, overseer of highways for road district No. ——— of the town of Brutus, in the county of Cayuga, do certify that the following is a true and correct list of all the inhabitants who are liable to work on highways, in said district No. ——— in said town.

BRUTUS, *June* 1, 1845.

John Smith, | Richard Roe,
George Johnson, | Thomas Ingraham.

JOHN DOE,
*Overseer road district No.*—.

---

### No. 20.

#### OVERSEER'S RETURN TO SUPERVISORS.

See *ante, p.* 108.

*To the Supervisor of the town of Brunswick, county of Rensselaer:*

The following is a list of all the resident land-holders residing in district No. 5, in the town of Brunswick, Rensselaer county, who have not worked out their highway assessment, or commuted for the same, with the number of days not worked or commuted for by each, at one dollar and fifty cents per day:

| Names. | No. of days. | Amount. |
|---|---|---|
| William Agan, .................... | 4 | $6 00 |
| John Riley, ....................... | 8 | 12 00 |

The following is a list of all the lands of non-residents and of persons unknown, which were assessed on my warrant by the commissioners of highways, or were added by me according to law, on which the labor assessed has not been paid, and the amount of labor performed or commuted for, and the number of days' labor unpaid by each, at one dollar and fifty cents per day:

| Description of lands. | Assessed value. | No. days. | Amount. |
|---|---|---|---|
| E. pt., L. 14, range 14, T. 9, 75 acres, ................ | $400 | 4 | $6 |

A. B., *Overseer of District No. 5.*

AFFIDAVIT TO SUCH LIST.

RENSSELAER COUNTY, *ss:*

A. B., being duly sworn, says, that he is overseer of highways of road district No. 5, in the town of Brunswick, in the county of Rensselaer, and that he has given the notices required by the thirty-second, thirty-third and thirty-fourth sections of title 1, chap. 16, of part first of the Revised Statutes, and that the labor for which such persons and lands are returned has not been performed or commuted. A. B.

Subscribed and sworn to before me this 7th day of September, 1870.

J. D., *Justice of Peace.*

## No. 21.

### COMMISSIONERS' LIST OF NON-RESIDENT LANDS.

See *ante*, *p.* 91.

The following is a list and statement of the contents of all lots, pieces or parcels of land within the town of Lansingburgh, in the county of Rensselaer, owned by non-residents therein. Made this third day of April, 1870, by the commissioners of highways of said town:

| NAME OF TRACT OR PATENT. | No. of lot. | Part. | No. of section. | No. of township. | No. of range. | No. of acres. | Valuation. | | No. of days. | No. road district. |
|---|---|---|---|---|---|---|---|---|---|---|
| Holland Company,..... | 1 | | 2 | 1 | 1 | 200 | $500 00 | | 5 | 3 |
| do ..... | 2 | | 2 | 1 | 1 | 200 | 500 00 | | 5 | 3 |
| do ..... | 3 | | 2 | 1 | 1 | 200 | 600 00 | | 6 | 3 |
| do ..... | 4 | | 2 | 1 | 1 | 200 | 400 00 | Bounded N. by A. B., | 2 | 3 |
| do .... | 5 | North | 2 | 1 | 1 | 100 | 200 00 | E. by C. D., S. by E. F., | 1 | 3 |
| do ..... | 6 | part. | 2 | 1 | 1 | 50 | 100 00 | and W. by G. H. | ... | ... |

Signatures.

---

## No. 22.

### ASSESSMENT OF HIGHWAY LABOR.

See *ante*, *p.* 93.

The undersigned commissioners of highways of the town of Pittstown, in the county of Rensselaer, having met at Johnsonville, in said town, for the purpose of ascertaining, estimating and assessing the highway labor to be performed in said town the ensuing year; all the commissioners being present and having deliberated thereon (or all the commissioners having been duly notified to be present at this said meeting, for the purpose of deliberating thereon), do hereby ascertain, estimate and assess such labor as follows:

1. The whole number of days' work assessed for the year is *twelve hundred*, being at least three times the number of taxable inhabitants in said town.

2. Every male inhabitant above the age of twenty one years (excepting ministers of the gospel and priests of every denomination, paupers, idiots and lunatics), there being *four hundred and fifty-three*, is assessed one day (*or two days, etc.*)

3. The residue of such work being seven hundred hundred and forty-seven days, is assessed as follows, to wit:

| | No. of days. |
|---|---|
| William Akin, ............................ | 4 |
| John Scott, ............................... | 6 |
| Anthony Snyder, ......................... | 7 |

The lands in said town owned by non-residents are assessed as follows, to wit: [Insert description and assessment as in preceding form.]

In witness whereof, we have hereto set our hands this 3d day of April, 1870.

Signatures.

---

**No. 23.**

OVERSEERS' ASSESSMENT OF PERSONS OMITTED.

See *ante*, *p.* 96.

The following named persons having been left out of the list of persons assessed to work on the highways in road district No. 6, in the town of Hoosick, in the county of Rensselaer (*or having become inhabitants of road district No.* 6 *in the town of Hoosick, in the county of Rensselaer, since the list of assessments of highway labor for said district was made*).

Now, therefore, I, James Allen, overseer of highways of said district, according to the statute in such case made and provided, do hereby assess and rate the said persons in proportion to their real and personal estate, to work on the highways, as others are rated by the commissioners on such list, subject to an appeal to the commissioners, which said assessment is as follows, viz.:

| | No. of days. |
|---|---|
| George Brownell, ........................... | 4 |
| James Kinnear, ........................... | 3 |

In witness whereof I have hereto set my hand this 9th day of April, 1870.

JAMES ALLEN, *Overseer.*

### APPEALS TO COMMISSIONERS FROM ASSESSMENT OF OVERSEERS.

*To the Commissioners of Highways of the town of Pittstown, in the county of Rensselaer:*

The undersigned having been assessed by the overseer of road district No. 3, in said town, four days' labor on the highway, on the ground that he is a new inhabitant of said district (*or that his name has been omitted by the commissioners in said town*), and conceiving himself aggrieved by said assessment does hereby appeal from said assessment so made by said overseer to the commissioners of highways of said town. A. B.

Dated, etc.

### APPEALS BY NON-RESIDENTS.

See *ante, p.* 98.

TOWN OF PITTSTOWN, *Rensselaer county.* } *ss:*

A. B., a non-resident owner of lands in said town, considering himself (*or* C. D., agent of A. B., a non-resident owner of lands in said town, who considers)

A. B. aggrieved in the assessment for highway labor by the commissioners of highways of said town, upon the following described lands, to wit: (*here insert the description as in the list or statement made by the commissioners*,) doth hereby appeal from the assessment of said commissioners, to the honorable Jeremiah Romeyn, county judge of Rensselaer county, that being the county in which said lands are situated.

A. B.

or A. B. by C. D., *Agent.*

Dated, etc.

---

**No. 24.**

OVERSEER'S ANNUAL ACCOUNT.

See *ante*, *p.* 88.

*To the Commissioners of Highways of the Town of Schodack, Rensselaer County:*

The undersigned, overseer of highways of road district No. 3, in said town, pursuant to law, renders the following annual account:

1. The names of all persons assessed to work on the highways in said road district No. 3 are as follows:

| Names. | No. of days. |
|---|---|
| John Jones, | 5 |
| Job Frost, | 6 |

2. The names of all those who have actually worked on the highways, with the number of days they have worked, are as follows:

| Names. | No. of days. |
|---|---|
| John Jones, | 5 |
| Job Frost, | $4\frac{1}{2}$ |

3. The names of all those who have been fined, and the sums in which they have been fined, are as follows:

| Names. | Sums. |
|---|---|
| John Greer, | $1 50 |
| John Ross, | 5 00 |

4. The names of those who have commuted are as follows:

| Names. | Days. | Amount. |
|---|---|---|
| George Ingraham, | 5 | $5 00 |

The manner in which the moneys, arising from fines and commutations, have been expended by me is as follows:

| | | |
|---|---|---|
| Whole amount received from fines and commutation, as above stated, | | $41 50 |
| Expended for scraper, by order of commissioners, | $23 00 | |
| Expended for repair of bridge over Muskrat creek, | 13 50 | |
| | | 36 50 |
| Leaving balance in my hands of, | | $5 00 |

5. The list of persons whose names he has returned to the supervisor as having neglected or refused to work out their highway assessments, with the number of days and amount of tax so returned for each person, is as follows: (*insert copy of list.*)

The list of all lands which he has returned to the supervisor for non-payment of taxes, and the amount of tax on each tract of land so returned, is as follows: (*insert copy of list.*)

JOHN GREEN,
*Overseer of Highways Dist. No.* 3.

Dated, etc.

RENSSELAER COUNTY, *ss.:*

John Green, overseer of highways for road district No. 3, of the town of Schodack, in said county, being duly sworn, says that the foregoing account is, in all respects, true. JOHN GREEN.

Subscribed and sworn to before me this 6th day of April, 1870. }

JOHN WILLIAMS,
*Commissioner of Highways.*

---

### No. 25.

#### APPLICATION TO LAY OUT ROAD.

See *ante*, *p.* 116.

*To the Commissioners of Highways of the town of Halfmoon, in the county of Saratoga:*

The undersigned, residents of said town (*or* owning lands in said town), and liable to be assessed for highway labor therein, hereby apply to the said commissioners of highways to lay out a road in said town, commencing at the *northwest corner of a lot of land in the possession of Abraham Rowan*, and running, etc. (*describing the proposed road*), which proposed road will pass through the inclosed, improved and cultivated lands of L. M. and M. O.

G. G.

---

### No. 26.

#### ORDER FOR LAYING OUT A HIGHWAY.

See *ante*, *p.* 118.

At a meeting of the commissioners of highways of the town of Wilton, in the county of Saratoga, at Doe's Corners, in the said town, on the 29th day of January, 1870, all the commissioners having met and deliberated on the subject-matter of this order (*or if but two of the commissioners met, say*, all the commissioners having been duly notified to attend the said meeting, for the purpose of deliberating on the subject-matter of this order), upon the application of Daniel Gailor, a resident in said town, and liable to be assessed to work on the highways therein for the laying out of the highway hereafter to be described, and on the certificate of twelve reputable free holders of said town, convened and duly sworn after due public notice, as required by the statute, certifying that such highway is necessary and proper; and notice, in writing, of at least three days, having been given in due form of law to S. M. and R. S., occupants of the lands through which such highway is to run, that the undersigned commissioners would meet at this time and place, to decide on the application aforesaid; and we having heard all reasons offered for and against laying out such highway, it is ordered, determined and certified that a public highway shall be, and the same is hereby, laid out pursuant to said application, whereof a survey has been made, and is as follows, to wit: beginning, etc. (*as in the survey*), and the line of said survey is to be the center of said highway, which is to be three rods in width.

Witness our hands this 29th day of January, 1870.

Signature.

---

**No. 27.**

CONSENT OF OWNER.

See *ante*, *p.* 119.

Whereas, a highway is proposed to be laid out by the commissioners of highways of the town of , in the county of , on the application of , commencing at (*insert description*), and which will run through my *orchard;* therefore, I do hereby consent that such road be so located, opened, worked and used through my said *orchard.*

Witness my hand this day of 18

A. B.

---

**No. 28.**

NOTICE OF APPLICATION TO LAY OUT HIGHWAY.

See *ante, p.* 125.

Notice is hereby given that the subscriber, a person liable to be assessed for highway labor in the town of , in the county of , has applied to the commissioners of highways of said town, to lay out a highway in said town, beginning (*insert a description of the proposed road*), which said highway is proposed to be laid through the improved lands of John Doe and Richard Roe (*specify the several tracts of land through which highway is to be laid*), and that twelve reputable freeholders of the town will meet on the , *at* 10 *o'clock* A. M., *at the dwelling-house of* , to examine the ground through which the said highway is proposed to be laid.

Signed.

---

**No. 29.**

FREEHOLDERS' CERTIFICATE TO LAY OUT ROAD.

See *ante, p.* 127.

COUNTY OF } *ss.:*
*Town of* }

We, the undersigned, being freeholders of the town of Brownville, in said county, and not inter ested in the lands through which the highway hereinafter described is proposed to be laid, nor of kin to the owner thereof, having met on the day and date hereof at , in the said town, and having been first duly sworn, and having personally examined the route of the said proposed highway, and heard the reasons offered for or against the laying out a highway, pursuant to the application of E. F., commencing at, etc. (*here insert the description as in the application and notice*) and which highway will pass through the improved (*or inclosed, or cultivated*) lands of A. B. and C. D., do hereby certify to the commissioners of highways of said town, that we are of opinion that such highway is necessary and proper.

In witness whereof, we have hereunto subscribed our names the 10th day of September, 1870.

Signatures.

---

**No. 30.**

NOTICE TO OCCUPANT.

See *ante, p.* 128.

To WILLIAM SMITH:

Take notice that we, the undersigned, the commissioners of highways of the town of , in the county of , shall meet at , in the said town, on the 10th day of October, 1870, at 10 o'clock in the forenoon, to decide on the application made by A. B., to us, to lay out a highway, commencing at, etc. (*here give the description as in the application*), and which will pass through your inclosed (*or improved, or cultivated*) lands; twelve freeholders having certified that it is proper and necessary to lay out said highway.

Dated, etc. Signatures.

## No. 31.

### ORDER LAYING OUT HIGHWAY.

See *ante*, *p.* 129.
See form No. 26.

---

## No. 32.

### NOTICE OF HIGHWAY ACROSS RAILROAD TRACK.

See *ante*, *p.* 134.

*To the Albany & Boston Railroad Company:*

Take notice, that the commissioners of highways of the town of Schodack, in the county of Rensselaer, have duly laid out a highway, commencing at (*insert description*), and that said highway crosses the railroad track of your said company *five rods north of your depot at Schodack*, and that said road will be opened for use after the expiration of thirty days from the service of this notice upon you. You are therefore required to cause the said highway to be taken across your said track, as shall be most convenient and useful for public travel, and to cause all necessary embankments, excavations and other work to be done on your road for that purpose, as by the statute provided. Yours, etc.,

Dated, etc. Signatures.

---

## No. 33.

### APPLICATION FOR THE ALTERATION OF A ROAD.

See *ante*, *p.* 142.

*To the Commissioners of Highways of the town of Hector in the County of Tompkins:*

The undersigned, residents of said town (or owning lands in said town), and liable to be assessed for highway labor therein, do apply to said commissioners to alter the highway leading from the house of Burton White to the Northern turnpike in said town, as follows: (*Insert particular description of the proposed alteration by known boundaries or objects, or courses and distances.*) The proposed alteration passes through lands which are not improved, inclosed or cultivated (or passes through the lands of John Doe and Samuel Johnson, who give their consent to said alterations). T. R.

Dated, etc. C. D.

---

**No. 34.**

APPLICATION TO DISCONTINUE OLD ROAD.

See *ante*, *p.* 142.

*To the Commissioners of Highways of the Town of Volney, in the County of Oswego:*

The undersigned, residents of said town, and liable to be assessed for highway labor therein, do hereby apply to you, the said commissioner, to discontinue the old road in said town, beginning, etc. (*insert general description*), on the ground that said road has become useless and unnecessary.

Dated, etc. Signatures.

---

**No. 35.**

SUMMONS FOR JURY TO DISCONTINUE ROAD.

See *ante*, *p.* 144.

ALBANY COUNTY, *ss.:*

To JOHN SMITH — You are hereby summoned and required to appear at the house of William Wait, in the town of Watervliet, in said county, on the 7th day of September, 1870, to make a jury of freeholders to consider, examine and certify in regard to the propriety of discontinuing the highway between (*insert description of road to be discontinued*). Hereof fail not. Witness our hands, etc.,

Dated, etc.

J. B.
G. F.
J. L.
*Commissioners.*

---

**No. 36.**

FREEHOLDERS' CERTIFICATE TO DISCONTINUE A ROAD.

See *ante*, *p*. 145.

The subscribers, disinterested freeholders of the town of Corinth, in the county of Saratoga, having met at the dwelling-house of Hiram Clothier, in said town, in pursuance of a summons from the commissioners of highways of the said town, to examine and certify in regard to the propriety of discontinuing the highway from (*describe the highway to be discontinued*), and having been duly sworn, and having viewed the said road, do therefore certify that we are of opinion that the same is useless and unnecessary.

In witness whereof, we have hereto set our hands this 10th day of June, 1870. Signatures.

---

**No. 37.**

ORDER TO ALTER ROAD.

See *ante*, *p*. 145.

The undersigned, commissioners of highways of the town of , in the county of , having met at the dwelling-house of , in the said town, to decide upon the application of , a resident of said town, liable to be assessed for highway labor therein, for the alteration of the road between the chair shop of Norman Neff and Shumla. All the said commissioners being present, and having deliberated (*or all the said commissioners having been duly notified to attend this meeting of the commissioners, for the purpose of deliberating*) on the subject of this order, do hereby order that the line of the said road be, and the same is hereby, so altered as to run from a point *thirty* feet south of the southeasterly corner of said *Neff's chair shop*, in a straight line; south, thirteen degrees east, till it strikes the present center of the road, thence along the present line thirty rods, and thence continuing in a straight line sixty rods to the center of the present road on the summit of the hill north of Shumla, the said line to be the center of the road, which shall remain of the width of three rods. And it is further ordered, that such parts of the present road as are not included in the above description be, and the same are hereby, discontinued.

Dated, etc. Signed, etc.

---

## No. 38.

### ORDER FOR DISCONTINUING A ROAD.

See *ante*, *p.* 145.

At a meeting of the commissioners of highways of the town of Carmel, in the county of Putnam, at Benton, in said town, on the 14th day of December, 1867, all the commissioners having met and deliberated on the subject of this order (*or all the commis-*

*sioners having been duly notified to attend the said meeting, for the purpose of deliberating on the subject of this order*) upon the application of George White, of said town, for the discontinuance of the road hereinafter described, and on the certificate of twelve disinterested freeholders, duly summoned and sworn, who have in due form certified that said road is useless and unnecessary; and the said commissioners having caused a survey of said road to be made as follows, viz.: (*here insert the survey or description.*) It is ordered and determined by the said commissioners, that the said road be, and the same is hereby, discontinued.

In witness whereof, we have hereto set our hands this 9th day of June, 1856.

Signatures.

---

### No. 39.

#### ORDER REFUSING TO DISCONTINUE A ROAD.

At a meeting of the commissioners of highways of the town of Pittstown, in the county of Rensselaer (*as in last form*). It is ordered and determined by the said commissioners, that the said application of the said A. B., to discontinue the said road, be refused.

In witness, etc.

---

### No. 40.

#### DESCRIPTION OF ROAD ABANDONED.

See *ante*, *p.* 146.

At a meeting of the commissioners of highways of the town of , in the county of , at , in said town, on the day of , 1870, all the commissioners being present, and having deliberated on the subject of this order (*or all the, etc., as in No.* 37), ordered that, whereas, the highway hereinafter described has been abandoned by the public, and is no longer used as a public road, the same is discontinued; and that the following is a description of the said road so abandoned: (*Insert description.*)

In witness, etc.

---

### No. 41.

#### APPEAL FROM ORDER LAYING OUT, ALTERING OR DISCONTINUING HIGHWAY.

See *ante*, *p.* 148.

*To the* HON. JEREMIAH ROMEYN, *County Judge of Rensselaer County:*

I, John Doe, of the town of Berlin, in said county, conceiving myself aggrieved by the determination of the commissioners of highways of the town of Berlin, in said county, made on the first day of August, 1865, in laying out (*or altering, discontinuing, refusing to lay out, alter or discontinue*) a highway in the said town, from (*describe the road as in the order of the commissioners*), upon the application of John Guy, do hereby appeal from the said determination of the said commissioners, and pray the appointment of referees, according to the form of the statute in such case made and provided, to hear and determine my said appeal.

The ground upon which this appeal is made is, that (*here set forth the cause of complaint*), and said appeal is brought to reverse entirely the determination of the commissioners (*or if part only, then*) to reverse the determination, etc. (*specifying the part sought to be reversed*).

Dated, etc. JOHN DOE.

**No. 42 a.**

APPOINTMENT OF REFEREES.

See *ante, p.* 148–151.

RENSSELAER COUNTY, *ss.:*

Whereas, A. B., of the town of Pittstown, in said county, has appealed from the determination of the commissioners of highways of the said town, made on the 30th day of December, 1867, in (*laying out, altering, discontinuing, refusing to lay out, alter, discontinue*), a highway in said town, which highway is particularly described in said appeal hereto annexed (*and, whereas, Richard Bailey and John Smith have also appealed from the same determination of the commissioners, which said appeals are also hereto annexed*), and sixty days having elapsed after such determination has been filed in the office of the town clerk of the said town;

Now, therefore, I, Jeremiah Romeyn, county judge of the said county, to whom the said appeal was (*or appeals were*) addressed, according to the form of the statute in such case made and provided, do hereby appoint James Monroe, of the town of Schaghticoke, William Otis, of the town of Lansingburgh, and Henry Myrtle, of the town of Hoosic, three disinterested freeholders, who have not been named by the parties interested in the appeal, and who are residents of the county, but not of the town wherein the road is located, as referees, to hear and determine all the appeals that have been brought in relation to the said determination of the said commissioners.

Given under my hand this 3d day of June, 1867.

JEREMIAH ROMEYN.

### No. 42 b.

### APPOINTMENT OF REFEREES BY JUSTICE OF SESSIONS WHEN JUDGE IS DISQUALIFIED.

See *ante*, *p*. 148–151.

RENSSELAER COUNTY, *ss.*:

Whereas, on the 10th day of June, 1867, C. D., of the town of Nassau, in the said county of Rensselaer, appealed to the Hon. A. B., county judge of the said county, from the order and determination of E. F., commissioner of highways of the said town, made on the 30th day of December, 1867, laying out (*altering, or as the case may be*) a highway in the said town, which highway is particularly described in the said appeal hereto annexed, and sixty days having elapsed after such determination has been filed in the office of the town clerk of the said town, and whereas the said county judge is a resident of said town of Nassau (*or whatever the disability may be*), now, therefore, in accordance with the statute in such case made and provided, I, the undersigned, one of the justices of the sessions of the said county of Rensselaer, do hereby appoint I. J., K. L., and M. N., all residents of the said county of Rensselaer, but not one of them residents of the said town of Nassau, referees to hear and determine the said appeal (*or appeals*).

Given under my hand this 10th day of March, 1868.

---

### No. 43.

### NOTICE BY REFEREES TO THE COMMISSIONERS OF HIGHWAYS.

See *ante*, *p*. 152.

To E. F., C. D. and J. G., *Commissioners of Highways of the town of Pittstown, in the county of Rensselaer*:

Take notice that we have been duly appointed referees to hear and determine an appeal made to A.

B., county judge of the county of Rensselaer, by C. L. of the town of Pittstown, from your determination contained in your order, made on the 10th day of July, 1867, and filed and recorded in the office of tho town clerk of the said town, on the 13th day of July, 1867, refusing to lay out, etc. (*as in the appeal*); and that we shall attend at the house of M. N., in said town, on the 5th day of October next, at 10 o'clock in the forenoon of that day, to hear and determine such appeal.

Signed,

Dated, etc. *Referees.*

---

**No. 43 a.**

NOTICE TO COMMISSIONERS, OF APPEAL.

See *ante*, *p.* 152.

To A. B., C. D. and E. F., *Commissioners of Highways of the town of Pittstown, in the county of Rensselaer:*

Take notice, that I have appealed to the county judge of the said county of Rensselaer, from the determination made by you on the first day of August, 1865, laying out (*altering, or as the case may be*) a highway in said town, beginning (*insert description*), and that said appeal is brought on the ground, etc. (*insert ground*), and is brought to reverse entirely your said determination (*or if part only*), to reverse your determination in so far — (*specifying the parts to be reversed*).

Dated, &c. Signature.

## No. 44.

### NOTICE TO OCCUPANTS OF LAND.

See *ante, p.* 153.

To A. B.:

Take notice that we shall attend at the house of J. R., in the town of Pittstown, in the county of Rensselaer, on the 6th day of October, 1867, at ten o'clock in the forenoon of that day, to hear and determine the appeal made by C. D., of said town, to G. L., county judge of the said county, from the order and determination of E. B., A. C., and D. L., commissioners of highways of the said town of Pittstown, made on the 3d day of April, 1867, and filed and recorded in the town clerk's office of the said town, on the 16th day of April, 1867, refusing to lay out, etc. (*as in the appeal*). Signed,

Dated, etc. *Referees.*

---

## No. 45.

### SUBPŒNA FOR WITNESS UPON AN APPEAL.

See *ante, p.* 155.

COUNTY OF RENSSELAER, }
TOWN OF BERLIN, } *ss.:*

To E. F. and J. K.:

You, and each of you, are hereby commanded, in the name of the people of the State of New York, to appear before the undersigned, referees, appointed by the county court of Rensselaer county, at the house of L. R., in the town of Berlin, county of Rensselaer, on the 3d day of July, 1870, at ten o'clock in the forenoon, to testify respectively in a matter of a certain appeal from the decision of the commissioners of highways of the said town of Berlin to the said county court, and then and there to be heard on the part, and in behalf of E. F. appellant (or of the said commissioners as the case may be).

Given under our hands this 20th day of June, 1870.

Signatures.

---

**No. 46.**

DECISION OF REFEREES ON APPEAL.

See *ante*, *p.* 159.

Whereas, Holloway Long, of the town of York, in the county of Livingston, on the first day of July, 1848, appealed to the Hon. Scott Lord, county judge of said county, from the determination of the commissioners of highways of the said town, made on the 15th day of June, 1848, in (*laying out, altering, discontinuing, refusing to lay out, alter, discontinue*), a highway in the said town, which highway is particularly described in the said appeal hereto annexed (*and whereas, Richard Bailey and John Smith also appealed from the same determination of the said commissioners, which said appeals are also hereto annexed*), and whereas, after the expiration of sixty days after such determination had been filed in the office of the town clerk of the said town, the said county judge, according to the form of the statute in such case made and provided, appointed us, James Johnson, of the town of Avon, Hiram Dennison, of the town of Lima, and James S. Wadsworth, of the town of Geneseo, three disinterested freeholders, who had not been named by the parties interested in the appeal, and who are residents of the county, but not of the town wherein the road is located, as referees, to hear and determine all the appeals that had been brought in relation to the said determination of the said commissioners, which said appointment is hereto annexed, and we having given notice pursuant to law, to the said commissioners of highways (*and to John Rogers, an applicant for such road*), specifying the 25th day of August, 1848, as the time, and the dwelling-house of Jacob Howe, in the said town of York, as the place, at which we would convene to hear the appeal, which notice was duly served at least eight days before the said time of convening, to wit: on the 16th day of August, 1848, and we having convened at the time and place specified in said notice, and before proceeding to hear said appeal (*or appeals*) having been duly sworn by an officer authorized to take affidavits to be read in courts of record, to wit: Robert Jones, Esquire, a justice of the peace of the said county, faithfully to hear and determine the matters referred to us, have heard the proofs and allegations of the parties, and do thereupon order, determine and adjudge that the said determination of the said commissioners of highways be and the same is hereby reversed (or affirmed, or reversed in so far [*stating part reversed*], and affirmed as to the residue, [*and, if the road is to be laid out by the referees add*]), and we do further order and determine that the said highway be laid out in accordance with the application of the said A. B., and the same is hereby described as follows: (*insert description.*)

Witness our hands this 25th day of August, 1848.

Referees' Signatures.

### No. 47.

NOTICE TO REMOVE FENCES.

See *ante*, *pp.* 138, 162.

Whereas, the undersigned, commissioners of highways of the town of Wilton, in the county of Saratoga, have laid out a public highway, by an order dated November 25, 1870, and duly filed with the town clerk of said town, which said road passes through inclosed lands, owned (*or occupied*) by you (*insert route as in survey*); and, whereas, our determination in the matter of laying out such road has not been appealed from: Now, therefore, please to take notice, that you are required to remove your fences from within the bounds of said highway, within sixty days after service hereof.

Yours, etc.

Dated, etc.

---

### No. 48.

AFFIDAVIT FOR CERTIORARI.

See *ante*, *p.* 164.

RENSSELAER COUNTY, *ss.:*

J. G., being duly sworn, says that he is a resident of the town of Berlin, in said county, and liable to be assessed for highway labor therein; that on the 3d day of July, 1870, G. L. and D. S., two of the commissioners of highways of the said town of Berlin, on the application of E. C., made an order laying out a highway in said town, commencing, etc., (*insert description*), which said order was filed and recorded in the town clerk's office of said town, on the 5th day of July, 1870, and is in the words and figures following, to wit: (*insert copy of order*) that the highway so laid out passes through the improved and cultivated lands of this deponent, and of M. N. and O. P. And this deponent further alleges that the said road so laid out, as aforesaid, was laid out without the certificate of twelve freeholders; and that W. D., one of the alleged freeholders who certified to the necessity and propriety of the said road, had, at the time of making such certificate, no legal title to any real estate. And this deponent further alleges, that the said order laying out the road, as aforesaid, was made by the above named two commissioners, without the intervention of G. D., one of the commissioners of highways of said town, and without any notice to him to attend the meetings of the commissioners for the purpose of deliberating on the subject of such order; and that the order laying out said road does not show that the said G. D., participated in the proceeding, or was notified to do so.

Sworn, etc. J. G.

---

**No. 49 a.**

WRIT OF CERTIORARI.

See *ante, p.* 164.

*The People of the State of New York:*

To A. W., J. W. and W. H., referees appointed by the county judge of Washington county, on the 3d day of June, 1870, to hear and determine the appeal of John McFarland and William McFarland, from the determination of the commissioners of highways of the town of Salem, in said county, in refusing to lay out a highway in said town.

We, being willing, for certain causes, to be certified of a certain decision made by you on a certain appeal of *John McFarland and William McFarland*, from the determination and decision of the commissioners of highways of the town of *Salem* in the county of *Washington*, aforesaid, in refusing to lay out a road in said town, under and by virtue of the statutes made and provided, we command you, that the said appeal, together with the testimony given, and offered to be given, on the hearing thereof, with your decision thereon, with all things touching and concerning the same, by whatever names the parties thereto are called, before our justices of our Supreme Court, at *the City Hall of the city of Albany*, on the first Monday of May next (*time and place of the next general term*), you send, under your hands, together with this writ; that our said court may further, thereupon, cause to be done therein what of right ought to be done.

Witness, Henry Hogeboom, one of the Justices of our Supreme Court; at the court-house in the city of Hudson, this 10th day of January, 1870.

JOHN WILEY, *Clerk.*

(*Indorsed.*) On the application of Edward Long, counsel for the applicant, and on the affidavit of J. G., dated the 3d day of July, 1870, I allow the within writ of certiorari to issue; and let said affidavit be filed in the office of the clerk of Columbia county.

HENRY HOGEBOOM.
*Just. Sup. Court.*

---

**No. 49 b.**

RETURN TO WRIT OR CERTIORARI.

See *ante, p.* 164.

WASHINGTON COUNTY, *ss.:*

By virtue of and in obedience to a writ of the people of the State of New York, hereunto annexed, and directed and delivered unto us, A. B., C. D. and E.

F., referees, appointed by the county judge of Washington county, on the 3d day of June, 1870, to hear and determine the appeal of John McFarland and William McFarland, from the determination of the commissioners of highways of the town of Salem, in said county, in refusing to lay out a road in said town. We do hereby certify and return that on the 3d day of June, 1870, we were appointed, by the county judge of Washington county, referees to hear and determine the appeals of William McFarland and John McFarland, from the order and determination of the commissioners of highways of the town of Salem, in refusing to lay out a highway in said town, which order and determination were made on the 5th day of April, 1870, and filed and recorded in the town clerk's office of said town of Salem, on that day, and that the order appointing us is in the words following, to wit: (*insert copy order appointing*). We do further certify, that the appeal of the said William McFarland and John McFarland, and which was delivered to us by the said county judge, is in the words following (*insert copy of appeal, proceed giving a detailed statement of every step taken, with copies of all orders, papers, evidence, etc.*).

In testimony whereof, we have respectively, to these presents, affixed our seals and subscribed our names, this 20th day of July, 1870.

Signatures, [L. S.]

---

No. 50 a.

APPLICATION TO COUNTY COURT TO APPOINT COMMISSIONERS TO ASSESS DAMAGES.

See *ante*, *p.* 166.

*To the County Court of Albany County:*

Whereas, we, the commissioners of highways of the town of Watervliet, in said county, by an order dated

September 20th, 1870, have laid out a highway in said town, beginning, (*insert description as in the order*).

Now, therefore, we the said commissioners, do hereby apply for the appointment of commissioners to assess the damages occasioned by the laying out of said highway, pursuant to the statute in such case made and provided.

Dated, etc. Signatures.

---

No. 50 b.

ORDER APPOINTING COMMISSIONERS TO ASSESS.

See *ante*, *p.* 166.

At a term of the county court of Albany county, held at the court-house in the city of Albany, in said county, on the 25th day of January, 1870.

Present—Hon. JOHN DOE, *County Judge*.

In the matter of the application of the Commissioners of Highways of the town of Watervliet.

On reading and filing the application of E. G., H. B. and N. B., commissioners of highways of the town of Watervliet, in said county, setting forth the laying out of a highway in said town, beginning, (*insert description*), and praying the appointment of commissioners to assess the damages ascertained thereby, it is ordered that F. G., H. J. and L. M., of said town, be and they are hereby appointed such commissioners, whose duty it shall be to take the oath of office prescribed by the constitution, and to proceed, on receiving at least six days' notice of the time and place, to meet the said highway commmissioners and take a view of the premises, hear the parties and such witnesses as may be offered before them, and to administer oaths to such witnesses; and they shall all meet and act, and they or a majority of them shall assess all damages which may be required to be assessed on the said highway, and shall deliver their said assessment to the said commissioners of highways.

---

### No. 50 c.

#### NOTICE OF MEETING OF COMMISSIONERS TO ASSESS DAMAGES.

See *ante*, *p.* 168.

To JOHN COLE:

Sir — Take notice that the commissioners appointed by the county court, by an order bearing date on the 25th day of January, 1870, to assess the damages occasioned by a highway laid out by the commissioners of highways of the town of Berlin, in the county of Rensselaer, beginning, (*insert description of road*), will meet for the purpose of making such assessment, at the house of William Wood, in said town, on the 13th day of February next.

Signature.

Dated, etc.

---

### No. 51.

#### ASSESSMENT BY COMMISSIONERS.

See *ante*, *p.* 170.

Whereas, the undersigned, Walker Gilbert, Daniel Gailor and Ira Wood, were appointed by an order of the county court, of the county of Saratoga, made on the tenth day of September, 1870, on the application of E. G., H. B. and N. R., commissioners of highways of the town of Wilton, in said county, commissioners to assess the damages occasioned by the laying out of a highway in the said town, beginning, (*insert description as in the order*), which highway passes through the improved lands of P. D., D. C. and J. I., and was laid out by the commissioners of highways of the said town, by an order dated November twenty-fourth, 1870.

Now, therefore, we, the said commissioners, having taken the oath of office prescribed by the constitution, and having all met and acted on the matter committed to us, at the residence of P. D., in said town, this twenty-fourth day of November, 1870, pursuant to a notice from said commissioners of highways, of at least six days, according to law, and having taken a view of the premises, and heard the parties and such witnesses as have been offered before us, do, thereupon, determine and assess the damages required to be assessed on the said highway as follows, viz: We assess the damages of P. D. at one hundred dollars; we assess the damages of D. C. at one hundred and fifty dollars, etc.

Witness our hands this 24th day of November, 1870.

Signatures.

---

**No. 52.**

NOTICE OF DRAWING OF JURY TO RE-ASSESS DAMAGES.

See *ante*, *p.* 170.

Notice is hereby given that I, John Doe, conceiving myself aggrieved by (*or we, the commissioners of highways, feeling dissatisfied with*) the assessment of damages made by H. F., H. C. and J. S., commissioners appointed by the county court of the county of Rensselaer, to assess damages occasioned by the laying out of a highway in the town of Berlin, in said county, beginning, (*insert description*), which said assessment was filed in the office of the town clerk of the said town, on the 10th day of September, 1870, do hereby ask for a jury to re-assess the said damages, and such jury will be drawn at the clerk's office of the town of Nassau, in said county, adjoining the said town of Berlin, on the 25th day of September, 1870, at ten o'clock in the forenoon of that day, by the town clerk of the said town of Nassau.

Dated, etc. Signature.

---

No. 52 a.

NOTICE TO ADJOINING TOWN CLERK OF DRAWING OF JURY.

See *ante*, *p*. 171.

*To* J. K., *town clerk of the town of Nassau, in the county of Rensselaer:*

Take notice that the undersigned, feeling himself aggrieved by the assessment of certain commissioners appointed by the county court of said county to assess damages occasioned by the laying out of a highway in the town of Berlin, in said county, and having asked for a jury to re-assess such damages, such jury will be drawn by you at the town clerk's office in said town of Nassau, on the 25th day of September, 1870, at ten o'clock in the forenoon of that day.

Dated, etc. Signature.

---

No. 53.

TOWN CLERK'S CERTIFICATE OF DRAWING OF JURY.

See *ante*, *p*. 171.

RENSSELAER COUNTY, *ss.:*

I. J. K., town clerk of the town of Nassau, in said county, do hereby certify that the following twelve names were this day drawn by me from a box containing the names of all such persons, now residents of said town, whose names are on the last list filed in the town clerk's office of said town, of those selected and returned as jurors, pursuant to the Revised Statutes, who are not interested in the lands through which a road in the town of Berlin was laid out by the commissioners of highways of said last-mentioned town, on the 25th day of January, 1870, or of kin to either or any of the parties, and that the said twelve names were so drawn by me to make a jury to re-assess the damages occasioned by the laying out of the said highway.

A. B., E. F.,
C., D., G. H.,
etc., inserting the twelve names.

Witness my hand this 3d day of September, 1870.

R. P., *Town Clerk.*

---

No. 54.

SUMMONS FOR JURY.

See *ante, p.* 172.

RENSSELAER COUNTY, *ss.:*

*To* WALTER SCOTT, *one of the constables of the town of Berlin in the said county:*

You are hereby directed to summon (*name the twelve persons*) to appear at ———, in the said town, on the 25th day of September, 1870, to make a jury to re-assess the damage occasioned by the laying out of a highway in the said town, by the highway commissioners thereof, on the 10th day of August, 1870. Hereof fail not.

Witness my hand this 3d day of September, 1870.

J. B., *Justice of Peace.*

### No. 54 a.

OATH OF JURY.

You, and each of you, do solemnly swear, in the presence of Almighty God, well and truly to determine and re-assess such damage as shall be submitted to your consideration.

---

### No. 55.

VERDICT OF RE-ASSESSMENT.

See *ante*, *p*. 173.

We, the subscribers, a jury duly drawn and sworn to determine and re-assess the damages occasioned by the laying out of a highway in the town of Berlin, in the county of Rensselaer, by the highway commissioners thereof, on the 18th day of September, 1867, which said highway runs from (*describe the highway as in the order, and state whose lands it passes through*), having taken a view of the premises, and heard the parties and such witnesses as have been offered by them and sworn before us, do hereby determine and re-assess the said damages as follows, viz.: We determine and re-assess the damages of H. B. at one hundred dollars. (*Specify each person's damages passed upon.*)

To be signed by the six Jurors.

RENSSELAER COUNTY, *ss.:*

I, J. B., the justice of the peace, by whom the within (*or above*) named jury were summoned, drawn and sworn, do certify that the within (*or above*) is the verdict of re-assessment rendered by the jury, pursuant to the said proceedings, this 28th day of September, 1867.

J. B., *Justice of Peace.*

## No. 56.

### AGREEMENT OF OWNER AND COMMISSIONERS AS TO DAMAGES.

See *ante*, *p*. 166.

Whereas, the commissioners of highways of the town of Pittstown, in the county of Rensselaer have, by an order dated the 10th day of January, 1868, laid out a highway in said town, beginning (*describe it is in the order*), which said highway passes through the improved lands of John Clark: Now, therefore, the damages of the said John Clark, by reason of the laying out of said highway, are hereby ascertained by agreement of the said John Clark, and the said commissioners of highways, at the sum of *one hundred dollars*.

In witness whereof we, the said parties, have hereto set our hands this 12th day of January, 1868.

Signatures.

---

## No. 57.

### RELEASE OF DAMAGES BY OWNER.

See *ante*, *p*. 166.

A highway having been laid out, on the day of the date hereof, by the commissioners of highways of the town of Rome, in the couny of Oneida, on the application of John W. Tallmadge, through the improved land of me, Henry Palmer, commencing at, etc., (*insert the description of the road as in the order*.)

Now, know all men by these presents, that I, the said Henry Palmer, for value received, do hereby release all claim to damages by reason of the laying out and opening the said highway.

Witness my hand and seal the 1st day of December, 1867. HENRY PALMER. [L. S.]

No. 58.

NOTICE OF APPLICATION TO SUPERVISORS.

See *ante*, *p.* 181.

Notice is hereby given that the undersigned, E. G., of the town of Berlin, in the county of Rensselaer, will apply to the board of supervisors of said county, at their next annual meeting to be held at the court-house in the city of Troy, in said county, on the 3d day of December, 1868, to be caused to be levied, collected and paid to the treasurer of the said county of Rensselaer, such sum of money as may be necessary to construct and repair bridges in said county, and to prescribe upon what plan and in what manner the moneys so raised shall be expended.

Dated, etc. C. A.

---

No. 59.

COMMISSIONER'S ORDER TO REMOVE ENCROACHMENTS.

See *ante*, *p.* 211.

Whereas, a highway was laid out in the town of Berne, in the county of Albany, on the 10th day of July, 1870, by the commissioners of highways of the said town (*or by E. G., C. D. and E. F., referees, etc.*), beginning (*insert description as in the order, including a statement of the width of the road*), which road is encroached upon by the fence of R. C., to the extent of (*state how much*), on the *north* side (*describe where*).

Now, therefore, we, the commissioners of highways of the said town (*state the attendance of, or notice to all the commissioners, unless they all sign the order*), do hereby order that such fence be removed, so that such highway may be of the breadth originally intended.

Dated, etc. Signatures.

### No. 60.

#### NOTICE TO REMOVE ENCROACHMENT.

See *ante*, *p.* 211.

To Mr. R. C.:

Sir — Please to take notice that an order, of which the annexed is a copy, has been duly made by the commissioners of highways of the town of Berne, in the county of Albany, and that you are hereby required to remove the fence therein specified, as encroaching upon the highway, within sixty days after service hereof.

Dated, etc. Signatures.

---

### No. 61.

#### DENIAL OF ENCROACHMENT.

See *ante*, *p.* 213.

*To the Commissioners of Highways of the town of Pittstown, in the county of Rensselaer:*

Take notice that I hereby deny that the fences mentioned in the order and notice heretofore served on me, and dated June 3d, 1867, encroach upon the highway mentioned in said order and notice.

Dated, etc. Yours, etc.,
G. W.

---

### No. 62.

#### APPLICATION TO JUSTICE THEREON.

See *ante*, *p.* 213.

To T. R., *Justice of the Peace of the town of Pittstown, in the county of Rensselaer:*

An order having, on the 3d day of June, 1867, been made by the commissioners of highways of the said town of Pittstown, of which the following is a copy (*insert copy*), and notice of said order having been duly served on A. B., one of the persons named therein, and through whose land said highway runs, requiring him to remove within sixty days according to said order, his fences therein mentioned as an encroachment upon the said highway, and said A. B., having in writing denied that said fences encroached on said highway, therefore, I, E. G., one of the commissioners of highways of the said town of Pittstown, do hereby apply to you, T, R., one of the justices of the peace of said county of Rensselaer, for a precept, directed to any constable of the said town of Pittstown, to summon twelve freeholders thereof, to meet on the 5th day of September, 1867, at the dwelling-house of M. N., in said town, to inquire into the premise, according to the statute in such case made and provided.

Dated, etc. Signature.

---

No. 63.

SUMMONS TO FREEHOLDERS IN CASE OF ENCROACHMENT.

See *ante, p.* 213.

ONEIDA COUNTY, *ss.:*

*To any constable in the town of Camden, in the said county:*

You are hereby commanded to summon twelve freeholders of said town to meet on the 5th day of July, 1867, in the dwelling-house of E. J., in said town, to inquire into the matter of an alleged encroachment upon the highway in said town leading from (*here describe the place and the alleged encroachment, as in the order*) and you are to give at least three days' notice to the commissioner of highways of said town and to C. D., of the time and place at which such freeholders are to meet.

J. W.,

Dated, etc. *Justice of the Peace.*

---

**No. 64.**

OATH OF JURY.

See *ante, p.* 214.

You and each of you do solemnly swear, that you will well and truly inquire whether any encroachment has been made, and by whom, on the highway now in question.

---

**No. 65.**

OATH TO WITNESS.

See *ante, p.* 214.

You do swear, that the evidence you shall give, in relation to the encroachment on the highway now in question, shall be the truth, the whole truth, and nothing but the truth.

---

**No. 66.**

CERTIFICATE OF JURY WHEN ENCROACHMENT IS FOUND.

See *ante, p.* 214.

ONEIDA COUNTY, *ss:*

The undersigned, freeholders of the town of Camden, in said county, having met on the day of the date hereof, at the dwelling-house of E. J., in said town, pursuant to a summons from J. W., Esq., a justice of the peace of the said county, to inquire into the matter of an alleged encroachment on the highway, in said town ; specified in an order of the commissioners of highways of said town, dated January 3d, 1867, a copy whereof is hereto annexed, having been duly sworn, and having heard the proofs and allegations which were submitted, do certify* that an encroachment on the said highway has been made, and that the same was made by John Jones, the present occupant (*or by Samuel Smith, a former occupant*).

Witness our hands this 13th day of July, 1867.

Signatures.

CERTIFICATE WHEN NO ENCROACHMENT IS FOUND.

(*As above to**, *continuing*,) that no encroachment has been made, as was alleged, and we also ascertain and certify the damages which John Jones, the present occupant, has sustained by these proceedings at *ten dollars*.

Witness our hands this 13th day of July, 1867.

Signatures.

---

**No. 67.**

ASSESSMENT BY OVERSEER OF ADDITIONAL LABOR.

See *ante*, *p*. 115.

Whereas, the labor in road district No. 9, of the town of *Schodack*, in the county of Rensselaer has been worked out, commuted for or returned to the supervisor, and the highways of said district, are obstructed by *snow* (*or as the case may be*) and written notice has been given to me by two or more inhabitants of the town, liable to payment of highway tax, requesting the removal of such obstruction.

Therefore, I do hereby further assess the following named persons — actual residents in said district — the amount of labor set opposite their respective names, being in the same proportion, as near as may be, to the original assessment of labor on said highways for the year.

| Names. | Days. | Names. | Days. |
|---|---|---|---|
| James Holt ...... | 6 | John Jones....... | 4 |

Witness my hand this 9th day of January, 1870.

JOHN JAY, *Overseer.*

---

No. 68.

NOTICE OF COMMISSIONER'S RESIGNATION.

See *ante, p.* 26.

To A. B., C. D., and E. F., Esqrs.,
*Justices of the Peace of the Town of Greenbush.*

Take notice that I hereby tender my resignation of the office of commissioner of highways of the said town of Greenbush, for the following reasons: (*Give reasons.*)

Dated, etc. L. J.

---

No. 69.

COMPLAINT TO COMMISSIONER AGAINST OVERSEER.

See *ante, p.* 88.

*To the commissioners of highways of the town of Greenbush:*

The complaint of A. B., a resident of the town of Greenbush, respectfully showeth that C. D., the overseer of highways for road district number five, in said town, *has neglected and refused to warn E. F. to work on the highways, in said district, after having been required so to do by the commissioners, or one of them.* And the said A. B. hereby requires the said commissioners of highways to prosecute the said C. D., for said offense.

Dated, etc. A. B.

---

### No. 69 a.

#### SECURITY TO COMMISSIONERS FOR PROSECUTING OVERSEER.

See *ante, p.* 88.

Whereas, John Doe has made complaint to the commissioners of highways of the town of Pittstown, that John Doe, overseer of highways for road district number 2, in said town, has neglected and refused to (*insert matter complained of*).

Now, therefore, we J. D. and W. H., of said town, do hereby undertake, pursuant to the statute in such case made and provided, that we will well and truly indemnify and save harmless the said commissioners of highways against any costs which may be incurred in prosecuting for the penalty annexed to such refusal or neglect.

Dated, etc. A. B., [L. S.]
C. D., [L. S.]

---

### No. 70.

#### COMPLAINT OF OVERSEER ON SEIZURE OF CATTLE.

See *ante, p.* 238.

John Doe of the town of Grafton, in the county of Rensselaer, makes complaint to George Ring, one of the justices of the peace in said town, and alleges that this complainant is overseer of road district, No. 7, in said town; that, on the 3d day of June, 1870, this complainant found running at large in the highway leading from the northern turnpike to John Roy's in said road district, one brindle cow, with the horn on left side broken; that thereupon this complainant, as such overseer, seized and took into his possession said cow, and keeps the same to be disposed of according to law. That this complainant has no knowledge, information or belief, as to who is the owner of the said cow. This complainant, therefore, prays said justice to issue a summons, under his hand, requiring the owner of said cow, or any party having an interest in the same, to show cause, before such justice, why said animal should not be sold, and the proceeds applied as directed by the statute in such case made and provided.

JOHN DOE.

RENSSELAER COUNTY, *ss.:*

John Doe, the above complainant, being duly sworn, says, that the facts set forth in the above complaint are true.

JOHN DOE.

Sworn to before me this 5th day of June, 1857.

PHILIP SLADE,
*Justice of Peace.*

---

**No. 71.**

SUMMONS.

See *ante*, *p.* 239.

RENSSELAER COUNTY, *ss.:*

Whereas, John Doe, overseer of highways of road district No. 7, in the town of Grafton, in said county, has made complaint, on oath, before me, a justice of the peace of said town, that he has siezed and taken into his possession, and keeps to be disposed of according to law, *one brindle cow with the horn on the left side broken*, found running at large in the highways in his said road district, contrary to the statute in such case made and provided. Therefore, the owner of said animal, or any party having an interest in the same, is hereby required to show cause, before me, at my office in said town, on the 20th day of June, 1870, why said animal should not be sold, and the proceeds applied as directed by "An act to prevent animals from running at large in the public highways, passed April 23, 1862," and the acts amending the same.

Given under my hand this 5th day of June, 1870.

PHILIP SLADE,
*Justice of the Peace.*

---

**No. 72.**

WARRANT FOR SALE OF ANIMALS.

See *ante, p.* 241.

RENSSELAER COUNTY, *ss.:*

*To any Constable in the town of Grafton, in said county:*

You are hereby commanded to sell at public auction, for the best price you can obtain therefor, one brindle cow, with the horn on the left side broken, heretofore seized and taken into possession by John Doe, overseer of highways of road district No. 7, of said town, and now in his possession, and make return thereof to me, at my office in said town, on the 5th day of July, 1870.

Given under my hand this 20th day of June, 1870.

PHILIP SLADE.
*Justice of the Peace.*

## No. 73.

### CONSTABLE'S RETURN OF SALE.

See *ante, p.* 241.

RENSSELAER COUNTY, *ss.:*

To PHILIP SLADE, *one of the Justices of the Peace, of the town of Grafton, in said county:*

I, John Jones, one of the constables of said town, and to whom was delivered a certain warrant, issued by you, and directed to any constable of the said town of Grafton, commanding him to sell, etc. (*as in the warrant*) do hereby certify and return, that by virtue of said warrant I did, on the 28th day of June, 1870, having given at least five days' public notice of the time and place of such sale, sell at public auction, in said town, the brindle cow mentioned and described in said warrant, to John Doe, for the sum of fifty-nine dollars, he being the highest bidder, and that being the highest price bid therefor.

JOHN JONES,
*Constable.*

Dated, etc.

---

## No. 74.

### APPEAL FROM DECISION OF JUSTICE.

See *ante, p.* 244.

JUSTICE'S COURT:

In the matter of the application of John Doe, overseer of Highways.

Take notice that I appeal to the county court of Rensselaer county, from the finding or determination of Philip Slade, justice of the peace of the town of Grafton, in said county, made on the 20th day of June, 1870, that cause existed for the sale of *one brindle cow, with the horn on the left side broken off*, alleged to have been found running at large in the public highways of road district No. 7 of said town, and seized and taken into possession by John Doe, overseer of highways of said road district, and that the following are the grounds upon which this appeal is founded:

That the justice erred in refusing to dismiss the proceedings, as the defendant requested, on the ground that the summons, issued by him therein, had not been served as required by law, etc.

The justice is hereby required to return all the evidence and proceedings in the matter, and to certify that he has done so.

Dated, etc.

JOHN SMITH, *Appellant.*

To PHILIP SLADE, *Justice*, and
JOHN DOE, *Complainant.*

---

**No. 75.**

APPLICATION FOR A PRIVATE ROAD.

See *ante, p.* 261.

*To the Commissioners of Highways of the town of Mendon, in the county of Monroe:*

The subscriber, a resident of said town, and liable to be assessed for highway labor, hereby makes application to you to lay out a private road for his use, beginning, etc. (*insert description, specifying its width and location, courses and distances*), that said road runs through the lands of Henry Barton and John Jones.

Dated, etc. A. B.

## No. 76.

### NOTICE TO OWNER OR OCCUPANT.

See *ante*, *p*. 262.

*To* LEMON GRIPPEN:

Please take notice that on the 20th day of July, 1868, at 10 o'clock in the forenoon, at the house of James S. Forbes, in Wilton, a jury will be selected for the purpose of determining upon the necessity of the road asked for in the application, of which a copy is annexed, and to assess the damages by reason of opening the same. Signatures,

Dated, etc. *Commissioners.*

---

## No. 77.

### CERTIFICATE OF JURY UPON APPLICATION FOR A PRIVATE ROAD.

See *ante*, *p*. 264.

We, the undersigned, being disinterested freeholders of the town of Green, in the county of Erie, having met on the 23d day of May, in the year 1867, at the residence of Anson Boice, in said town, having been duly sworn, well and truly to examine and certify with regard to the necessity and propriety of the road described in the annexed application of A. B., and having viewed the lands through which it is proposed to be made, do certify, that in our opinion it is necessary and proper to lay out a private road for the use of the said A. B., pursuant to his said application, and we do assess the damages as follows: to John Hall, $100.

In witness whereof, we have hereunto subscribed our names, this 23d day of May, 1867.

P. W.,
S. T., etc.

### No. 78.

### ORDER FOR LAYING OUT A PRIVATE ROAD.

See *ante*, *p.* 264.

At a meeting of the commissioners of highways of the town of Mendon, in the county of Monroe, at the residence of Anson Boice, in the said town, on the 23d day of November, 1867, all the said commissioners having met and deliberated on the subject of this order (*or if but two of the commissioners met, say*, all the said commissioners having been duly notified to attend the said meeting, for the purpose of deliberating on the subject of this order), upon the application of A. B., for the laying out of the private road hereafter described, and on the certificate of twelve reputable freeholders of said town, convened and duly sworn, after due notice to the owner (*or occupant*) of the lands through which said road is to pass, as required by the statute, certifying that such road was necessary: It is therefore ordered and determined by the said commissioners, that a private road be laid out for the use of the said A. B., pursuant to his application, the courses and distances whereof, according to a survey thereof which the said commissioners have caused to be made, are as follows: (*insert the survey.*) And it is further ordered, that the line above described, shall be the center of said road, and that said road shall be of the width of two rods.

In witness whereof, we have hereunto subscribed our names, this 23d day of November, 1867.

A. B.,<br>C. D.,<br>E. F., } *Commissioners.*

### No. 79.

### COMMISSIONER'S CONSENT TO WORK IN ANOTHER DISTRICT.

See *ante*, *p.* 100.

Whereas, A. B., a resident of road district No. 7, in the town of Hoosic, in the county of Rensselaer, is assessed six days' labor in district No. 3, in said town, for lands situate therein, therefore at his request we hereby approve of his applying the work so assessed in respect to such lands in said district No. 3, where the same is situated. (Signed.)

Dated.

---

### No. 80.

### NOTICE TO AGENT OF NON-RESIDENT.

See *ante*, *p.* 102.

*To* C. D., *Agent of* A. B., *a non-resident owner of lands in the town of Brunswick, in the county of Rensselaer:*

Take notice that A. B., a non-resident of the said town, is assessed four days' labor in road district No. 5, in said town, and that said labor is required to be performed on the road between the house of J. K. and Millville in said district, on the third day of May next and the days following.

Yours, etc. J. D., *Overseer.*

Dated, etc.

---

### No. 81.

### NOTICE IN CASE OF NON-RESIDENTS.

See *ante*, *p.* 102.

Notice is hereby given that the highway labor assessed on the following described parcels of land in the town of , county of , owned by non-residents, is required to be performed from the 5th to the 12th days of June next, in road district No. 2, in said town, on the highway leading from (*describe locality with reasonable accuracy*).

| Owner's names. | Description of lands | Assessment. |
|---|---|---|
| Jared Rust,.... | N. pt., L. 10, 100 acres. | 10 days. |

A. B., *Overseer of Dist. No.* 2.

Dated, etc.

---

**No. 82.**

OVERSEER'S COMPLAINT FOR REFUSAL TO WORK, ETC.

See *ante*, *p.* 105.

SENECA COUNTY, *ss.*:

A. B., being duly sworn, says, that he is overseer of highways of road district No. 9, in the town of Ovid, in said county; that on the 17th day of June, 1848, he gave C. D., who resides in said district, and is assessed to work on the highways therein, notice to appear on the 19th day of June aforesaid, with a (*state what kind of team or implements were required*) on the road (*state where*), to do such work; and that the said C. D. did not appear nor furnish any one in his stead (*or did not bring such team or implement as was required, stating it; or when he so appeared was idle, or hindered others from working, or whatever the complaint is*), and has not paid the commutation money for said work, nor rendered a satisfactory excuse for such neglect. A. B.

Subscribed and sworn to before me this 3d day of July, 1848. }

T. R., *Justice of Peace.*

### No. 83.

SUMMONS.

See *ante, p.* 105.

SENECA COUNTY, *ss.:*

*To any Constable of the Town of Ovid, in said County:*

Whereas, A. B., overseer of highways of road district No. 9, in said town, has made complaint on oath before me, a justice of the peace of said town, that C. D., a resident of said road district, and assessed to work on the highways therein, after being duly notified to appear on the 19th day of June, instant, with (*state what team or implements were required*) to do such work; and that the said C. D. (*stating the matter of the complaint*), and has not paid the commutation money nor rendered a satisfactory excuse.

You are, therefore, hereby required to summon the said C. D. to appear forthwith before me at my office in the said town, to show cause why he should not be fined according to law for such refusal (*or neglect, or misconduct*). G. H., *Justice of Peace.*

OVID, *June* 21, 1848.

### No. 84.

CONSTABLE'S RETURN ON SUMMONS.

See *ante, p.* 105.

The within summons, personally served on Richard Roe, by reading the same to him, this 22d day of June, 1851. JOHN DOE,

**No. 85.**

JUDGMENT THEREON.

See *ante*, *p.* 105.

In the matter of the complaint of A. B., overseer of highways, *vs.* C. D.

The said C. D., having been duly summoned to appear before me, J. B., the justice of the peace to whom the said complaint was made, to show cause why he should not be fined, according to law, for the refusal (*or neglect, or misconduct*) set forth in said complaint; and no sufficient cause having been shown by said C. D., I do therefore impose upon the said C. D. a fine of *three dollars* for said offense, together with two dollars for the costs of the proceedings under the said complaint.

G. H.,
*Justice of Peace.*

Dated, etc.

---

**No. 86.**

WARRANT TO LEVY FINE.

See *ante*, *p.* 105.

SENECA COUNTY, *ss.:*

*To any Constable in the Town of Ovid, in the said County:*

You are hereby commanded to levy of the goods and chattels of C. D. *four dollars and eighteen cents;* being *one dollar* for fine imposed by me, for (*specify the neglect or misconduct*), as set forth in the complaint of A. B., overseer of highways of road district No. 3 in the said town; and also *three dollars and eighteen cents*, for the cost of the proceedings on said complaint; and bring the said sum of money before me without delay.

G. H., *Justice of Peace.* [L. S.]

OVID, *June* 23, 1851.

# INDEX.

www.ingramcontent.com/pod-product-compliance
Lightning Source LLC
LaVergne TN
LVHW021251110826
845151LV00002BA/386

* 9 7 8 1 4 2 5 5 3 9 1 7 7 *